INTO THE NEW IRON AGE : MODERN BRITISH BLACKSMITHS

Cheltenham

INTO THE NEW IRON AGE :

*'Fire Welding' limited edition Wood
Engraving by Rachel Reckitt.*

MODERN BRITISH BLACKSMITHS

AMINA CHATWIN

PART I INTO THE NEW IRON AGE

LOOKING BACK TO THE PAST   1

WHAT MIGHT HAVE BEEN   7

CHARLES RENNIE MACKINTOSH   15

HOW IT ALL BEGAN   23

BABA EXHIBITIONS 1982-3   38

MOVING FORWARDS   44

EIGHT SMITHS   Richard Bent, Adam Booth,   61
Philip Johnson, John Creed, Paul Margetts,
Peat Oberon, Brian Russell, Anthony Wootton.

WHAT *IS* MODERN IRONWORK?   74

PART II MODERN BRITISH BLACKSMITHS
Monographs on eighteen of our finest Designer
Ironsmiths.

TERRENCE CLARK
ALAN DAWSON
ALAN EVANS
THEO. GRUNEWALD
STUART HILL
JAMES HORROBIN
ALAN JACK
GIUSEPPE LUND
MICHAEL MALLESON
CHARLES NORMANDALE
PETER PARKINSON
DAVID PETERSEN
MELVIN PINNOCK
       and the Nailbourne Forge
WALENTY PYTEL
RICHARD QUINNELL
       and the Rowhurst Forge
RACHELL RECKITT
MICHAEL ROBERTS
ANTONY ROBINSON

Published
by
Reardon Publishing
PO Box 919, Cheltenham, GL50 9AN

by
Amina Chatwin

Author of:
'Cheltenham's Ornimental Ironwork'
&
History of Iron Making in Britain

The engraving shown on cover is from a
woodcut by **Rachel Reckitt**

ISBN**: 9781901037265**

THIS BOOK IS DEDICATED
TO HIS ROYAL HIGHNESS
THE PRINCE OF WALES

Who has said:

"I want to see laymen and professionals working together; developers, architects and craftsmen understanding each other."

A Vision of Britain.

The Worshipful Company of Blacksmiths
London

FOREWORD

From time immemorial there have been blacksmiths.

Who tempered the iron and fashioned the tools to make the masterpieces of the world? Names that have been forgotten, but of more recent times many names have been remembered for their practical contribution to the craft of Blacksmithing and are referred to in part I of this book.

Whose names will go forward and become the history of tomorrow? Some are featured in this book and others will surely follow.

The Worshipful Company of Blacksmiths has been the mentor and arbiter of the craft for over six hundred years and names like Elwood, Lister, Tucker, Day, Bent, Allen, Lloyd and others have been involved with the Company in setting standards by which modern blacksmiths are judged.

We are proud and honoured to be associated with this book. The author is not a blacksmith, but the research that she has undertaken to produce this work warrants its recognition as an authoritative reference book for the present and the future.

Raymond C. Jorden
Learned Clerk
The Worshipful Company of Blacksmiths.

The origins of the Worshipful Company of Blacksmiths are lost in time. The main charters of the Company were granted in 1571, 1604 and 1639, enabling it to become the fully fledged Livery Company that it is today, but its earliest written records go back to 1496. The Worshipful Company exercised complete control over every aspect of the craft. A blacksmith could only trade within the walls of the City, and take apprentices, if he possessed the Freedom of the City. As soon as an apprentice had served his indenture and learnt his craft he could obtain the Freedom of the Company.

However, by the late 18th century the Company's influence over the Craft had diminished, just as many of the privileges attached to the honour of the Freedom of the City had been eroded through time. In recent years the Worshipful Company has begun to develop relationships with other blacksmithing associations and to operate a system of awards at all levels from apprentices to teachers. The awards are open to everyone whether connected with the Company or not.

It is hoped in this way that it will be possible to re-vitalise the craft to the glories of the past and to progress forward with the new revival of creative contemporary smithing.

INTRODUCTION AND ACKNOWLEDGEMENTS

Blacksmiths are no longer the "village smith" of popular concept — today they carry mobile phones in their back pockets and often design their ironwork on computers.

Their new creative thoughts on design, and their assimilation and acceptance of modern techniques, has finally brought ironwork into the 20th century.

Their lives and their personalities are as varied as their work. I hope this will be evident from the monographs I have written. They have one thing in common, the same motivation and the same love of hot iron as their forbears.

The last fifteen years have been exciting ones and it has been a privilege to follow the development of this revival of creative smithing. To see it build on an illustrious past, and open-up to the future.

I should like to thank His Royal Highness the Prince of Wales for allowing me to dedicate to him this work on ironsmiths. I feel it is a singular honour for us all. I thank also the Worshipful Company of Blacksmiths for providing the Foreword.

Then there are the smiths themselves, I want to thank them for their patience, in finding time to talk to me and answer my questions; replying to my letters, and providing photographs; always when they were pressed for time. It seemed as if they had always deadlines to meet and work to be done — if there were times when I pressured them I hope they will forgive me. I must thank also their wives, who added their entreaties to mine, if weeks slid into months, and reminded their hardworking husbands of letters not yet written and photographs not yet found and sent.

Many friends have given me their help and advice and I thank them all sincerely. First, Norman Hodgkinson F.I.Mech.E. who has acted as my technical adviser, and been a great support throughout. Richard Quinnell M.B.E., whose recollections augmented "How it all began"; and Peter Parkinson for reading and commenting on the section "What is Modern Ironwork". Michael Pountney, personal computer consultant, without whom I should never have learnt to operate my Apple Macintosh; and for various help Kenneth Pinnock, David Bick, Roy Day, Michael Grange and Yankel Mandel. Rachel Reckitt for allowing me to reproduce her powerful engravings and all the people who have let me use their photographs (see also page 215) and quote from their writings and lectures. I should also like to thank everyone at BAS Printers for their patience and help.

Amina Chatwin

LOOKING BACK
TO THE PAST

Detail of the Capel Garmon firedogs. National Museum of Wales.

Since Celtic times there have been blacksmiths of supreme skill in Britain. One has only to look at the Capel Garmon Fire Irons in the National Museum of Wales, the quadrangular frame with ox-head terminals in the British Museum, or the pot-chain in the Museum of Archaeology and Anthropology, The University of Cambridge, to be immediately aware of the lively creativity of the native smiths who were already working here before the Romans came to this country.

Although a number of Celtic fire-dogs exist those from Capel Garmon (c 50BC–50AD)

found in a Denbighshire peat bog, are of exceptional beauty; while the quadrangular frame from the British Museum, found in a Belgic burial from Welwyn, Hertfordshire (50–10BC), represents an extraordinary technical tour-de-force on the part of the blacksmith, when one realises that with the small primitive furnaces used for producing iron at that time, each upright 1.69m high, and at the lower part, 11cm wide by 4.5cm thick, would require several blooms of iron, of the size then produced, to be heat welded into a single upright, even before the actual shaping by forging began.

The Cauldron chains, of which various remains have been found, were about 12ft (1.658m) long and used some 30lbs of iron. When made as carefully and decoratively as the Cambridge example they must have been objects of considerable prestige to their owners.

Equally from the Middle Ages sufficient examples of ironwork remain, for us to see how in those times, the blacksmiths mind, eye, and hand, worked to produce products of great immediacy and aesthetic satisfaction. There is a grille from Chichester Cathedral (13c), now in the Victoria and Albert Museum,

Far left: Hector Cole who now specializes in Medieval ironwork. Blacksmiths working by hand at the anvil have changed little over the last two thousand years,

of round scrolls linked in an unusual way. There are the remains of the *St. Swithin's Grille*, now used as gates in Winchester Cathedral, where very small scrolls are grouped into leaf forms. Then there is the unique *Eleanor Grille* in Westminster Abbey, made by Thomas de Leghtone in 1294 which is swaged (stamped or moulded) and scrolled, and has little forged animal heads on the lower border. There are many great hinges on church doors, whose utility as strengthening bars, in no way detracts from the patterns of the designs. I suspect, though we have no means of knowing, that all these pieces were conceived by the minds of the blacksmiths as surely as they were made by their hands and hammers;

these smiths were what today we should call artist-blacksmiths or designer-metalsmiths— they evolved their own forms. I sometimes think that up to this time we can see more affinity with smithing of the last fifteen years, in this country, than at any later period in our history.

With the 15th and 16th centuries came what we know as The Age of the Locksmith when much of the iron was worked cold by piercing, chiselling, and filing, as well as being forged while hot. Door locks and bolts of great intricacy were made. The style was often architectural, as the screen to the Henry V chapel in Westminster Abbey; made by Roger Johnson in 1428. The lower part is an intricate diaper pattern, built up in layers of forged crosspieces backed by cut plate, cut slightly

larger giving an effect of depth and richness. The supreme example, however, of this style can be seen in the massive gates and screen (c 1482-3) to the chantry of Edward IV in St. George's Chapel, Windsor, and thought to have been made by John Tresilian. While we can marvel at the perfection of this incredible ironwork, there is no denying that it is colder and more precise than the work of earlier centuries. It is as though a little of the heart has gone out of it, it no longer has the immediacy which comes from working only at the anvil with red hot malleable metal.

By the early 17th century ironwork in this country had lost something of the delicacy of the early, and the perfection of the late, middle ages. There was a certain naivety about it, but a lot of strength and gusto—one feels that it was made in a straight forward way with great enjoyment. Nowhere is this quality better shown than at the Warburton Chapel in St. John's Church, Chester. There is a screen of rails between the chapel and the main body of the church and a pair of gates with narrow side panels at the entrance. There are twisted rails, a decorative element much used in the 17th century, and a riot of fleur-de-lis, derived from the lily or iris flowers, a popular form in the middle ages.

By the late 17th century ironwork was already becoming more elegant and more elaborate, so to some extent it was ready for the arrival of the frenchman Jean Tijou, who was to have such a great influence on English Ironwork design. He was already at the height of his skills and is first heard of, in this country, working for the Duke of Devonshire at Chatsworth in March 1688. Soon he was working for William and Mary, the new monarchs, at Hampton Court. His work on the Fountain Screen in the garden near the river, is flamboyant in the extreme. He was a great worker in repoussé (embossing) and although

Top above: Lively forging on Hinge from Mere Church, Somerset.

Above: Detail of Screen to Henry V Chapel in Westminster Abbey.

Far left: Detail of the Warburton ironwork in St. John's Church, Chester.

scrolled panels set in the wooden screen dividing the choir from the aisles. There are the more elaborate screens and gates around the Sanctuary, in the centre of which, in the north aisle, are set four exquisite repoussé plaques, of the evangelists, surely Tijou's personal work, and of a technical perfection previously unkown in this country.

Jean Tijou and his confreres, of whom John Gardom, William Edney, and a little later Robert Bakewell, are the most outstanding, were producing new forms in the white heat of their enthusiasm. The designs were new and vital and that is why they were so good.

Far Left: Detail of the Fountain Screen in the garden of Hampton Court Palace.

many of the more delicate parts have, by necessity, been replaced (the Satyr head is in the V & A Museum) enough remains to be very impressive. The gauge of iron is thick and the garlands and acanthus leaves must have been forged hot on the anvil, not cold worked as was frequently the case in later european repoussé. Tijou had assistants and operated a workshop at Hampton Court. They were not solely concerned with producing exotic ironwork as we know they made window frames for St. Paul's Cathedral, and the great chain, within the stonework, to girdle the dome. Inside the Cathedral some of their finest work can still be seen. There are beautiful

Left: Detail of repoussé plaque of Evangelist in the Sanctuary Screen in St. Paul's Cathedral.

Left: Scrolled panels set in wooden screen in St. Paul's Cathedral. From the workshop of Jean Tijou.

There is an affinity here with what modern blacksmiths are trying to do today, just like Tijou, they are producing new forms, to revitalise and continue a living art.

In the later 17th and early 18th centuries English ironwork had reached a pinnacle of perfection, both artistic and technical. However, as time went on, financial considerations as well as fashion, dictated a certain simplification of the designs. We arrived at a style that was very English and very elegant, but already beginning to settle into a formula. Unfortunately ironwork in this country crystallised at this point and remained there for the next two hundred years. If anything is continually copied it loses its vitality until it becomes a pale shadow of its former self.

There was another element that to some extent debilitated wrought ironwork, and that was the introduction in the later part of the 18th century, of more cast iron. The Adam brothers, architects, used ironwork to great effect, but they seemed to care little whether their balconies and gates were produced in cast or wrought iron, and indeed they usually opted for a combination of the two. Their designs were distinctive and led to much elegant cast work in the Regency period. Indeed by the early 19th century cast iron was in the ascendancy and by Victorian times it was to be found everywhere, not only gates, balconies, and railings were cast, but even fountains, plates, clocks and chairs.

Victorian fine art was naturalistic rather than creative, and when it came to architecture and crafts they were eclectic—they borrowed the designs of previous centuries, rather than seeking to create their own style. It was not thought in any way strange that a cabinet maker might produce a Gothic or a Louis XVI sideboard, rather than creating something new for his own time. While craftsmen in many disciplines chased about after numerous styles, they came up with little that was recognisably and typically Victorian; unless it was in being heavily overdecorated. Their craftsmanship could be technically excellent, they could reproduce any style, but they thought more of applied decoration than of the basic shapes of the objects. When it came to ironwork, really cast iron was king. Skilled moulders could cast almost anything, from

Far Left: Detail of Sword Rest by William Edney in the Lord Mayor's Chapel, Bristol.

Below: Overthrow to the Chancel Screen at Staunton Harold, Leicestershire, by Robert Bakewell.

Below: Detail of the Staircase by John Gardom at Chatsworth House, Derbyshire.

5

It even seems as if some of the smiths were aware of this lack of a contemporary style. J.A.R. Stevenson, a Devonshire smith, writing "The Din of a Smithy" in 1932 writes in his introduction that a letter had appeared in The Architectural Review saying that education was teaching people to be Strangers to the age we live in, and encourages us to continue building preposterous shams of the dead past. He goes on to say that although a critical appreciation of past ironwork is helpful. It is not enough. You must come in contact with the metal.

"We think it poor fun to be tied down to periods and styles. When I design a piece of ironwork I am much more ready to be guided by the possibilities and limitations of the metal, as I have learned them, and by the peculiarities of the site and of its environment, as I see them, than by any polite consideration of the need to make a copy of some other example of ironwork . . . The happiest examples of smithcraft are those of the twelfth, thirteenth and fourteenth centuries, when smithing was a virile craft, unencumbered by much 'designing' and unprejudiced by consideration of other styles." Admirable sentiments, yet the strange thing is that even he, judging by the photographs of work in his book, seems to have been overwhelmed— either by his clients or the general outlook of

Far left: Adam ironwork on Chandos House, Queen Ann Street, London.

whole buildings, to openwork plates and delicate bracelets. I have a charming small Victorian wall clock, but it is basically in an 18th century style! It was not until the Art Nouveau Movement began, that a truly distinctive style could really be said to have been born since Regency times.

The industrial revolution must have taken many blacksmiths from their forges into the factories. After World War I, when the use of horses was declining and the motor car growing in popularity, many village blacksmiths must have gradually become motor mechanics. By the 1920s and 30s smiths were spoken of, with some justification, as a dying breed. For the average blacksmith a decorative job was rare and neither the smith or the client would expect the design to be anything other than 18th century based scrolls and rails. This does not mean that there were no good smiths working in the 1930s and 40s, on the contrary there were many doing technically excellent work—but they were rare, and the patterns they used were based on the past.

Left: Design for one of their standard gates by W.G.Banks & Son, Westonbirt, Tetbury, Glos. Such firms made excellent hand crafted gates, but continued into the late 20th century to look back some 200 years for their design inspiration.

the time—the vast majority of his gates were still composed of rails and scrollwork as used in the 18th century.

It was the tradition for more important ironwork commissions, often handled by larger firms, to be designed by architects. Having studied the history of art and architecture they were familiar with suitable ironwork for various types of buildings. However, often they did not understand the behaviour of hot metal, so there was little incentive for creativity, and they were content to design in the styles of the past. Even today this is a situation that often pertains.

Another element that worked against ironwork was that the most avant garde modern buildings of the 20th century tended to be so bare, both inside and out, that ironwork as a decorative element was never entertained.

In this way, fantastic as it may seem, we reached the last quarter of the 20th century before, with perhaps a very few exceptions, contemporary ironwork began to be noticed or created here. It could so easily have happened eighty years earlier, when Charles Rennie Mackintosh designed the Glasgow School of Art, at the turn of the century. There was new and interesting ironwork both inside and out, far in advance of its time—why did the seeds fall on stoney ground? Perhaps it was because the design was by an unusually gifted architect, rather than being created from the grass roots at the hands of the blacksmiths.

WHAT MIGHT HAVE BEEN

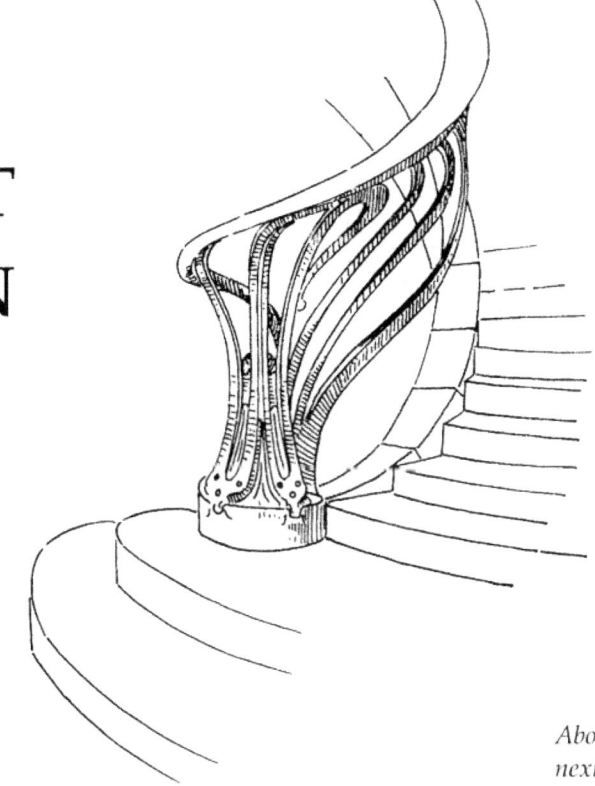

In the years between 1899 and 1909 Charles Rennie Mackintosh, artist and architect, designed the Glasgow School of Art, and incorporated both inside and outside, some of the most amazing ironwork that had ever been seen in this country. It is safe to say that it was beyond its time, and ahead of public appreciation. One must remember that at that date the flowing lines of Art Nouveau were the up to the minute style. Mackintosh's ironwork did not have graceful flowing lines it was hard, almost barbaric, with an economy of shape that marks it out as the forerunner of **modern** ironwork today.

There was ironwork everywhere. In the actual structure of the building; on the outside, railing panels integrated with the stonework, and window supports; and inside grilles and light fixtures; while the finials with globes and birds on the roof turrets are perhaps the most exciting of all.

One could say, that the grouped plant forms that rise above the stanchions on the north

Above left and on next page: Illustrations from "Éléments d'Architecture Moderne" par H.Sauvage et Sarazin. Charles Schmid, Editeur 51, Rue des Écoles, Paris. 2 Vols. No date.

facade, owe something to the Art Nouveau style, but even these have an untypical angularity. Indeed it is on record that Mackintosh disliked the softness of Art Nouveau and "fought against it with straight lines".[1]

England never had the strong Art Nouveau Movement that pertained on the continent. France had a similar fine tradition in 18th century ironwork, yet smiths there seemed more open to innovation and new designs than those in this country. In France, as in

England, cast ironwork became popular in the 19th century to the detriment of fine forging. However, towards the end of the century the Art Nouveau style in art brought forwards something of a rebirth of forging particularly in France and Belgium.

French master smiths who were also fine artists, of whom Emile Robert was the best known, began to forge designs of their own time. Robert in particular took as his subjects foliage and flowers and the sinuous forms that were typical of Art Nouveau.

It was around 1900, in some places a few years before, that ironwork on the continent began to break loose from the constraints of the past. An architect who confronted one of the major problems of the time, which is still relevant today, was another Frenchman Hector Guimard, and the problem was how to unite architecture with decoration. He found his solutions in abstract sculptural forms and effective use of line. He lavished ironwork on his early buildings and designed the famous early french Metro Station entrances. Like the Belgian architect Victor Horta he "banished the leaf and the flower and seized the stem" as his style motif. [2]

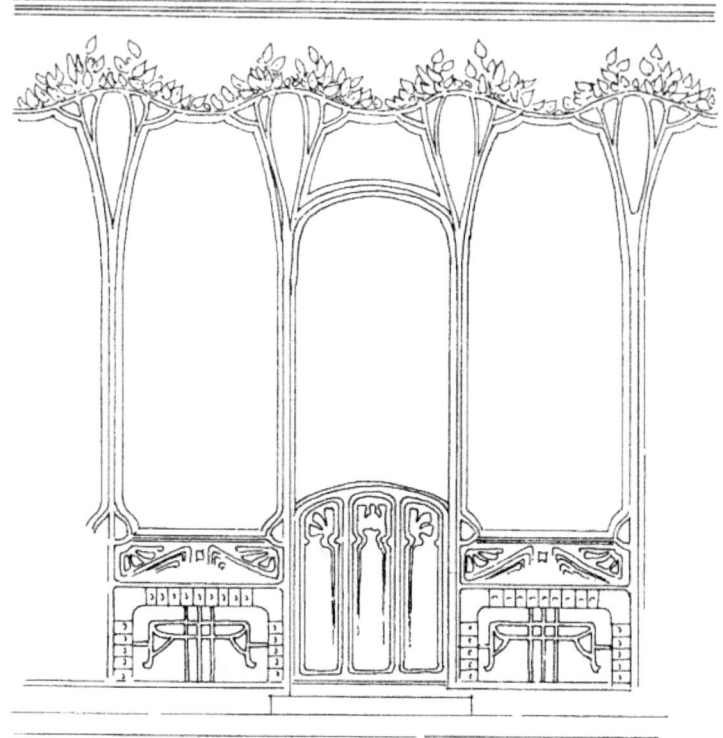

Meanwhile in Spain there was a whole new and very advanced style of ironwork evolved by architect Antoni Gaudi (1852-1926) and his collaborators, mostly in Barcelona. He was the son of a copper smith[3] and his grandfather and great grandfather had been potters. He seems to have been much influenced by both these crafts and ceramic and ironwork are to be found as an integral part of almost all his architectural projects.

He served an apprenticeship to a blacksmith[4] and the nuns at the Teresian Teaching College, which was one of his earliest commissions, maintain that the massive wrought iron gate and grille to the entrance porch were made by his own hands.

The ironwork on the Vicens House (1878-1885); the strange *Dragon Gate* at the Guell Pavilions (1884-87), an extraordinarily innovative work; and the two very large heavy grilles in the entrance arches to the Guell Palace (1886-91) all belong to the first, rather eclectic, phase of his development. They were all made in the workshop of Juan Onos[5]. Some have seen an Art Nouveau influence in these works, though whether he was following or leading the style is debatable.

Left: A rare example, in England, of an Art Nouveau lamp standard. It is on the corner of the churchyard in Painswick, Glos. Erected in 1904 to commemorate the reign of Queen Victoria.

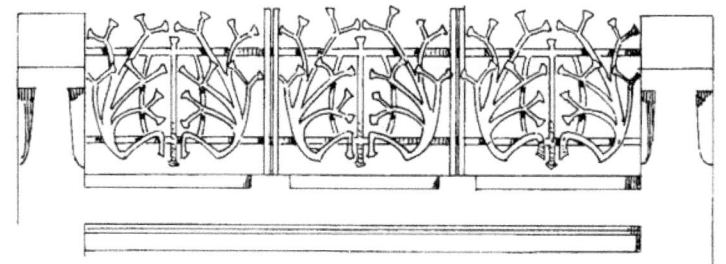

After the turn of the century it is as though his ironwork takes on a new dimension, as indeed did his buildings. He had fully developed his own personal style and was concentrating on his ecclesiastic commissions, while exploring the organic and structural aspects of nature in relation to his architecture. Many of the decorative elements he was leaving to his assistant, and one time student, Jose Mª Jujol; who designed many of the ceramic collages and who is said to have been responsible, under the general direction of Gaudi, for the balconies on the Mila House. He continued to work as an architect long after Gaudi's death. There is an Art Nouveau staircase on his building Torre de la Creau, Sant Joan Dispi, 1913-1916, with a very beautiful stair rail of fine *knotted* iron bar and forged plate which looks like a loose ribbon.

In Gaudi's alterations, 1904-06, to an old building, in the paseo de Gracia, Barcelona, the Battlo House, the stair rails are very accomplished and typical Art Nouveau curves. On the façade of the house the mask-like balconies introduce an infill of narrow plate with a loose twist. This technique re-appears on the balconies of the inner courts of the Mila House, and on the interior stair rails. It is also found on the fence around the Sagrada Familia and in the examples of what are obviously innovative, but low cost, boundary railings now to be found in the garden of the Museum in Güell Park

However, the balconies on the great cliff-like façade of the Mila House, 1906-1912 are something else again. The ironwork integrated into this sculptural building transcends Art Nouveau—it is as modern in outlook as anything that has been made in recent years. The curving walls are complimented by ironwork balconies that form an integral part of the building design.

There are some thirty of these exterior balconies and all appear to be different; surely much of the detail must have been created by the smiths themselves. The technique is that of cut plate forged into curvilinear forms and riveted together.

It is a stupendous concept—who knows what was in the minds of those who created it—a great troglodite cliff on whose ledges grow luxuriant plant forms, or a stone sea washing up succulent flat twisting ropes of seaweed.

Today all these works find echo in the designs of our modern designer metalsmiths, yet strangely, at the time British smiths seemed impervious to these influences.

Organic plant forms began to be joined by the abstract, the asymmetrical and the curvilinear as Art Nouveau slid into Art Deco. About 1910, in France, Emile Robert joined forces with the firm of E. Bordel which led to more industrialisation of the metalwork. His pupil Raymond Subes carried on working with the

Above: Exterior of the Battlo House with its mask-like balconies.

Below: Interior stair balustrade with typical Art Nouveau curves.

the softness of Art Nouveau but are marked by the firmer heavier forms that bring them into the realm of Art Deco. There are also ornate lamp standards on the Beursplein and various bridges over the canals from this time —but in Britain one looks almost in vain for ironwork dating to this period.

What England did have was the Arts and Crafts Movement, of which William Morris had been the founding father. It is true that the firm of William Morris & Co. did show several pages of wrought iron in fairly stereotyped Art Nouveau patterns, in their catalogue, but the majority of metalwork that seems to have been produced in the Movement was small-scale, jewellery, silverwork, furniture mounts, and hearth furniture, rather than architectural ironwork.

Far left: The interior court of the Mila Building with many balconies.

Below: Close up of these ribbon-like twisted balconies.

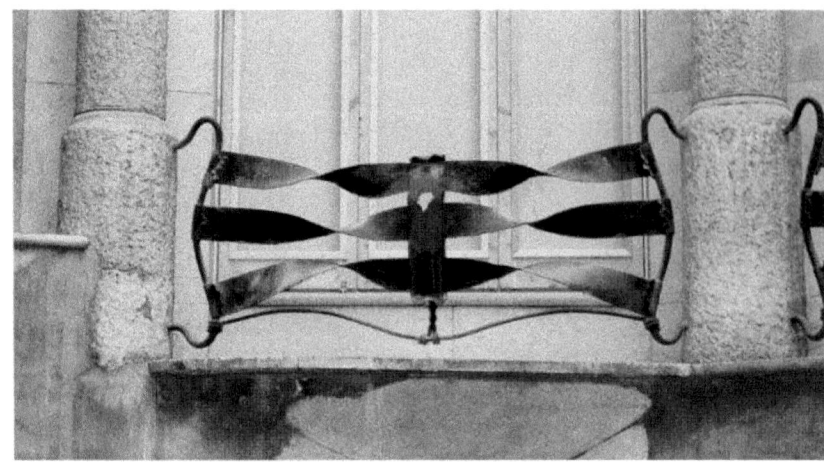

firm in later years, while Gilbert Poillerat, Charles Piquet, Pierre Garnier, Szabo and Schenck et Fils, all operated into the Art Deco period. Edgar Brandt was one of the best known exponents of the style producing very highly finished metalwork in the 1920s.[6]

In Amsterdam the ironwork on Van der Mey's Scheepvaarthuis of 1913-16 and the Tuschinski Cinema by de Jong in 1918-21 no longer have

Left: One of the balconies on the front façade. Freely interlacing writhing organic forms; almost unbelievably made in 1912.

There are, however, some examples of ecclesiastic ironwork. There are two churches of the Arts and Crafts period in London both furnished with extraordinarily rich interiors— Holy Trinity, Sloane Street, Chelsea, and St. Cuthbert, Philbeach Gardens, Earl's Court.

Holy Trinity, 1888-90, was by J.D. Sedding, a pupil of G.E. Street, who gathered around him a body of artists and craftsmen. He designed the ironwork between the chancel and the nave. It has a heavy coat-of-arms on the gates and large ancanthus leaves form a scrolling top to both the gates and wings. The part of the work which seems the most *Arts and Crafts* in style is the delicate infill of flowers and leaves.

There is rather similar foliage with flat iron scrolls and coarse flowers and leaves in brass on the stair to Sedding's Pulpit; these were made by Longdens.

Sedding's closest pupil and successor was Henry Wilson (1864-1934) who designed the strapwork screen, round the organ, behind the altar of the Lady Chapel; and the railings outside on Sloane Street.[7] Both are made by straps of wrought iron enriched with vine

leaves and lively tendrils all riveted together. On the screen are also groups of circles to form bunches of grapes. Both the screen and railings were made by Nelson Dawson. The roof was destroyed during the blitz in 1944 and the present electroliers were made up from salvaged fragments.[8]

The other great Arts and Crafts church of extraordinary richness is St. Cuthbert, Philbeach Gardens, 1884-1887, by H.R. Gough. Here the maker of most of the metalwork was William Bainbridge-Reynolds, well known in the Movement both for ironwork and church plate. He was a member of the congregation and was largely in charge of the interior decoration for some ten years. When he began to work there he was with John Starkie Gardner's firm.[9]

He made the Communion rails (in low repoussé), the lectern, the Altar rails and screens of the Lady Chapel, the wall clock, the baptistry screen, the screen on the west side of the organ and the hanging Royal Arms.

The lectern is rather extraordinary, but heavy, with a lot of copper about it. The organ screen is decorated with cast brass birds, teals, in

reference to the Rev. William Teale in whose memory the screen was presented. It is heavy strap work of a type not unlike that in Holy Trinity. On the opposite side of the church is the screen to the Lady Chapel. Most of it is twisted bar and pierced work, very medieval in feeling; but the top of the screen is unusual and attractive, it seems to represent the wall of

Amsterdam.
Above left: One of the ornate lamp standards on the Beursplein. The rivet heads are bright red giving a rather jewel-like quality (on the central spine).

Above right: One of the canal bridges.

Left: The Tuschinski Cinema. There are also elaborate metal light holders further down the façade.

some medieval town and is sheathed in copper.

Some of the liveliest ironwork is the hanging repoussé Royal Arms which form a memorial to Queen Victoria.

William Bainbridge-Reynolds is said to have "studied deeply" in Spain and certainly two of his three magnificent wrought iron screens in York Minster are based on the designs of Spanish *rejas*.[10]

William Bainbridge-Reynolds died in 1935, and was buried in St. Paul, West Street in Brighton[11] but his firm continued to operate until about 1960.[12]

Charles Robert Ashbee, one of the best known architects in the English Arts and Crafts Movement, did design and build in 1898-9 number 39 Cheyne Walk, Chelsea. The house has interesting ironwork, probably made by the Guild of Handicraft, which he had formed in 1888. There are graceful simple rails and massive standards topped with balls on each side of the steps. The gate to the basement area is simple and clear cut, but retains something of the feel of 18th century work, which is also apparent in the building itself and is suitable to its surroundings. Lurking in the shadows beneath the porch canopy, above the door, is an impressive peacock, a motif much used by Ashbee in his jewellery. I do not know if Mackintosh and Ashbee were known to each other or not, even if they were, the dates of the designs for 39 Cheyne Walk and the Glasgow

Arts and Crafts Movement. Above: Handle and latch from a cupboard in the Debenham House, 8 Addison Road, London W14. c 1900. Below: Top of Lady Chapel screen by W. Bainbridge-Reynolds in Holy Trinity church.

School of Art are so close, that who knows if either one influenced the other.

Here was a house, in London, of considerable merit, and next to Ashbee's own architectural office; one might have expected it to have some influence on other architects and smiths, but it seems to have had no more lasting influence than the ironwork of Charles Rennie Mackintosh.

10. "The Ironwork of the Minster" by E. Milner-White.

11. "Buildings of England. Sussex" Nairn and Pevsner.

12. Information from C.A.H. Tucker.

Arts and Crafts Movement ironwork on the Charles Ashbee house, 39 Cheyne Walk, Chelsea, London.

Top left: Detail of a balcony railing on the back of the house. The little "heart shaped trees" are typical of motifs found in textiles and jewellery of the period.

Top right: The peacock above the door.

Left: The ironwork of the steps and gate to the basement. Probably made by the Guild of Handicraft c 1888.

Sources and Notes

1. Anthony Jones, *Charles Rennie Mackintosh* page 21. Studio Editions 1990.

2. "L'Architecture" 15 April 1899, pp126-133. quoted in *Architectural Monographs 2.* Hector Guimard page 2. Academy Editions.

3. James Johnson Sweeney and Josep Lluis Sert. *Antoni Gaudi.* The Architectural Press 1960.

4. ibid.

5. George R. Collins *Antoni Gaudi.* Mayflower London 1960. Note 91.

6. Henri Cloüzot *Ferronnerie Moderne* Editions d'Art published by Charles Moreau, Paris. Nouvelle Serie. No date.

7. There are drawings of the railings and gates in *Details* No 2 Vol 1. Feb. 1909.

8. Holy Trinity Church Sloane Square. A Brief Guide and History.

9. Information from the Rev. John Vine.

THE IRONWORK OF CHARLES RENNIE MACKINTOSH

Charles Rennie Mackintosh was born of a Scottish highland family in Glasgow in 1868, the son of a superintendent of the Glasgow police. He decided early that he wanted to become an architect and enrolled at the Glasgow School of Art at the age of fifteen. The following year he became an articled apprentice to the architectural firm of John Hutchison, though he continued to be a part time student at the art school for the next ten years. He would attend class in the early morning, work at his office during the day, and return to the Art School again in the evening. It was here that he was later to become friends with the Macdonald sisters, Margaret and Frances, and Herbert MacNair; together they were to be the prime movers in the creation of "The Glasgow Style". MacNair married Frances, and Charles in 1900 married Margaret.

Mackintosh was a very successful student, carrying off medals and prizes throughout his time at the school. In 1890 he won the coveted Alexander (Greek) Thomson Travelling Scholarship of £60 which he used, the following year, for an extensive tour of Italy travelling by way of Paris, Brussels, Antwerp, and London.

In 1889 he joined the architectural practice of Honeyman and Keppie. In the years that followed he was helping, with other members of the firm, to design buildings, and making the drawings for them with incredibly fine draftsmanship. These included the Glasgow Herald Building, Queen Margaret's Medical

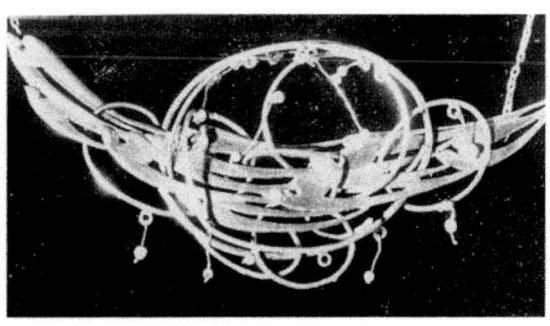

College, and the Martyr's Public School. This last drawing features a most elaborate street lamp, quite unique in design, outside the building. Perhaps it was natural that he should pay attention to such detail for both he and his wife had interests which covered a wide spectrum; designing posters, embroideries, stencils, embossed metalwork panels, hangings, and furniture. A pendant of silver and pearls designed by Mackintosh, made by his wife, and owned by the late Mrs Mary Newbery Sturrock is possibly their only surviving jewel. It serves to show the extraordinary *avant garde* nature of all their designs—it would be some half a century before jewellery entered into such free form design.[1] Their interiors would come to be shown at a number of exhibitions and to excite considerable acclaim, though more in Europe than in Britain.

In 1896 Mackintosh began a long association designing tea rooms for Miss Catherine Cranston who owned several such establishments in Glasgow. He first designed a series of large murals for premises in Buchanan Street, and then created one of his most striking chairs for the Argyle Street Tea Room. These bold high backed chairs have become, in the course of time, absolutely synonymous with his name.

At the age of 28 he submitted a design to a competition for the new Glasgow School of Art. After all his years as a student in the cramped old school it follows that he knew better than anyone what was needed, and he

Collection
Glasgow School of Art

Above: Iron sculpture on top of one of the turrets of Glasgow School of Art.

Left: Pendant of silver and pearls, designed by Mackintosh and made by his wife Margaret.

designed "from the inside out" a maxim he would follow throughout his architectural career. The site was difficult and the budget modest yet his winning design was stupendous, and has been called "the first truly modern building". Yet it was rooted in the tradition of the Scottish baronial period that he so much admired. The studio windows are walls of glass set in stone walls that have all the strength and massive nobility of a medieval castle. Enveloped by strong winds, the building broods almost grimly, on top of its hill overlooking the city. Approaching upwards along Dalhousie Street one is aware only of the narrow east side, austere in the extreme, and the almost cubist back of the building. High above can just be seen the weathervane-like iron sculpture on top of the east tower. The main façade faces north on to Renfrew Street with the entrance in the centre. Owing to financial constraints the building was completed in two stages; the wing to the east of the entrance was built in 1897-99 and that on the west in 1907-09.

The facade is subtlely asymmetrical. In the centre, above the entrance, is a balcony, with simple disc finials to the standards, and graceful upward curves at the ends. The most immediately noticeable ironwork feature is the front railing set on a wall built in a wave-like series of curves. This is punctuated by eight stanchions with openwork disc finials above. These serve both to strengthen the railings and to provide the main ornamental element at

Right and above right:
The north façade of the
Glasgow School of Art
on Renfrew Street.
The balcony, the window
supports, the front
railings and the disc
finials.

street level. The uprights are six grouped heavy plain flat bars, from which rises a decorative group of plant or stamen-like forms, in the round. (The fact that they cannot be painted inside has given rise to rusting problems.) These bunches of stems, with small leaf-like forms at the top, are perhaps the nearest Mackintosh ever comes to Art Nouveau design, but even these have an angularity not normally associated with that style. (The band around the plant group is a later addition to prevent vandalism; as also are the second line of straight main upright rails set slightly back from their fellows.) The plant-like groups are integrated to the horizontal top of the railings with a large flat semi-circular flat piece of iron. A single round rod then rises up from the centre holding aloft a pierced disc. Although the effect is in no way heavy, the whole forms a fairly massive screen; the top of the highest uprights being some seventeen feet from the pavement while the discs are almost two feet across. Some have seen in these banner-like creations allusions to Japanese heraldry and family crests. Certainly the work of Charles Rennie Mackintosh is known to have been influenced by Japanese Art and Architecture.

At first floor level there is another wealth of Ironwork. The windows here are twenty feet in height and are braced at the lower part by brackets which seem to grow, like fantastic flowers, from horizontal bars or "branches" sticking out from the wall below the windows. Their purpose is eminently practical, serving not only as spring braces, but also as holders for planks and supports for the ladders of window cleaners. It has been pointed out that the round sculptural forms on the top of the braces, some twelve inches in each direction, are reminiscent of the great basket hilts of Claymore swords, Scotland's national weapon; though perhaps Mackintosh saw in these attenuated forms no more than a reflection of the flowing stems and flowers that were so characteristic of his drawings and paintings. There are four braces to each window and the design of the hilt-like tops are different at each of the seven windows. Those on the eastern part of the facade are slightly more elongated in shape and more strongly made than the later ones on the west, which could be said to be looser and more freely designed. In the earlier examples the bar fastening the top of the brace to the window, passes through a hole drifted in one of the main iron bars in the sculptural form, but in the later versions it

simply rises from the centre of the form without such strengthening attachment.

There is an interesting screen to the sub-basement on the west facade. It shows Mackintosh's liking for tall, slender uncluttered forms, being largely composed of plain vertical bars. It is asymmetrical and divided by broad vertical flat bands and extra bars in a manner completely consistent with his designs for many room interiors. The grouped uprights carry basket-like structures at subtley varying heights, composed of interwoven oval section bars, except on the gate where they are flat, almost resembling a plaque. There are also three shield shapes, the whole producing something of the feeling of African art, which one could also say of the disc finials on the main façade. It must be imagined without the security mesh which is a later addition. Smaller versions of the shield shapes appear in the geometric gates and

Below: Grouped stems on the railing of the north façade.

railing screen at Scotland House School which he designed in 1903.

The culmination of the exterior ironwork are two Turret Finials, one fairly central at the north side, and the other, and most exciting, above the east facade. Both are wonderful sculptural shapes on the theme of the Arms of the City of Glasgow, with stylised birds on the top. They were probably intended as weather vanes as one originally had horizontal cross-pieces fixed below the cage structure. They are of course very much larger than they appear from the ground; that on the north turret is 224cm x 48.4cm (96" x 23") and the one on the east tower 224cm x 76cm (96" x 30"). The amazing thing is that they were designed and made in 1899 yet they would cause quite a stir if made today.

Ironwork inside the building is no less innovative than that on the exterior. Ascending the main staircase to first floor level it is possible to look down the stairwell on to a delightful gilt wrought iron bracket, whose purpose is to suspend a cast iron bell. The design again is based on the Arms of the City of Glasgow and the story of a fish who retrieved a ring belonging to a princess. The concentric circles represent the tree, the clappers the bell, and the horizontal bars below the fish. The bracket was badly damaged and both the bird and the fish are modern reconstructions. A photograph has now been found of the original bird, and it is hoped to restore the bracket to its original form.

The east and west staircases contain much simple ironwork which, although obviously designed in a very practical way, with safety in mind, is enlivened by unexpected details.

There are fairly massive, strongly designed, curved balconies of plain upright bars; these are strengthened by a broad, flat section, bar in the centre curving upwards from below the floor to the top rail.

The staircases, bare and uncluttered, have a medieval austerity which is enhanced by lattice screens reminiscent of a portcullis or the traditional Scottish Yett. These were defensive iron doors of stout horizontal and vertical bars passing through each other alternately. In this version the horizontals are checked, to house the verticals, and rivetted. The ends of the horizontal bars take varied and unusual forms, either of a flat curve or, on

the east stair, of angular flat scrolls. Where vertical bars descend above an opening, two pairs of rails are extended beyond the bottom horizontal and broadened to form decorative flattened curves.

Even in the basement Mackintosh still has surprises in store. In one of the sculpture studios the ends of T girders supporting elaborate roof timbers have been split, by sets and strikers, and forged into various sculptural forms; each "sculpture" about 35 cm in length. The difficulty of the procedure, is said to have caused a strike among the blacksmiths; although one suspects that it was more because they

thought it a senseless waste of time, because they could not see the point of such designs. Today it is not unusual to use rolled steel sections to cut and forge into sculptures, but once again Charles Rennie Mackintosh was ahead of us.

Throughout the building there are metal light fittings designed by Mackintosh. Some are original to the building and others have come from Windyhill House, Kilmacolm, commissioned by William Davidson, which Mackintosh completed in 1901. In the board room there are wrought iron circular chandeliers with hanging shades of hammered copper. Perhaps the most

inpressive of the designs is the great fall of lights in the library. There are thirteen hanging lamps of pierced copper and coloured glass. Each lamp shade is an angular cubist shape like some fantastic skycraper.

Mackintosh seems always to have been aware of ironwork and sometimes, when out sketching, included drawings of rough homely pieces, like bolts or fastenings among his more finished studies of vernacular architecture. Although at first he was primarily an artist and draughtsman, it sometimes seems as if even in his watercolours there are the lines of ironwork trying to escape. He and his wife were past

Above: The central fall of lights in the library.

Opposite page above: Screen on the west façade.

Below: One of the shaped girder ends.

masters at simplification, they reduced everything to the elemental, and in so doing created interiors that were quite amazingly beautiful in their elegant simplicity—entirely at variance with the usual cluttered interiors of their time.

When designing buildings he seems never to have forgotten ironwork details but always to a purpose and a use. Even if there is nothing more remarkable, the drawings almost always show weather vanes, lamp standards and gates. Even at Queen's Cross Church (now the Charles Rennie Mackintosh Society Centre) I found a well designed side gate of iron. His house interiors include metal lamp fittings and elegant steel fireplaces, in a variety of shapes. Sometimes the hearth furniture forms part of the fireplace design, as in the drawing room at Hill House, Helensburgh, where the bright steel fire irons are suspended from hooks, in a mosaic surround, on each side of the fireplace. More often the fireplace is a simple, but graceful, design of plain straight low bars, set on a flat or curved plane, across the front of the opening. There are also two flat discs, either circular, triangular, or square set to the side front of the bars, which I take to be kettle stands (or is there toast for tea!)—as always Mackintosh was a designer for people and practicality. One of these fireplaces is in the hall at Hill House, and another version of the type can be seen in the dining room of "The Mackintosh House" (recreated as part of the Hunterian Art Gallery) where it is flanked with painted box-like metal finials rising to the ceiling cornice.

A larger fireplace, beautifully proportioned, with a flat steel front can be seen in the Studio/Library part of the combined Studio and Drawing Room in "The Mackintosh House". The lower part of two broad flat verticals cross two narrower, closer spaced, horizontals which hold the low bars of the fire front. The lower end of the verticals support two square stands pierced with nine square holes a decorative device much used by Mackintosh. Where the top of the verticals meet the wall there are three similar holes, but only the centre one takes the fixing, the other two being decorative.

Hill House, Helensburgh, well north of Glasgow, is a wonderful building overlooking the Firth of Clyde. It was commissioned by Walter W. Blackie, the publisher, in 1902 and after the Glasgow School of Art is Mackintosh's most famous work. Throughout

Above and below: Gates and lamp post at Hill House.

The commitment to Miss Cranston's tea rooms was on-going over many years. The interiors that Mackintosh designed for them epitomised his belief in "the total work of art". He designed not only the decor but the furniture and even the cutlery. In 1904 the best known of them "The Willow Tea Rooms" in Sauchiehall Street was opened. There is an interesting band of ironwork across the front facade with two ironwork rondels on a background of square lattice. The circular motifs are outlined with sparse leaves and contain a similar bird, or little beast head, to that used in 1899 on the railing disc at the Glasgow School of Art. Above, on each side, are brackets for name-signs which again incorporate the bird and bell theme of the Glasgow legend.

Far left: Detail of the gates to Hill House.

The ground floor of the building is now a jeweller's shop. On entering one finds an ironwork screen on the left with hanging bells of green glass. In the rectangular openings in the border at the top there were once central lines of round glass balls, seven in each.

Another screen high up at the end of the shop, with a band of pierced squares along the base, probably once had glass pieces on the hooks. Elongated open ironwork shapes are balanced by pairs of lozenge-shaped stained glass. Mackintosh has again used the device of joining pairs of rods at the base as

Below left: Ironwork above shop window; formerley the Willow Tea Rooms.

the house there are lamps, fireplaces and furniture fittings of interest; the window catches are simple traditional shapes.

The entrance gates at Hill House are typical Mackintosh ironwork using straight plain bars, piercings and disc finials. What we have not seen in his work before are the looped elements at the top of the decorative forms composed of closer set rails; one should perhaps also notice that he seems to have been aware of the possibilities of changing the design from different angles of vision: the form of the flat ovoid pieces at the sides of the close set rails not being readily apparent from the front but clearly visible when the gates are open. Near the gates, at the side of the road, is a cast iron "Mackintosh" design lamp standard.

In 1988-9 an architectural student discovered drawings of lamps, seven different designs, by Charles Rennie Mackintosh, in Strathclyde University. They had been in the collection of Sir Patrick Geddes. One of these designs has been fabricated by Adam Booth and placed outside the Glasgow School of Art by Scott Street. (Information from Adam Booth)

on the Glasgow School of Art staircase. Upstairs in the tea-rooms he uses a wealth of decorative stained glass. There is such similarity between his designs for ironwork and glass in leaded lights it is sometimes difficult to distinguish between them.

Charles Rennie Mackintosh was an incredibly creative artist, far ahead of his time in everything he touched. His buildings were the first to be truly modern in concept and his furniture was unlike anything that had ever been designed before; while his interiors included built-in furniture and all white rooms. In ironwork he anticipated so many ideas which we regard today as forward looking and modern: simplification, stylisation, abstraction, forging of steel sections, integration of glass with iron and forms altering in shape from different viewpoints—it has taken us more than half a century to catch up with him.

What little recognition Mackintosh received was from abroad; and like many people who are in advance of their time he met with much antagonism and ridicule, especially in this country. By 1914 he was deeply depressed and the architectural practice was dissolved. He and his wife left Glasgow for Suffolk where he started work on a series of flower studies which were to be published by a German press, but this project ended with the advent of the first World War. They later moved to Chelsea and in the 1920s spent some years in France where he worked on watercolour painting. He died in London in 1928.

In recent years the pendulum has swung full arc and Charles Rennie Mackintosh is now as much revered as he was once reviled or ignored. The house where he and his wife lived from 1906-14, which was later demolished, has been recreated as part of the Hunterian Art Gallery; and there is now a project in hand to actually build "A House for an Art Lover" designed in 1901 and never built.

It was a tragedy for the 20th century that Mackintosh's designs in iron did not spark off a resurgence of creative ironwork in this country, as it might so easily have done, and that we had to wait another eighty years before the Modern Renaissance began.

Left: and left below: Grilles in the former Willow Tea Rooms.

Left: Sign outside the former Willow Tea Rooms, the ironwork designed by Mackintosh.

The Glasgow School of Art, Renfrew Street, is still very much a working school, but inside the main entrance is a small shop, and there are times when the public are allowed to take a short guided tour of the building.

"The Mackintosh House" is built alongside, and as part of, the Hunterian Art Gallery, University of Glasgow, 82 Hillhead Street. Tel. 0141 330 5431.

The Charles Rennie Mackintosh Society has a centre at Queen's Cross Church, 870 Garscube Road, Glasgow. Tel. 0141 946 6600

Note 1. This jewel was illustrated in "Modern Jewelry" by Graham Hughes in 1963 Studio Vista Ltd.

Source Bibliography.

Anthony Jones *Charles Rennie Mackintosh* 1990 Studio Editions Ltd.

Charles Rennie Mackintosh Ironwork and Metalwork at the Glasgow School of Art 1968 & 1978 with an introduction by H. Jefferson Barnes Director of the Glasgow School of Art.

HOW IT ALL BEGAN

A NEW BEGINNING OF CREATIVE IRONWORK IN THIS COUNTRY.

If one can date the new beginning of creative ironwork in this country to any one time, I believe it was born at the International Conference on Forging Iron in 1980. It is to the great credit of The Crafts Council, whose then Chairman was Robert Goodden CBE RDI and Director Victor Margrie, that they sponsored and organised this conference. It was held at the Hereford Technical College, from July 22nd to 28th, and the arrangements were made by Caroline Pearce-Higgins who was then the Crafts Council's Education Officer.

The following report I wrote immediately after the conference as an addendum to Newsletter 10 of the Historical Metallurgy Society. I reprint it here feeling it has more immediacy than anything I could write today.

THE INTERNATIONAL CONFERENCE ON FORGING IRON Hereford July 1980.

The influence of the International Conference on Forging Iron, held at Hereford, is likely to be far reaching. Smiths were present from all over the world, France, Germany, Italy, Finland, Austria, Czechoslovakia, America, Canada, Australia, New Zealand and Japan, as well as from England, Ireland and Wales. Language difficulties there may have been, but at the forge all were as one. Delegates varied from smiths working alone in comparative isolation, to heads of large commercial firms. One might say that links were forged on all levels.

Days were filled from 9 a.m. to 10 p.m. and only a few of the many speakers can be here mentioned. The first day was given to the Americans; Jack Andrews of the Philadelphia College of Art spoke on Samuel Yellin, the founding father of American blacksmithing. His was a classic success story, a young apprentice immigrant smith from Galacia, coming in 1907 to the United States; later to become one of the most honoured citizens of Philadelphia employing, at the height of his success, some three hundred workers, two hundred of them smiths. Not only an artist at the forge he also had great organising ability. From the beginning works were completed on time, and he once wrote, "Whatever leaves my shop must satisfy my conscience." One of the most complete ironworking commissions ever undertaken in modern times, and worth fifteen hundred thousand dollars, was for the Federal Reserve Bank in 1917. It included making 155 lamps, strong rooms, and grilles, some of which were 300ft in length. During the last ten years of his life, unable to work at the forge, he drew constantly, and influenced by natural forms, began to develop a completely new design form to his ironwork.

We then turned to modern America with Albert Paley of Rochester. First a highly original goldsmith, of international renown, he was the first designer since the makers of Roman fibulae, to attempt to integrate the pinstem into the general design of brooches. Later he turned, as a self trained blacksmith, to monumental works in iron and steel. Major commissions include iron gates for the Smithsonian Institution in 1974, which were immediately followed by a fence of free flowing curved forms, between the old and new sections of Chattanooga Foundation for the Arts, Tennessee. Difficult to describe a design so fresh and new, though perhaps here were the swirling forms of water eddying into pools, just as one can sense the feel of flames in his eleven foot high candlesticks, which seem almost to gesture to each other. He is continually exploring the interrelationships between forms and the aesthetics of the iron. There were some who found Al Paley's work slightly disturbing, perhaps because it is so very much ironwork for our own time.

Far left below: Samuel Yellin, especially towards the end of his life, was influenced by natural forms.

Below: By Albert Paley ; one of two pairs of gates of steel, brass and bronze, commissioned by the State of New York for the Senate Chamber, Capitol Building, Albany, 1980.

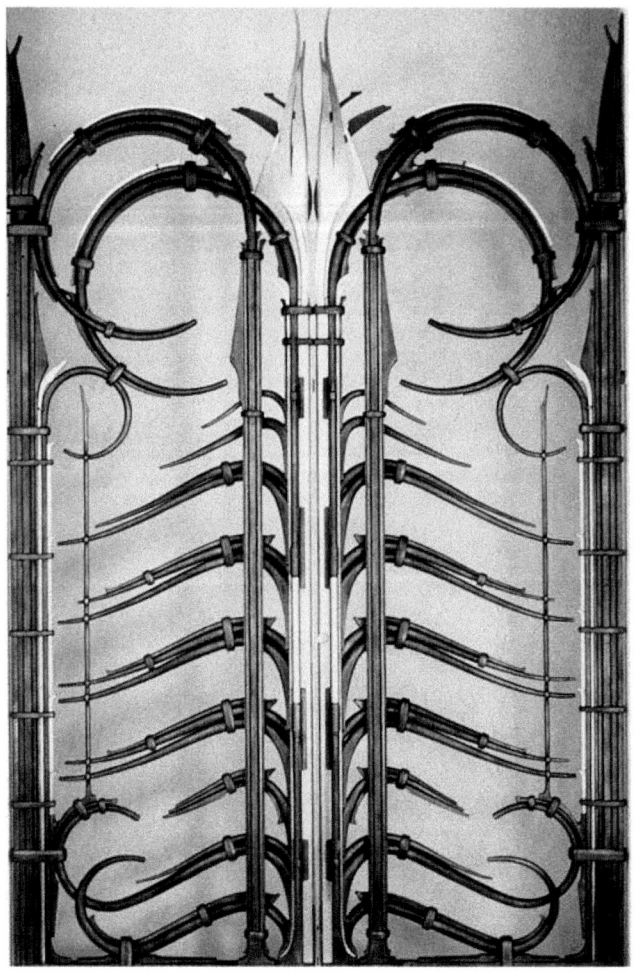

Paley Studios

Above: Albert Paley at the International Conference on Forging iron.

Below: Plant Stand 1989. Boston Museum of Fine Arts.

Above: Steel, brass and copper gates for the Smithsonian Institution. (The Renwick Gallery) 1974. Below: Detail of unusual scroll treatment.

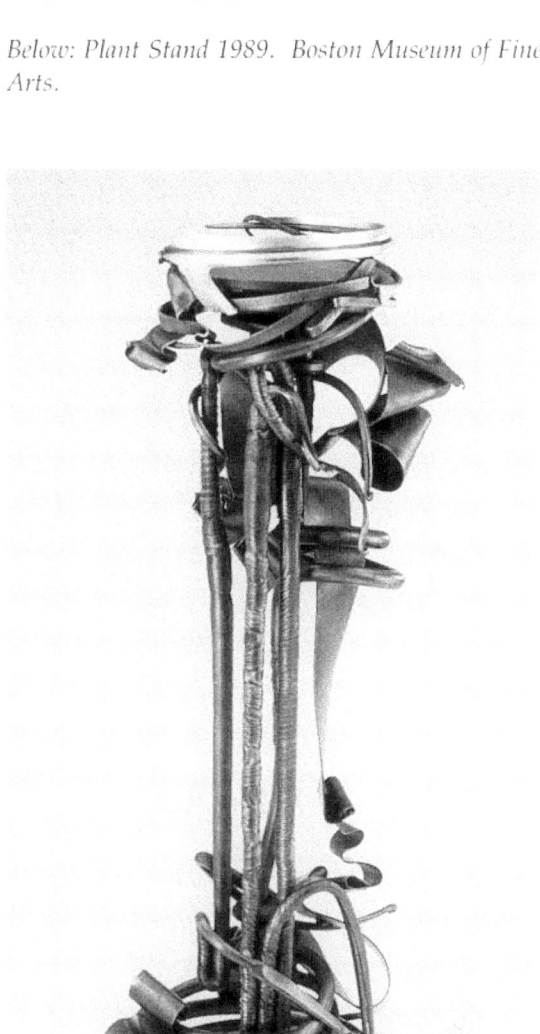

Paley Studios Ltd

Paley Studios Ltd.

25

Demonstrations in the afternoon, which were a daily feature, included Ivan Bailey of Savannah, Georgia, inlaying metals into forged iron. A talk on the Artist Blacksmiths Association of North America, rounded off a very enlightening day. It is clear that the Americans have made a virtue out of necessity; untrammelled by tradition, they are utilising every modern facility in tools and processes to produce work of thrusting vitality.

It was noticeable how each day produced an entirely different character, dependent on the various countries responsible for the lectures and demonstrations. The French, on the second day, emphasised fine craftsmanship from the past and spoke of the Compagnons du Devoir. This association runs a network of great houses all over France, where boys train in all the building trades including smithing. Another speaker Serge Marchal, after three years at the University of Grenoble, worked with Souriou for two years, before continuing his training with the compagnons for a further eight years, and he now has his own workshop near Nimes. This long and dedicated training was typical of so many smiths present at the conference. One of his most important works, which stays firmly in the mind, is a massive sculpture, reaching from floor to ceiling, up a stairwell, of the house of the Compagnons in Nimes. This great sculpture grows treelike, its seven stem bars, representing the seven virtues of the compagnons. It is not one but many sculptures, since it is seen from such a variety of angles. In places natural stones are set in the iron, and on an upper floor, two great hands

hold a world-like sphere; the hands of the compagnons explain their basic philosophy, the union of hand and spirit. Hovering above all, that symbolic spirit, a flowerlike form, but as Serge explains "rather more worried".

Serge Pascal, an expert in repoussé work, is currently restoring the great gate arches and screens at Nancy. This ironwork by Jean Lamour, originally took eight years to construct and was given by the exiled king of Poland to the King of France. Some idea of the scale of the work can be gained when we realise that the frame of each gateway weighs six tons; the hanging brackets are as tall as a man; and one of the single surmounting crowns contains as many as 500 rivets. We were able to watch Serge Pascal working at the craft of repoussé. He explained the processes which turned flat cut out leaf shapes into the familiar finely moulded acanthus foliage of 18th century work. It was all in the skill, working the iron cold, and hammering it into a hollow he had made in a piece of wood.

Below: The central part of "Creative Hands" in the Maison des Compagnons du Devoir, Nimes, by Serge Marchal. Height overall 11m. Forged steel and steel plate. 1976

Above left: The flowerlike form on the top floor.

Photographs Serge Marchal

opulent Siemens memorial, with the stark, grim, simplicity of a concentration camp memorial door; the latter an example of his interest in lettering forged into the plate.

Achim Kühn continues and extends the work his father began; using modern technology to observe the innermost structure of steel he seeks to express in his work the essential element of the material. He continues to experiment with new techniques, particularly using other metals in flashing or spraying to colour surfaces, with great effect. Especially beautiful the sculptural modern doors of steel and repousse copper plate, with deeply textured surface, like the rough bark of a tree, set in Gothic arches at Marienkirche, Berlin, in 1970. An unusually successful blending of old and new architectural features.

Far left: Achim Kühn at the International Conference on Forging Iron.

Below left: Panel showing the strength of Fritz Kühn's design in lettering from the ornate to extreme simplicity.

Below: Experimental forms by Fritz Kühn.

Fritz Kühn

On Friday, the German day, we found ourselves in the presence of long tradition and efficient modern expertise. But it was really the day of the Kühns; Achim Kühn showed and explained much of his own and his father's work. Fritz Kühn, who grew up between the wars, sought to re-establish the identity of German ironwork, after its decline in the 1870s. In so doing he was in the forefront of the modern movement and did much to motivate the resurgence of the 20th century ironwork which is still spreading across Europe and America. We saw his sensitivity to time, in the use of rusted scrap iron to make a cross in 1961, when materials were scarce and life hard. Equally sensitive his awareness of place when we contrast his

Fritz Kühn

Fritz Kühn

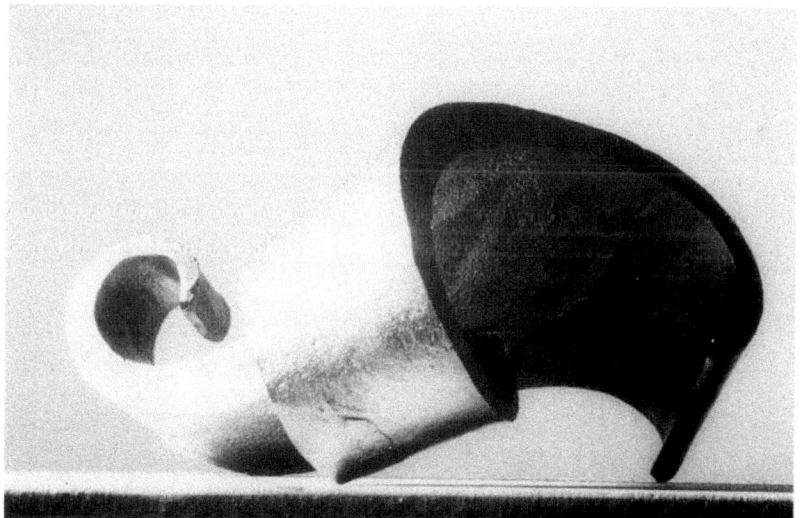

Achim Kühn

Above left: Fritz Kühn was renowned for his lettering in iron. Detail of the entrance door to the Berlin City Library made in 1965. Forged steel, enamelled copper, and gold leaf. (See also illustration on previous page.)
Below left: Screen "Swinging Steel" by Achim Kühn 1976/77. The curved pieces swing when set in motion; one of his lines of experimentation has been in moving sculptures. Another has been colouring iron with other metals, as in this door of textured steel, above. Below: Doors to a theatre in Karl-Marx-Stadt, Berlin, made by Achim Kühn in 1974.

Achim Kühn

The conference on this day had been thrown open to architects, but the response was negligible. Comments during a general discussion on Ironwork in Architecture further showed up the gulf which seems to exist between architects and smiths in this country. By tradition, at least since the 19th century the architect expects to design any ironwork to appear on his buildings; but since he usually has little understanding of the intrinsic life and fluidity of the metal, he has no incentive to make use of it. The fact that we still regard the ironwork, designed by Charles Rennie Mackintosh, for the Glasgow School of Art, seventy years ago, as modern, speaks volumes for the stagnation of architectural ironwork in the years between. On the other hand we have a new generation of smiths perfectly able to design their own works and desperately needing the opportunities that an architectural setting affords. The need for communication is obvious but how is this dialogue to be instigated?

Tranquillity returned in the evening when the Czech group showed a colour film, made by Vaclav Jaros, which received a standing ovation. It showed Alfred Habermann at work, the chief restorer of ironwork in Czechoslovakia, he appears as the very epitome of Vulcan. He has spent time with most of the well-known blacksmiths on the continent, and at one point in the film was shown at work with Professor Antonio Benetton of Italy who lectured on the following day. Professor Benetton founded the Accademia Internationale del Ferro in

Alfred Habermann

Above : A more recent work by Alfred Habermann incorporating blue glass.

Below: A room divider here becomes a sculptural component of architecture, forms build-up in richly articulated verticals. Hotel Medlov 1965.

Below left: House number.

Alfred Habermann

Alfred Habermann

Veneto in 1967 devoted to experimental three dimensional work in iron. Among the slides shown of historical works, it was interesting to see a medieval wrought iron chair dated to 1000 A.D. and an iron bed circa 1500. Professor Benetton considered decadence had set in by 1600.

Incredible inventiveness is shown in the iron sculptures of both Prof. Benetton and his son Simon Benetton. Many of these are extremely large, one in the centre of Altura, measuring some 5 metres by 6 metres. Yet so finely balanced and so carefully calculated are these enormous sculptures, that their great spines, often reminiscent of palm fronds, sway in every wind; anchored mobiles moving as trees move or the spread quills of bird wings soaring.

The last day of the Conference was spent with the Ironbridge Gorge Museum Trust—odd on reflection, there was a time when it was said "One day people will come from all over the world to see our iron bridge"—on Sunday July 27th they came, and the bridge was so shrouded in scaffolding and plastic sheets as to be quite invisible!

It was the day of forged iron in the Dale and we passed blast furnaces with scarcely a glance. The greatest focus of interest was the exhibition of modern ironwork in the Coach House Gallery by a small selection of smiths working in this country. Outstanding the work of Jim Horrobin from Carhampton, strong sculptural pieces, full of sound smithing, especially his set of hanging irons in forged, punched and firewelded steel, a combination of the functional and intrinsically decorative all too rare. There was the

Above top: Antonio and Simon Benetton during the visit to Ironbridge.

Above: Detail of the sculpture they made at Hereford in 1979.

Left: It was a time of camaraderie and goodwill; of forging links for the future. Left foreground, Mack Beal, (behind him) Jim Horrobin, (standing) Dick Quinnell. Right foreground, Richard Overs, (behind him) Vaclav Jaros and Eric Moebius. (At the far end of the table) Al Paley.

exploratory work of Giuseppe Lund; while Lindsay Miller in his graceful panel, with a dash of Art Nouveau, had translated the traditional floral piece into a modern idiom. Overheard comment by a sculptor "Now I feel I can happily go away and leave you fellows to get on with the job."

In the evening Stuart Smith and Friends of the Museum laid on a magnificent cold collation in Mawes Tile Works, which was much appreciated. As one American said "It was a wonderful experience to sit there eating strawberries and cream while listening to a Silver Band." As the evening wore on there was a marked inclination to participate, both with movement and sound. There was an amazing ingenuity in the creation of percussion instruments, energy was unbounded, and the Jackfield Silver Band exceptionally tolerant, if slightly surprised; they could hardly have met with an audience like this before.

In the semi-dereliction of Mawes Tile Works one fancied the revelries sufficiently isolated to cause no disturbance. Later, crossing the river, beneath a great plate of a harvest moon, it became apparent that half the Gorge must have heard the noise; it had surely been sufficient to wake the long dead spirits of all Coalbrookdale forgemen—doubtless their descendants will remember the night the smiths came to Ironbridge.

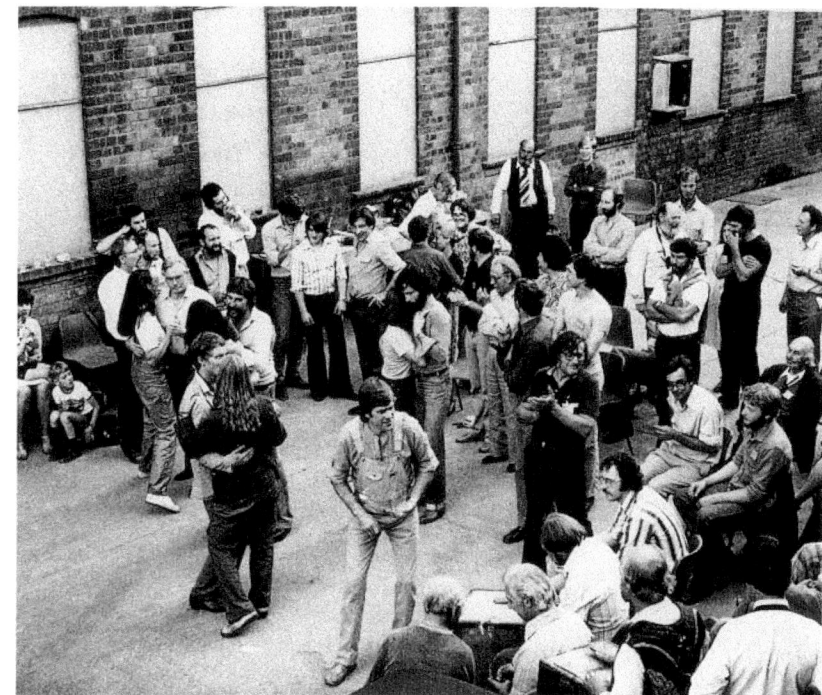

Michael Mallesson

It all entered our minds like a thunderbolt.
Up to that conference I had been interested in historic ironwork but modern work meant nothing to me, mainly because I had never seen any really good examples. In the years since then I have heard many smiths themselves say much the same thing. A few had taken tentative steps towards smithing in modern design, but most were working in the traditional way with patterns derived from

Above: The party at the Tile Works on the last night of the Conference.

Below left: Lunchtime picnic at Blist's Hill during the visit to Ironbridge.

the past. Some were perhaps already wondering, "Where next?", and feeling themselves dissatisfied with the craft where it then stood.

Already a few British smiths had heard the Siren voices. A touring exhibition "Forged Iron", organised by Ceolfrith Gallery, Sunderland Arts Centre, has already been mentioned in the report above. Some of the participants were jewellers but others were smiths. Lindsay Miller from Cumbria professed allegiance to traditional 18th century work but showed a floral firescreen of freely flowing lines which had grown out of his admiration for the work of Victor Horta.

Stuart Hill from Suffolk had not been restrained by a traditional training, and had already won the Organiser's Award at the 1980 International Exhibition at Lindau with his *Metamorphosis* table which was later bought by the Victoria and Albert Museum for their permanent collection. The flat top of the table almost undulates with uneven squares and from the centre, where it seems to ripple into life, rise the beginnings of frog shapes. These radiate out to the four corners by which time they have become four perfect small hand forged frogs. His fertile mind was already experimenting, at his Claydon Forge, with an almost bewildering range of possibilities in the working of iron. Before 1980 was out he would hold, at the Minories Gallery in Colchester, the first one man exhibition of contemporary ironwork to be held in this country.

The "Forged Iron" exhibition also showed some chunky experimental pieces by Giuseppe Lund. He had at first been doing traditional ironwork and feeling very restrained because the ideas he wanted to put into practice *broke the rules*. After travelling and working in Germany, amongst the smiths there, he no longer felt restricted. He is on record as saying "I saw shapes I recognised as my own half-formed ideas which I had pushed aside because they didn't seem to fit with the rules of the game".[1] From then on the restraint disappeared.

Jim Horrobin had been apprenticed to his father, in Somerset, and then carried on in partnership with him as traditional smiths. After his father retired he felt his isolation, in a village smithy, was preventing any broadening of his outlook and his work was becoming more and more mechanical. He had

come to a parting of the ways and was no longer sure he even wanted to go on being a blacksmith. He took a year off and spent much of his time wave-surfing in Woolacombe Bay. At the end of that time he knew he still had personal commitment to smithing, but this time it would be on his own terms, working the iron to his own designs. "The work I had done before that really belonged to other people. It was all based on 18th century ironwork. Now I have entered into a spirit of blacksmithing using my own mind."[2] From then on he offered his clients his own ideas and was surprised how often they liked them. One of his first modern works, shown in the "Forging Iron" exhibition, was *Hanging Irons*, inspired by the humble functional skewer holders to be found in early kitchens; but in his hands turned into an extraordinarily beautiful and decorative modern piece. It uses the finest traditional skills to create new forms and is a magnificent 1m long.

One other small exhibition was mounted during the conference "The Britsh Grate" in which ten British blacksmiths each created a modern firegrate. They were Ivan Smith, Stuart Hill, Tony Wootton, Tony West, Jim Horrobin, Denys Mitchell, Giuseppe Lund, Alan Evans, Alan Gwylt and Tony Robinson.

So that is about where modern British Blacksmithing stood at that time—suddenly these smiths, and many, many more, were brought together in one place with all the best modern smiths in the world. It was a revelation. Our eyes were opened to new techniques; to the cutting of steel plate with an oxyacetylene flame and opening it out into designs, as demonstrated by the Benettons; to the American attitude where smiths would use any modern aids, power hammers and any form of welding, to achieve their required ends. Above all we saw the old traditional ways of first class forging at the anvil but creating designs that were very much of the 20th century. I know that Hector Cole, Mike Roberts, Peter Parkinson, Alan Dawson, Alan Evans, and David Petersen were all inspired by what they saw, and there must have been many other smiths who took away a lasting impression that worked into their lives. I have never known any conference like it, the very air was electric—it is no exaggeration to say that it changed our lives. Everyone who was present felt that we had taken part in something momentous.

Perhaps there were two reasons why the conference was such a great success. First the word was coming from blacksmiths themselves, the inspiration was at the grass roots, not being imposed remotely by architects or designers; secondly, the time was right, the British smiths were ready for it.

Now nothing just happens one has to look quite closely to see how the forming of the British Artist Blacksmiths Association and the arranging of the International Forging Iron Conference came about. To unlock personal doors and look into minds, where every germ of an idea first takes place.

In 1975 Richard Quinnell, of the Rowhurst Forge, Leatherhead, was on the point of giving up the family business which had been started by his father, who had died when Dick was still a boy, and for ten years the firm had been run by his mother. He was feeling disillusioned and very isolated "I honestly thought we were the last firm of blacksmiths in the world."[3] He then received an unexpected invitation to a conference in the United States organised by the Artist Blacksmith Association of North America. He was amazed to find that ironwork there was thriving and was both experimental and creative.

This had not been the case a few years earlier; in fact blacksmithing in America had seemed on the point of dying out, just as it was in England. Alex Bealer had an old friend, who was half Cherokee Indian, and together they set out to find some of the pioneering breed of rural blacksmiths—of whom Judd Nelson was one. This led to Louis Brent Kington, a professor in the School of Art, Southern Illinois University, setting up a meeting with these blacksmiths and his students. As a result of these tentative beginnings the Artist Blacksmith Association of North America was formed, and in 1971-2 started having conferences. In 1974 they brought over Fritz Ulrich, from Germany, as demonstrator. So it was that in 1975 Dick Quinnell was invited to the ABANA Conference at Greenville, North Carolina to demonstrate; though he has no idea how he came to be chosen. By that time ABANA had 300 members and 100 of them were present. He knew no one, but soon met many people that he knows to this day. He laboured over a demonstration of making water leaves, which did not seem to go down very well; but later showed slides of work and that was well received.

The following year he returned to America, accompanied by his wife Jinny, to the ABANA Conference at Carbondale, Illinois. It seems to have been a watershed both for him and for Americans. He found it a tremendous experience, there were 500 members present, and there was a great exchange of ideas and techniques of smithing. This was the year that Albert Paley became well known and first made an important impact.

The outcome of this visit was that Dick Quinnell was inspired to see if it might be possible to form such an association in this country, and he and Jinny discussed it on the way back in the 'plane. Jinny was enthusiastic "...we have to do something like this". Throughout the early years she was well regarded and much loved by everyone associated with the craft, both in England and America. From then on, as Dick says, "...it was all waiting to happen".

The British Grate Exhibition 1980.

1. Tony Wootton

2. Jim Horrobin

3. Stuart Hill

4. Giuseppe Lund

5. Tony West

6. Tony Robinson

7. Ivan Smith

8. Alan Evans

9. Denys Mitchell

10. Alan Gwylt

Photographs by Chris Fairclough

    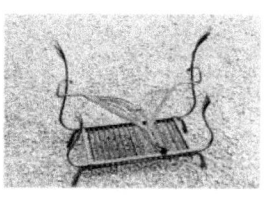

1   2   3   4   5

6   7   8   9   10

Already Ivan Smith, a blacksmith of great integrity and a passionate advocate of his craft, had also felt the need for change. He worked near Droitwich and was a teacher and lecturer of long experience. He was also closely in touch with adult students from courses on blacksmithing he was running at West Dean, Sussex. He recognised the need for a fundamental change in blacksmithing if it was to survive into the modern world. In 1977 he "... put the blacksmiths' dilemma to the Crafts Council in eloquent terms, stressing the enormous potential of this difficult craft, and the need for a new imaginative breakthrough." [4] This cry for help resulted in a small exploratory committee being set up composed of Ivan Smith, Richard Quinnell, Claude Blair (Keeper of the Metalwork at the V & A) Neil Cossons (Director of the Ironbridge Gorge Museum) Victor Margrie (Director of the Crafts Council) and Caroline Pearce-Higgins as Secretary.

Mention must here be made of CoSIRA, the Council for Small Industries in Rural Areas, which had formerly been the Rural Industries Bureau, but is now the Rural Development Commission. It had been formed in 1921 to assist the economy in rural areas and to encourage employment in the countryside. Its brief was to be more economic than artistic. Rural blacksmiths who were farriers and agricultural smiths were encouraged, especially during the depression, to augment their income by making saleable objects of wrought iron. Mr A.W.Elwood was the first wrought iron officer. He was Prime Warden of the Worshipful Company of Blacksmiths in 1924.

With the outbreak of World War II, and the need to grow more food, blacksmiths were then encouraged to concentrate on agricultural machinery repairwork. Engineers to the number of about eighteen were taken on to the staff and gas and arc welding, lathework, and bench fitting were the order of the day. Smithing became strictly practical, keeping tractors working and repairing agricultural machinery in the field. It was not really until after the end of the war that wrought ironwork was again encouraged. William E.C. Morgan became the senior craft officer; he was a fine draughtsman and the subject matter of designs was largely in his hands. The Book of Drawings or Design Catalogue as it was then called was inherited from pre-war days, but was much in use and frequently up-dated.

For many years the principal instructor was Augustino Zanni who had joined R.I.B. in 1937. He had been apprenticed as a wrought ironsmith at William Bainbridge Reynolds Ltd, Manor House Metalworks in Clapham Old Town. He broke his apprenticeship during World War I to volunteer for the Royal Flying Corps, but returned to Reynolds after the war; completing his improvers time under Fred Landon, the forge-shop foreman. He later worked for many well known firms including that of Starkie Gardner.

He was joined in 1949 by C.A.H. ("Tommy") Tucker. He had been apprenticed as an ornamental and general smith to George Edwards, Home Orchard Ironworks, in Dartford. After service in the Royal Navy as an engine room artificer during World War II

Above and opposite on next page: A CoSIRA course in action at Cannington, Somerset, under the direction of Frank Day.

he was discharged from the RN with an injured right leg. He set up his own business at Bexley Heath in 1946, where he still has an operating forge and workshop. However he liked the idea of working with A.Zanni, whose work he greatly admired, and thus began a partnership that lasted for fifteen years working for CoSIRA. "Tommy" continued for another fifteen years as Senior Forgework Officer. Together they trained other officers and organised both day and week-long courses in schools and colleges. An important part of this work was with blacksmiths, day release or short courses, and instruction on a one to one basis, training smiths in rural localities. Mr C.A.H. Tucker tells me that they gave considerable attention to contemporary design and on many occasions gave practical help with contemporary commissions. However, most of the training had of necessity to concentrate on scroll and leaf techniques suitable for restoration work, which was what the smiths wanted. Marketing contemporary design was at that time almost impossible and CoSIRA resources did not provide for much promotional activity for innovative modern design and it was this that led to the creation of The Crafts Council.

By the time of the International Forging Iron Conference CoSIRA had about six Technical Smithing Officers doing great work in teaching smiths and maintaining a high standard of workmanship. However, the Council neither expected nor encouraged smiths to design their own work. For a few shillings each smiths could purchase scale prints or working drawings from CoSIRA. These were mainly based on designs of the past, though by the sixties a few grilles seem to have been inspired by the work of Fritz Kühn. William Norris, who at that time had a workshop in Richmond Surrey, was a smith who brought the work of Kühn and other German smiths to their notice. In that the Council did not encourage creative design and saw no reason to put smiths in touch with each other, some have said that they were not so much encouraging blacksmithing as presiding over its decline. However it is clear to see, from the testimony of smiths in Part 2 of this book, how great a part CoSIRA played in their basic training and in many cases those who taught them are remembered with much respect and affection. Also co-operating Guilds were formed, notably the Guild of Wrought Iron Craftsmen of Wessex. Undoubtedly CoSIRA kept alive the

traditional techniques of wrought ironwork at a time when it might otherwise have almost died out and this it continues to do today. [5]

One of the technical officers 'Tommy' Tucker, gave Dick Quinnell the names of fifty smiths, and in 1978 Dick invited them to meet one week-end at his forge. Thirty turned up and by the end of the week-end they had formed themselves into the British Blacksmiths Association.

After this Smiths were no longer alone—as Alan Dawson has written:

"I was working in isolation in a collapsing cow shed thinking that I was the only decorative blacksmith in the world." [6] And as Jim Horrobin has set on record:

"It allowed people to talk about techniques, instead of having a diminishing vocabulary there was an explosion of ideas." [7]

Stuart Hill was the first editor of the British Blacksmith, which he felt to be of **"central importance to the revival of communications between blacksmiths in Britain."**

In the same year, with the help of a Churchill Fellowship and the British Council, Dick Quinnell and Caroline Pearce-Higgins visited thirty forges in Germany, Austria, Switzerland, Italy and France—a journey that was to bear fruit in the 1980 International Forging Iron Conference. The voice of Giuseppe Lund was also heard in these years encouraging action by the Crafts Council.

In 1979 the Crafts Council organised a small scale International Experimental Workshop at Hereford, where there were demonstrations by Simon Benetton of Italy, Eric Moebius U.S.A, Serge Marchal France, and Herman Gradinger Germany. Although there were only 25 people there it has been clear in talking to some of them how much they were affected by what they saw. BABA was also active, the association took a stand at the Royal Show, with thirty members in attendance; and later in the same year held their first conference at Ron Carter's Trapp Forge near Burnley, Lancs. It was on that occasion that Dick Quinell, transporting a power hammer to the forge, jack-knifed his car on the M1.

From now on there was development on two fronts, encouraged by both the Craft Council and BABA. The former with its organisation of the great Forging Iron Conference in 1980 meant that from then onwards British smiths were not only talking to each other but to smiths all over the world. Meanwhile BABA conferences were becoming more ambitious all the time. The second was held at Colin Day's forge at Stotfield, near Hitchin. In 1981 it included an exhibition, and was held at Sheffield Polytechnic, with Herman Gradinger as the principal demonstrator.

The same year Alfred Habermann and Vaclav Jaros from Czechoslovakia visited Wales for the month of October. They travelled the length and breadth of the Principality and demonstrated to schoolchildren, students, blacksmiths and the general public. They visited Colleges of Art at Wrexham, Cardiff and Hereford, and gave important demonstrations at the Welsh Arts Council Conference, on "Developing Ideas in Iron", at Dyfed College of Art where they also made a gate for the County Museum at Abergwili.

The whole movement continued to gain momentum, and 1982 was an important year—a lot was going on. Three limited design competitions for major commissions gave rise to gates for the Treasury of St. Paul's Cathedral by Alan Evans and gates to the Ironwork Gallery at the Victoria and Albert Museum by Jim Horrobin. These were two very fine modern works which few people could have forseen coming from British forges two years previously. The third work was to be made by Anthony Robinson, two pairs of gates for the Great Hall at Winchester,

Michael Mallesson

commissioned by Hampshire County Council as a gift to commemorate the wedding of the Prince and Princess of Wales. In fact Prince Charles was being well looked after; the town of Tetbury presented him with gates for his country home at Highgrove made by Hector Cole.

Dick and Jinny Quinnell opened the Fire and Iron Gallery, alongside the Rowhurst Forge, at Leatherhead. This was the first gallery in the country to be devoted entirely to exhibitions of ironwork where pieces could be seen and purchased by the general public.

In May a group of about a dozen british blacksmiths attended the conference of the Artist Blacksmith Association of North America at Ripley in West Virginia. Achim Kühn, and his wife Helgard, from what was then East Germany, were also able to join the group; and on arrival we were delighted to find Alfred Habermann had managed to obtain permission to make the trip from Czechoslovakia.

Most importantly that year there were two exhibitions; one was a travelling one called "Six British Blacksmiths", mounted by the Minories Colchester in association with the British Crafts Centre, and featuring the work of Alan Evans, Stuart Hill, James Horrobin, Ian Lamb, Peter Parkinson and Anthony Robinson. It showed first at the Fire and Iron Gallery. The other, a major exhibition, ran from May 12th to July 10th at the Victoria and Albert Museum. It was called "Towards a

Above: At Dulles Airport. Left to right, the author, Jim Horrobin, Eaman Kenward, Ian Lamb, Howard Robbins, John Dittmeier, Dick Quinnell, Dorothy Bosomworth, Helgard Kühn, Fay le çompte, Achim Kühn.

New Iron Age", and was the first international display of wrought ironwork to be seen in the country. At that time Sir Roy Strong was Director of the Museum and Claude Blair the keeper of the Department of Metalwork, assisted by Marion Cambell. It came about partly because Giuseppe Lund designed ironwork for an 11th c church in Godalming, which was seen by Claude Blair. Lund asked why there were no examples of modern work in the V & A galleries and showed him work by German smiths. This led to interest and the suggestion of an exhibition. Giuseppe Lund helped Paul Williams, the designer of the exhibition, with the setting up and organisation.

The influence of this exhibition must have been considerable. David Lyle, a partner in Whitfield Partners, London, was just one of the architects moved by it to take the plunge and commission artist blacksmiths for architectural ironwork.

"We had reached the conclusion that the design of metalwork in prominent positions—like fences, screens, gates, railings, grilles and the like—needed to be treated more seriously. Components of a building such as these, which are actually touched by people, and viewed from a very close range, needed to have life and interest on the tactile scale. It was not sufficient always to treat such things simply as minor elements in the general large scale composition of the building. Architects' own designs for such components tended to be neat, orderly, dull and mechanical: attempts to avoid the dullness were often either brutally out-of-scale or feebly extravagant. We concluded that the answer to the problem might be to employ a person who could apply artistic judgement not only to the overall design of the object but also to the execution of all its parts; this is, an artist-craftsman."

Naturally there were a certain amount of initial apprehensions ". . . the prospect of possibly heated arguments with muscular smiths, of determined artistic convictions at odds with our own, was a little daunting. And the cost—what about that? Would they be too expensive when compared with the routine metalwork contractors?" He found that in most cases the cost difference was insignificant while ". . . their knowledge of their materials opened up possibilities which had not occurred to us. They were able to make pleasing details in ways which we could

not have envisaged; and their designs were eminently practical, to a degree which rather shamed us, as supposed construction experts. In short, we learnt a great deal from them and envied the flexibility which makes such collaborations not only possible but a pleasure." [8]

In September 1987 BABA launched their own exhibition called "The New Iron Age" at The Building Centre which included a magnificent *light wall* of 95 large back-lit colour transparencies, which enabled the viewing of larger commissions than could be accommodated in the exhibition. This was opened by architect Edward Cullinan CBE who said:

"We have passed that period of modern architecture that liked only mass-production, smooth detailing and repetition, and we are re-discovering an earlier more profound idea of modern architecture that would craft buildings carefully to human needs and particular situations. An expressive architecture, desperately in need of artist craftsmen: it will be a much better future and it will especially need the work of smiths." [9]

So it all came about. We were firmly on our way—into the New Iron Age.

For the next three years I sent reports on the exhibitions held at BABA conferences to "The Anvils Ring", the Journal of ABANA; Having made good friends in America I thought they might like to know how we were going on in England. Since to write about these very early exhibitions today would be to write with hindsight; and feeling that they may be of interest in that they introduced, often for the first time, names that would later become very well known, I therefore reprint the following extracts in their original form.

Notes and Sources

1. Lesley Adamson *The Guardian* 19.7.80
2. Ibid.
3. *Richard Quinnell* article by Paul Tozer.
4. Caroline Pearce-Higgins *Forged Ironwork Today* in the catalogue of *Towards a New Iron Age*.
5. I am most grateful to Mr C.H.A.Tucker FWCB LWCB for providing information about CoSIRA.
6. *British Blacksmith* number 53.
7. Redfield Lecture.
8. David Lyle *British Blacksmith* number 45.
9. Edward Cullinan CBE *British Blacksmith 46*.

BRITISH ARTIST BLACKSMITH EXHIBITION 1982

The British Artist Blacksmith Association Conference was held in early September at the West Surrey College of Art, Farnham. The exhibition of work by members was set up by Mike Roberts; the entirely white backgrounds he provided, showing the work to the greatest possible advantage.

Most of the pieces were on a fairly large scale with plenty of breadth and vigour. The first work to meet the eye, on entering the exhibition hall, stood immediately beneath the association name board, and was a massive candle holder by 'Tommy' Tucker from Bexleyheath, Kent; no conference would be complete without his presence. It was noticeable how many older smiths, who have spent their lives with traditional styles, have opened their minds to modern work, and are turning their fine craftsmanship to experimenting with new forms.

Alan Dawson, a blacksmith of the modern school, from Cockermouth, Cumbria, exhibited a 3ft (900mm) tall lamp in the form of two flowers—a piece of quite exceptional beauty. It had been forged from wrought iron with mild steel for the tendrils; the electric flex cunningly housed in fine steel tube (normally used as petrol pipe for cars) which, after annealing was twisted around the stem giving

the impression of additional tendrils. There is more than a hint of Art Nouveau here, though Alan tells me he was not consciously influenced by that period. It appears that looking to natural plant forms he has arrived at a style in which we can see an affinity with such an illustrious predecessor as Guimard. Recent architectural ironwork he has undertaken has been in similar vein, though not always with quite the assurance of this exquisite piece. It is, however, possible to see the quite significant change in his style from his earlier work, *Gate with Singing Birds* also shown in the exhibition.

Exhibits tended towards the useful, rather than the purely decorative, which since iron as fine art can often appear facile, was probably all to the good. One work which could never fall into this category, since it carried great conviction, was *Worshipping Figure* by Rachel Reckitt; a sculptress living in Somerset, she had been able to study forging with the Horrobins, father and son.

Jim Horrobin came up with something rather new in his tall stands, with wrap around

Far left above: C.A.H. 'Tommy' Tucker FWCB, LWCB, EX R.D.C.

Above centre: General view of exhibition with candle-holder by 'Tommy' Tucker in foreground.

Above: Aluminium Panel by Mike Roberts. 5 x 10 inches

Chris Fairclough

bases, particularly suitable for holding floral arrangements in churches.

Terry Clark's flat *Village* depicted the houses and trees to be seen on a walk between his home and the local Public House, where its eventual resting place will be on the top of a low wall outside the building, where it will undoubtedly provide a lot of interest for the customers and passers by.

A massive pair of garden chairs, by M.J. Pinnock, had openwork profile-cut backs and forged arms, with a completely forged table.

It is impossible to enumerate all the items, but the illustrations may give some idea of the diversity of the exhibits.

It was a happy conference—I formed the impression that British Blacksmiths are a band of men who respect the past but whose sights are now firmly set on the future.

Ivor Nicholas

39

Right: Single or repeated double gate by M.Emm. Single gate .

Far right: Fire screen by Peter Parkinson.

Centre: Candle bowl by Eamonn Kenward.

Inset: Rachel Reckitt.

Below right: Worshipping figure by Rachel Reckitt.

Below: Bowl for standing or hanging by Derek Griffiths.

Below that: Detail of modern grille by Ian Lamb.

BRITISH ARTIST BLACKSMITH EXHIBITION 1983

The 1983 British Artist Blacksmith Conference was held, as in the previous year, at the West Surrey College of Art, Farnham. There were two important innovations, in that the exhibition was open to the general public and lasted for nine days in order to cover two weekends. Although it has proved a strain on the association's financial resources, it has long been felt that blacksmiths needed this contact with the public to show their work.

The results in sales and commissions were very encouraging.

During the last three years Mike Roberts has brought the setting up of the exhibition to an extraordinarily high standard. This year he included an introductory set piece with an anvil and the legend "These basic tools and man make what you are about to see and discover."

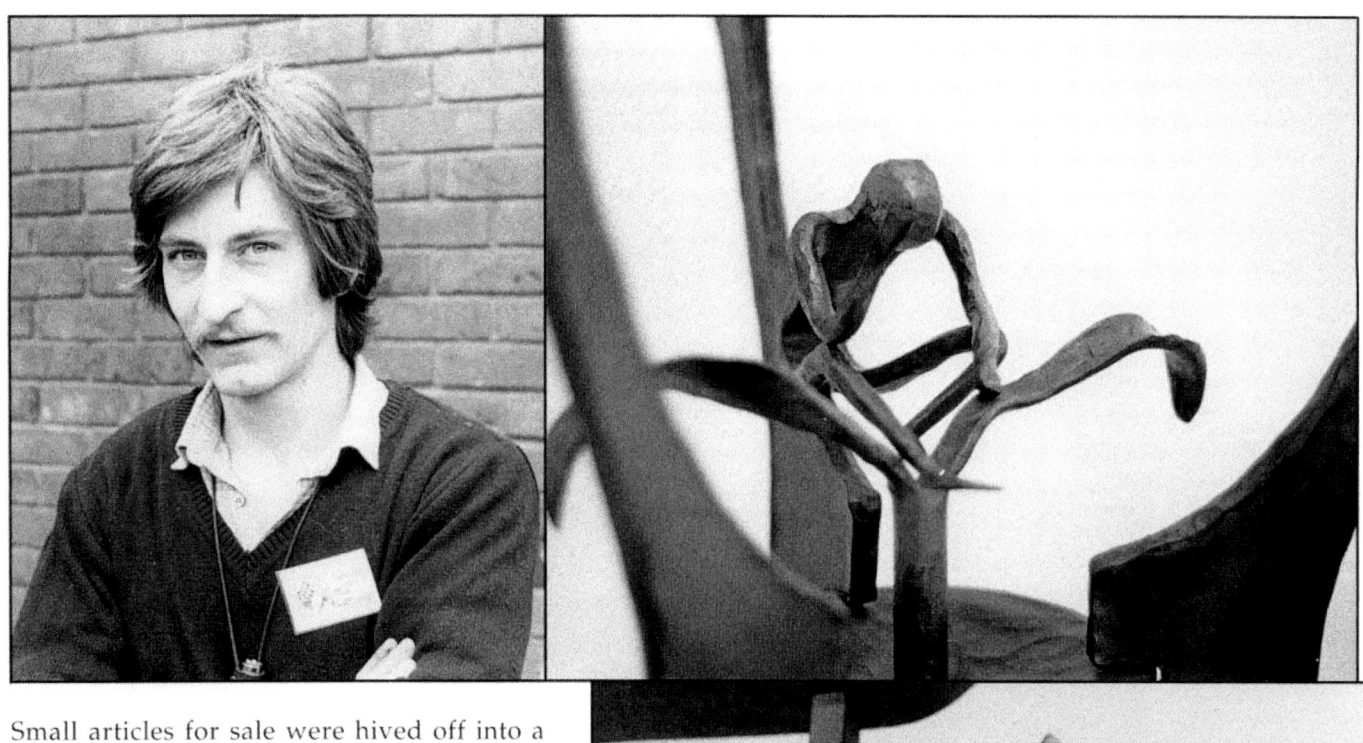

Small articles for sale were hived off into a special section to themselves, leaving plenty of breadth and space in which to show larger pieces. The first centrally placed work to meet the eye was a gate with elegant simple lines by Charles Normandale, Hampshire. M.J.Pinnock of Canterbury showed a section of a spiral staircase with particularly clean clear lines; while his apprentice, nineteen year-old Martin Reeves, exhibited an intricately forged bell pull with three leaves leading down to a delicate cage handle. He was honoured and delighted when it was purchased by Alan Dawson, who this year showed a boldly conceived and brightly coloured gate with one large flower as its central motif.

Mike Roberts' work included his forgings in bronze and copper, and a very unusual step balustrade formed of iron *briars* for a garden. Slightly sprawling in the exhibition environment, this would obviously find its ideal home in the beautiful garden for which it was designed.

Nice to have Tony Wootton in this country again, working at Sevenoaks. From his long sojourn with German smithing, one would expect a high quality of modern craftsmanship, and there was no way that viewers would be disappointed. He showed a very fine round coat stand, which drew high praise from our Czech visitors, Alfred Habermann and Vaclav Jaros; as well as a grille of Zimmerman-like forms evolved into interesting strapping. Also much commended by our distinguished demonstrators were mirrors by Peter Parkinson, a stainless steel

Top left: Tim Fortune. Top right: Thinking man by Richard Overs.
Centre: Detail of gate by Peter Walker. Above: Chess set by Terrence Clark.

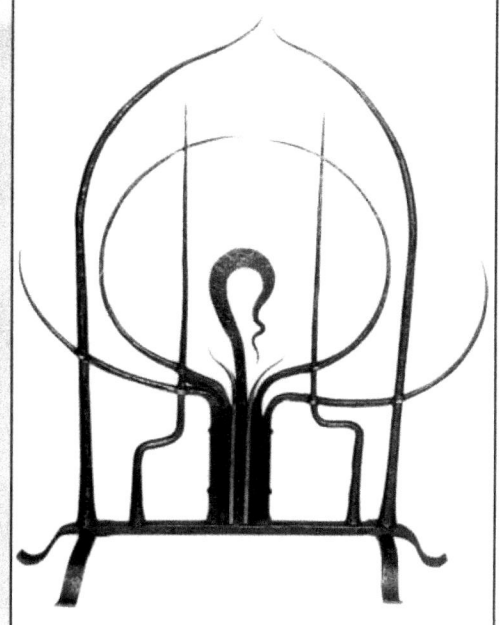

bowl by Anthony Robinson and the *fire* panel of a four section gate depicting the elements, from Richard Quinnell Ltd.

The Addy Taylor cup, presented by the Worshipful Company of Blacksmiths, was awarded to Terry Clark for his chess set and stand.

Tim Fortune from Gillingham, Dorset, showed an interesting group including a strongly designed low gate and a landscape wall panel. It was a free interpretation of an actual landscape, with lines engraved on the ploughed fields and copper fused in the fire on to mild steel sheet for colour and textures in trees and hedges. (The gate was later accepted for a Royal Academy Summer Exhibition and shown in the sculpture gallery.)

There were strongly designed fire grates by Mike Malleson and Alan Evans—the latter also showing a fairly massive gate with a very modern twist adaptation. Richard Over's *Table with thinking man* was unusual, and a small stainless steel ladle by Matt Galpin notable for its clean graceful lines. Among the more traditional designs—a semi-circular panel in the style of the 18th century by Tommy Tucker; *Gate with Roses* by Peter King; and a sturdy gate with stylised flowers by Peter Walker from Burton-on-Trent. Tom Hughes showed beautiful work in three bird pieces—a

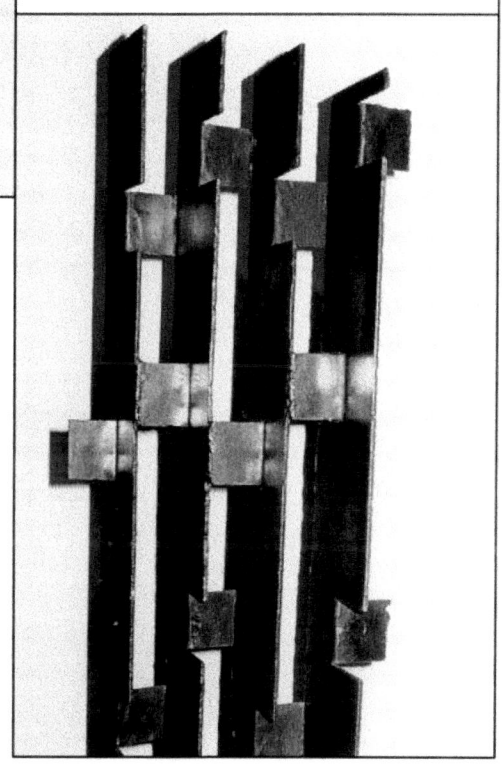

Peregrine Falcon and of smaller size, a Heron and a Mallard. Another of our best traditional smiths, Bill Norris from Cornwall, who made the ironwork for the Guard's Chapel in the crypt of St. Paul's Cathedral, also exhibited a finely wrought panel.

There was gratifyingly vigorous and proficient work by students of the West Surrey College of Art and Design; the metalwork section being under the direction of Peter Parkinson.

After the conference was over many of us lingered long in the exhibition hall. One young blacksmith spoke for us all when he said, "I can't drag myself away."

MOVING FORWARDS

These Conferences at the West Surrey College of Art in Farnham in 1982 and 83 codified the BABA Conference into a high degree of excellence, providing visiting Master Smiths from abroad to demonstrate their skills, and bringing the exhibition of members' work to a most professional presentation. The demonstrators for these two early years proved all time favourites, Paul Zimmermann, 1982, and Alfred Habermann, accompanied by Vaclav Jaros, 1983.

In 1984 there was a new departure, taking and amplifying a single theme—Design. It was a remarkably constructive and well developed conference, especially considering that it dealt with a subject so difficult to define. We had a series of talks, each completely different, which most competently covered every aspect of the theme. Particularly valuable were a series of design case histories in which six smiths each discussed the design origin, development and making of one of their recent major works. Three of these were of particular interest—Jim Horrobin on his gates for Crown Reach, Mike Malleson on his *Tree*, and Charles Normandale on the frieze for the Institute of Accountants (see part 2 under the names of the smiths).

Melvin Pinnock gave a most informative and helpful lecture on *Draughtsmanship and Presentation*, and the final lecture by Peter Parkinson was a masterly summing up. He sought to define the difference between the *decorated* and the *decorative*. He contrasted slides of a late 19th century stove, covered with pattern or in other words *decorated*, with objects of intrinsic beauty of form such as bronze-age axe heads and microlith arrow heads which were *in themselves decorative*. He discussed optical illusion, symmetry and the asymmetrical; the neat balance of black letter print; scale; the tradition of Celtic design; and the changing styles of fashion—such as Rococo. He questioned the well springs for inspiration—nature and close up photographs of plants—paths already trodden by Fritz

Kühn and Samuel Yellin with such great effect.

The visiting demonstrator and lecturer was Jan Dudesek from Switzerland. Slides of his early work showed grilles and grave crosses of a traditional Middle European nature. Some superb 18th century style signs with particularly lively cockerels forming part of the design. Gradually his work took on a modern look, candlesticks and fire tools of extreme grace and beauty, as indeed were those shown at the Victoria and Albert Museum Exhibition in 1982. The fire tools there rested on a large natural pebble as a stand. He was becoming particularly fascinated by the combination of iron and stone. One of his works at Lindau was an outdoor lamp of three stems with an enormous boulder standing apart from the iron but a necessary part of the group. It was possible to see how later iron gates of solid sheet form and often triangular shape, came to take the same relationship to stone gate posts; the work always becoming larger and more architectural. In something of the same way, his fire accoutrements, such as grilles or griddles, were also pared down to the essentials, taking on a definite end of the 20th century look.

Below: Fire Grate : Made by Julian Coode in 1984.

A series of slides showed his work for a cemetry, all the gates and barriers being based on triangular shapes and heavily symbolic. Movement by wind and the integration of water were also taking place.

The final set of slides showed pieces for a public park in Zurich; the work had become contemporary abstract sculpture—uncompromising stark tubes with a little carefully thought out colour. In one instance, a very long red tube was suspended, balanced over a river and, in a form of audience participation, passers by on the bridge above could, if they wished, swing round the tube by a hand wheel mounted on the side of the bridge rail.

Jan Dudesek can be said to be one of the most original blacksmiths working as a sculptor in the world today. His philosophy is that he doesn't like to see beauty spoilt; if a tube is all one could wish in elegance, why spoil it by bashing it about unecessarily! However, as when all modern art is taken to its logical conclusion, subtracting all that is irrelevant, one is in danger of arriving at something of a void.

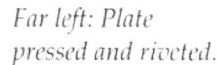

Far left: Plate pressed and riveted.

Left: David Tucker.

Below: Plate. Shaped, flanged and welded.

This is not an easily acceptable art. The latest work of Jan Dudesek is so stripped to the bare essentials that members found it difficult to accept the renunciation of his earlier style based completely on fine smithing.

A newcomer to the exhibition was David Tucker. He had just completed his BA (Hons) Metals Course at the West Surrey College of Art and showed several small and most unusual bowls. The whole group was interesting; the earliest made were boldly riveted together from a number of pieces of pressed plate, until in the progression the bowl shapes gradually refined and the rivets disappeared. One small bowl in particular presented a very unusual design, the form attractive and varied from all angles; it was made from three pieces of shaped plate, flanged and welded together. David had also evolved a unique method of colouring and patterning his work by the use of chemicals, heat and controlled rusting.

Hector Cole showed a small modern gate with all the refinement and elegance of 18th century work. (Illustrated on next page.)

Much as we enjoyed meeting at Farnham, it was not felt right to always hold conferences at the same place. For this reason 1985 saw the gathering take place at Coalbrookdale. An area steeped in iron history and with many exhibitions and remains under the jurisdiction of the Ironbridge Gorge Museum Trust; there was much to see and the Conference attracted a large number of delegates from Europe and the U.S.A.

Demonstrators included Americans Daniel Miller and, from Santa Fe, Tom Joyce. Six

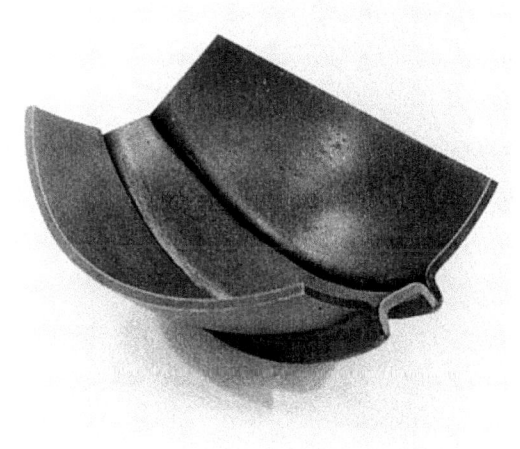

forging stations were set up under the arches of the viaduct, that runs alongside the old Darby works, and were in full use each day. Alan Dawson held a Masterclass and Mike Malleson led a Team Demonstration.

There were slide shows of work by Manfred Bredohl, Oscar Hafen and Jurgen Maurach; Dick Quinnell lectured on *Restoration* and Peter Parkinson on *Design*—in short there was a lot going on.

The exhibition posed especial problems, since it was a large marquee. This meant that all walls, sufficiently strong on which to hang ironwork had to be fabricated and self supporting. Lighting was another big problem, solved only with the much appreciated help and sponsorship of Mike Wood *Slick Systems*, who is more often to be

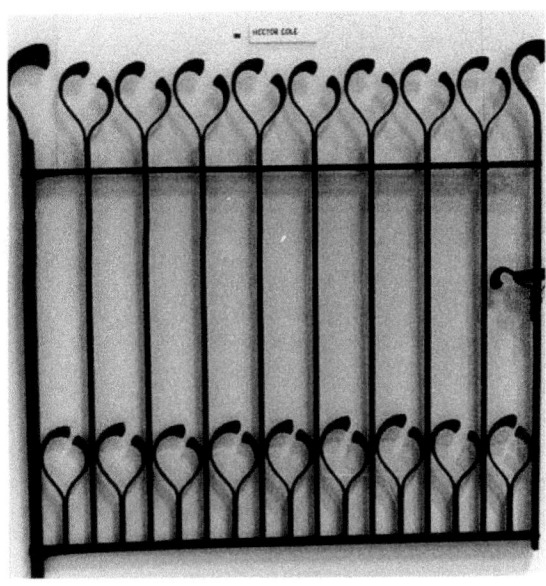

After a visit to the Victorian Streets with craft, trade and industry exhibits at Blist's Hill it was the venue for the end of Conference Barbecue, where no less than five barrels of Wem Bitter were consumed.

There was no doubt that the conferences were getting biger all the time, but at a cost—after Coalbrookdale all the organisers, and the greatest burden had fallen on Terry Clark, were so exhausted it was decided to hold conferences bi-annually instead of every year.

1987 saw the BABA Conference at Hereford to mark the seven years that had passed since the International Forging Iron Conference held there in 1980. It was a good opportunity, not only to look back, but to assess progress in the years between, which had been very considerable.

Our main British smiths were completing commissions of a standard undreamt of at that time. Younger smiths like Andy Rowe, Tony Wootton, Simon Robinson and Juian Coode had become journeymen in the true sense of the word, augmenting their training under great foreign masters, as at home in Germany as in their own country. In fact I found it quite confusing trying to sort out exhibitors to the exhibition, there were names like Theo. Grunewald working from Wales, while others with English names were sending work from Germany. To confuse matters further Saraj Guha a young Indian, Farnham trained, also came from the Principality.

Left: Gate by Hector Cole.

Left below: Dish by Duncan Reeves.

Below: Forging station at Coalbrookdale; Left to right —David James, Henry Pomfret, Michael Malleson, and Tim Fortune at the anvil.

found illuminating famous pop groups. In the early stages of arrangement the floor was a morass of mud; at one point a number of helpers were shovelling in gravel to cover the whole interior. One can begin to see from this some of the problems encountered. Anyone around seems to have given a hand, Americans chipping in, and French and German tongues could be heard solving the difficulties and getting the show on the road.

Many of the works exhibited are mentioned elsewhere in this book. But I particularly liked some pieces by Henry Pomfret which included delicate stainless steel fungi growths set into a wooden branch (which proved all but impossible to photograph). Also an unusual flaring bowl set on little celtic-like animal feet by Duncan Reeves from the Nailbourne Forge. Some of the more stalwart pieces were displayed in the open, towering in pride of place, a 17ft high sculpture by Antony Robinson called *Creation* in Corten-steel.

New names were surfacing, among them Jayne Wilson with some interesting work. There was altogether more breadth of outlook, a sculptural gate by Tim Fortune, shown at the BABA 1983 exhibition, had been accepted and shown in the Scuptural Gallery of the Royal Academy of Arts Summer Exhibition.

Henry Pomfret, who was the hard working forge master for the conference, showed, as usual, a wide range of work. A coloured and textured wall plaque *Sunset-Moonrise*; some forged heads rather in a medieval tradition; and his most ambitious piece to date *Waterwork* in which water rose from a lily-like central form and ran down outstretching gracefully curved projections, to return to the pebble covered water tank below. (See page 48.)

Of our guest demonstrators it was Alfred Habermann Jnr. and his wife Vera who won the hearts of their audience. Such was their co-ordination, Vera striking for her husband, that no word passed between them, the rhythm never faltered— the language of the anvil spoke more eloquently than words. It was a joy to watch, a reaction shared by all; at the end of a particularly long bout of concentrated hammer blows the audience burst into spontaneous applause (page 49).

Albert Paley gave a most informative lecture on the development of his smithing. Starting as a stone sculptor, he then became a goldsmith and his first essay in the use of steel was in making tools for his jewellery work. Compared with the materials he had been using, such as silver and platinum which work hardens, he found hot steel very malleable. He began to explore the possibilities of wrapping one hot piece of steel round a cold piece, which led before long to his making 6ft high candlesticks; a complete contrast to the minute scale of his jewellery. Coil, twist, wave, all were an evolutionary growth from the hot metal, and imprinting texture, as it defined the form, also helped, as he expressed it, to *read* the iron.

BABA members who visited America in 1982 had been able to see some of his newer work at Clydes Restaurant, Tysons Corner. Flowing rails which appeared very much Art Nouveau influenced, and steel trees with fairy lights. Briefly, he continued to let the iron evolve its own forms continually developing techniques of forging that had not been used before. Twisting has been in the smiths vocabulary

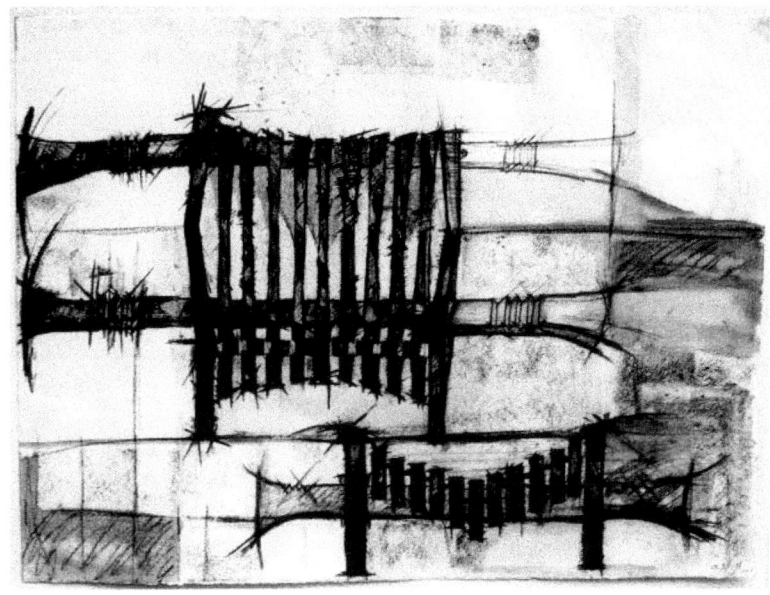

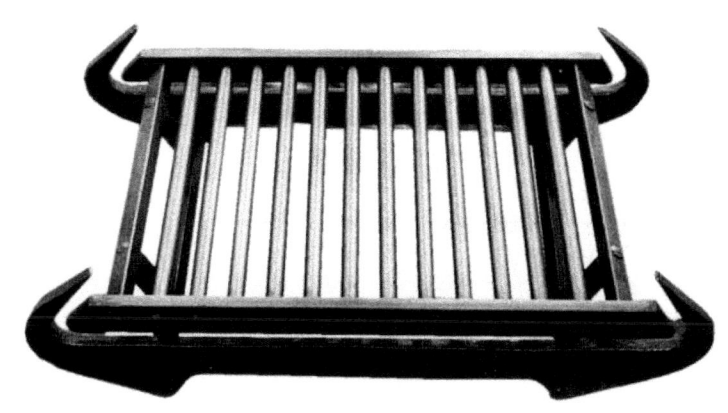

for hundreds of years, yet he did new things with it, twisting heavy bars so closely that the ridges produced were almost horizontal, upsetting, pressing the twist down, and sometimes allowing the steel to become so hot that edges burnt off into distinctive rough patterning.

Above: Drawing for Fire Basket by Jane Wilson.

Below: Fire Basket by David James.

Left: ". . . twisting heavy bars so closely that the ridges produced were almost horizontal."

Left and below:
Waterwork
by Henry Pomfret.

We heard of the Albany Gates for the New York State Senate Chamber in Albany, New York. This necessitated enlarging the workshop; whereas the Renwick gates has taken two men one year to make, these took eight people six and a half months, working flat out with pneumatic hammers, air grinders, heat and hammers, with no days off. His team were currently working on a tremendous commission for the Huston Performing Arts Centre. Fantastic sculptures,

made hollow because they were so large, fluttering ribbon shapes and a lot of colour, lined each side of a wide stairway. Even the handles to the entrance doors were 36 inches across. Albert Paley still forges the prototype but has twelve men fabricating the designs. He was currently designing an archway to go over a city street, by a slip of the tongue he first said *over a city*. The audience laughed a little but not too much, because I think we felt it was not beyond the bounds of possibility that this could be the next job!

Other demonstrators and lecturers were Dimitri Gerakaris, who spoke of his great Eagle Square archway in Concorde, New Hampshire; Kauko Moisio of Finland, and Serge Marchal from Nimes.

Far left: Kauko Moisio of Finland one of the guest demonstrators.

The BABA Committee never rested on its laurels. By now conferences had become impressive gatherings of smiths from many parts of the world, showing their enthusiasm and techniques and thereby bringing the craft forwards. What did not appear to be happening was spreading the word among laymen—they needed to bring the craft to the people. It was with this in mind that David Petersen took on the mammoth task of organising the International Festival of Iron held at Cardiff in 1989. BABA had never tackled so enormous a task as running this marathon get-together of blacksmiths from all over the world. It was not really possible to count them, some came for the week, some for days, some even for single events, but each day there were between 300 and 400 participants.

Three public forging stations were set up in pedestrian precincts in the middle of the City and an enormous tent, with seating for 600, was erected in the Castle precincts for the delegates forge. As I approached Cardiff I could hear the ring of the anvil and I noticed a new phenomenon, blacksmiths with walkie-talkies in their back pockets.

The proceedings officially opened on Sunday with an inaugural service at St John's Church, where a fine exhibition of ironwork had been set up. The occasion was impressive, the pomp and panoply of the church intermixed with that of Civic Dignitaries in velvet, gold, feathers and sable. When the Lord Mayor, preceded by two mace bearers, had taken his place followed by the Choir and then by Churchmen in their finest copes, there was a moments pause. Then Freddy Habermann, the quintessential blacksmith, in snow white shirt, breeches and leather apron, accompanied by his little shorn-headed daughter, walked slowly up the aisle carrying the tools of the blacksmiths trade. The Vicar placed the

hammers and tongs on the altar. After the representatives of church and state the simple homage of the craftsman was surprisingly moving. The Lord Mayor read the first lesson. "Every craftsman . . . who labours by night as well as by day," (I listened more attentively—the words seemed most apt) "So it is with the blacksmith sitting by his anvil; he considers what to do with the iron; the breath of the fire scorches his skin, as he contends with the heat of the furnace; he batters his ears with the din of the hammer, his eyes are fixed on the pattern; he sets his heart on completing his work, and stays up putting the finishing touches. . . . The work of their hands is their prayer."

The Chairman of BABA, David James, read

Above: Alfred Habermann Jun. with his wife Vera.

Below: Railing for Cardiff. Railing head by Noah Taylor.

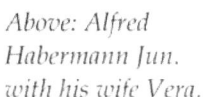

Right: One of the forging stations set up in Cardiff City Centre.

49

the second lesson. The Rev. M.R. Ellis, Vicar of St. John the Baptist, in his sermon tied in blacksmithing with the history of South Wales, whose prosperity was founded on coal and iron. At the end of the service the tools were returned to Freddy and the whole congregation followed him in procession from the church to the castle forging station. Policemen in white gloves held up the traffic for us—the Americans especially were impressed.

There were demonstrations by Achim Kühn, Dorothy Steigler, Albert Paley, Takayoshi Komine of Japan, Manfred Bredohl, Brian Russell, Charles Normandale and many others, while Alfred Habermann demonstrated with a team from Israel. There were lectures on African agricultural implements and Roman artifacts and a film on Christoph Friedrichs' forge in Switzerland, where he had restored an old hammer-mill where four wooden water wheels worked bellows, hammers, grinding wheels and mechanical saws. There were exhibitions in the Old Library, one of work by members, delegates and demonstrators, another by college students and a third of the work of Samuel Yellin and the Yellin Metalworkers Co. There were a number of other exhibitions, *British Forged Metal Sculpture* by Hamish Black, Anthony Caro. Katherine Gili, Richard Rome and Tim Scott; Sculpture by Igor le Floch, and an exhibition of photographs by Fritz Kühn. As well as all this there was a banquet in the Castle, a concert by the Welsh National Opera Orchestra and Chorus with Bryn Terfel, and a concert by the Rhymney Silurian Male Choir.

Wales was certainly making an impression on us and after a few days I began to feel that we were making an impression on Cardiff; there were many more people gathered round the forging stations in the streets, the banks were full of stetsons and, on one of the colder days, the smith from Alaska was wearing a fur-lined hat with ear muffs!

The blacksmiths made and presented an elaborate Sundial to Cardiff. Delegates had also been asked to make and bring with them a railing bar to their own design—each itself a minor work of art. These were afterwards set up at Cardiff Bay as a thank you from the blacksmiths to the City that, with its Castle and its Civic Centre had welcomed us in such an unforgettable way.

After Cardiff conferences could hardly get

bigger so events tended to become more diverse.

BABA had always organised *forge-ins* in different parts of the country. On these occasions members, or anyone who felt interested in the proceedings, would meet at someones forge. Everyone brought food for the communal lunch buffet and there was usually a competition to make some iron object during the day. They were informal meetings and many blacksmiths preferred them to the more formal conferences. At first they were usually for one day, then people began to stay over until next day, and gradually the forge-ins became longer and began to assume the importance of major events. There were also times when they could provide a wider public view of ironwork, such as when they were held at the Great Yorkshire Showground at Harrogate; in 1990 the *Smallholder Magazine* was holding an exhibition and over 4,500 people visited the showground over the two days. The following year it coincided with a large antiques fair.

In 1992 Bob Oakes organised a forge-in at

Above: Alfred Habermann with his daughter and Uri Hofi, from Israel.

Alford, Lincs., in connection with the Alford Craft Market in May. It was a two day event with an optional visit to look over the Frodingham Steelworks at Scunthorpe on the previous day. There were two exhibitions, one "A Festival of Light" in the church devoted to candlesticks and another, in a marquee, of general ironwork. Smiths worked hard during the weekend to forge an arch which was to be presented to Alford Manor Museum in whose grounds the whole event was staged. The evenings passed with music and drinking and a barbecue, in considerable conviviality.

*Some of the candlesticks shown in the **Festival of Light** in Alford Church.*

Left: By Bill Poirier.

Below: By Bob Oakes.

Below left: By Brian Russell.

Far left top: By Roy Thedvall.

Far left below: By Peat Oberon.

Left below: By Paul Margetts.

51

The idea of racing against time to produce a large communal work over the weekend seemed to fire imaginations; Alford being followed a few months later by a Conference at Gressenhall Rural Life Museum, in Norfolk, where double gates were made. In April 1993 a *Flowery Gate* was made at the first forge-in of the season at the Rural Development Commission Workshop on the Great Yorkshire Showground at Harrogate for the Yorkshire Agricultural Society, though on this occasion Brian Russell designed the gate and development work in advance.

Something completely different took place in November 1992, instead of a *Forge-in* a *Talk-in* at Redfield, near Winslow, Bucks. For once smiths were not exhausted by long hours at the anvil, they had time to think, and brought forward more ideas on their work and how to organise the future of blacksmithing than usually surface in half a dozen meetings.

During these years the east of Europe began to open up and British smiths were able to make contact with countries that had previously been inaccessible. In 1990 Phil Johnson and Bill Cordaroy and their wives, visited Estonia making friends with the blacksmiths of Estonia, Lithuania, the Ukraine, Finland, Eastern Germany, and from the Russian minority of Komi in the Soviet Arctic Circle.

David Petersen visited Russia in 1992 and Phil Johnson and Adrian Legge flew via Warsaw to Gdansk to attend an inaugural meeting of SPAK (Polish Art Blacksmiths Association) and once the contacts were made smiths from the East began to visit this country.

A major event organised by BABA was the sale at Sotheby's, in September 1991, of 20th century ironwork made by their members. It attracted more than 200 items. There was a preview exhibition at Quinnell's Fire and Iron Gallery in Leatherhead, with the subsequent sale at Summers Place, Billingshurst.

It was the first public auction devoted entirely to contemporary decorative ironwork and a wonderful opportunity to raise public awareness of modern work. More than 2000 visitors came to the gallery during the three weeks of exhibition. Many who came were amazed at the wide variety of work they saw. It attracted a number of articles in the press and as a public relations excerise was a great success. Although some of the finer works failed to reach their reserves, some £33,500

worth of ironwork changed hands. Not least there was a lot of publicity for all concerned and it helped to educate the public in understanding modern ironwork.

Twelve Scottish members of BABA organised a travelling exhibition "Fireworks" in 1992-93. The exhibition was attached to the Edinburgh Festival Fringe, where it was held outdoors in an architect's courtyard off the Royal Mile. It was also linked with the Glasgow School of Art with a competition amongst students to design an outdoor piece which would become a permanent feature of the school. It travelled to nine different venues and was highly

Above top: "All go" at Alford. Peat Oberon and Terry Clark, with Hazel Moore in the background.

Above below: Carol Oakes and Adrian Legge talk to Elspeth Bennie and Shona Johnson at work on a rondel for the communal gate project.

successful in bringing modern Scottish ironwork to the attention of architects and the general public.

In spite of the great deal of work necessary to mount such an exhibition such is the organisers' enthusiasm that they are now setting up a travelling BABA exhibition for England *Fe–An Exploration of iron through the senses* to exhibit in eleven galleries over a period of two years. The intention being to encourage both the viewer and the maker to explore the tactile qualities inherent in iron

Photographs P. Johnson & Co.

From 'Fireworks'
Far left above:
Stainless steel Angel
by Robert
Hutchison.
Above: Tall Plant
Stand by Jolyon
Havinden.
Below and left below:
Organic Forms by P.
Johnson & Co. in
Council Car Park ,
Cupar, Fife.

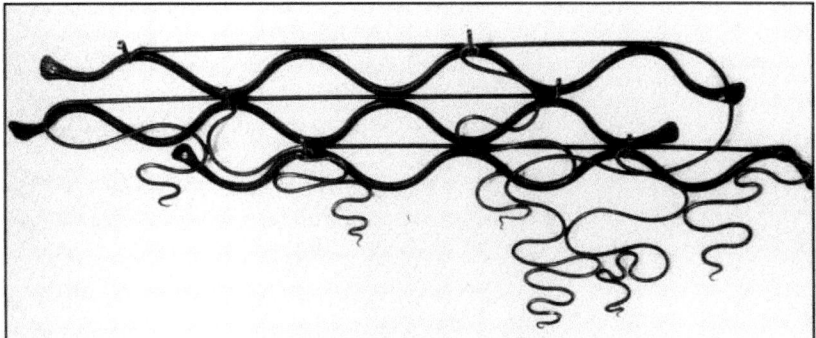

but rarely explored. The use of texture, shape, movement and balance, finishes of various natures, and sounds created by striking and blowing, all offer an exciting way to take iron forward.

WORK FROM THE SOTHEBY'S EXHIBITION.

In August 1994 I was able to see the sixty pieces that had been selected for the *Fe* exhibition—the difficult brief imposed has ensured carefully considered ironwork, much of which breaks new ground. I shall remember a lifesize figure of a woman selling papers, painted in red, by Bill Cordaroy; a sculpture by Dick Qiunnell, dedicated to his wife, entitled *You and I*; and a large head *Portrait of Naomi Campbell* by Mark Tilley which, while I recoiled in horror, I could only admire—this is going to be an exciting exhibition.

All photographs on this page by Glynn Clarkson.

Above: Trailing Coatrack, hand forged and welded in steel with beeswax finish 105 x 65 cm by Ivan Yates Colbert.

Far left above: Mirror Frame by Heather Burrell. Its openwork abstract patterns were inspired by entangled vines and twisted thickets, asymmetrical but beautifully balanced.

Far left below: A Chair in Gothic style forged in mild steel. Seat straps rolled over the front and back frame, the back formed of four broader straps rolled over the sides, by Graeme Hopper.

Left centre: Bowl with stand, in steel with clear laquered finish supported within a tapering coiled forged steel base, with waxed finish, 18 x 8 cm, by Bill Cordaroy.

Left below: A Fruit Bowl, segmented forged plates laced to an oval frame, 60 x 25 x 15 cm by Derek Griffiths.

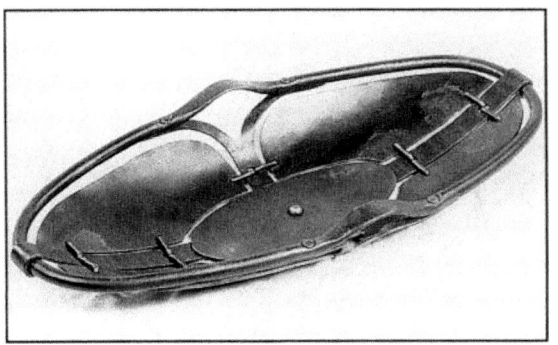

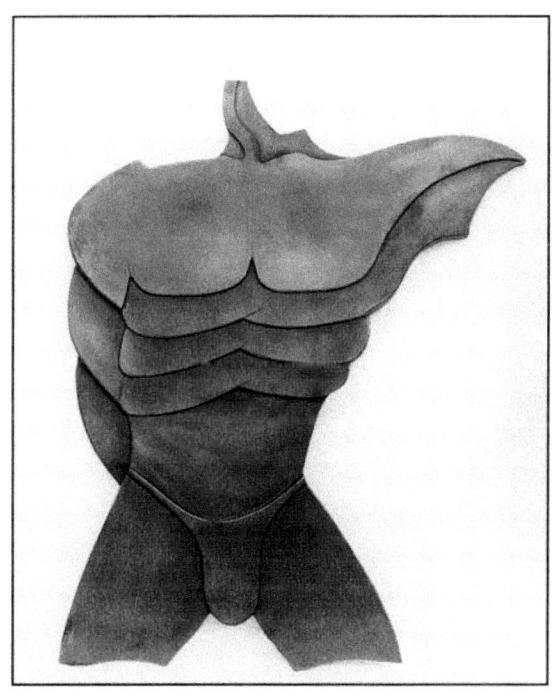

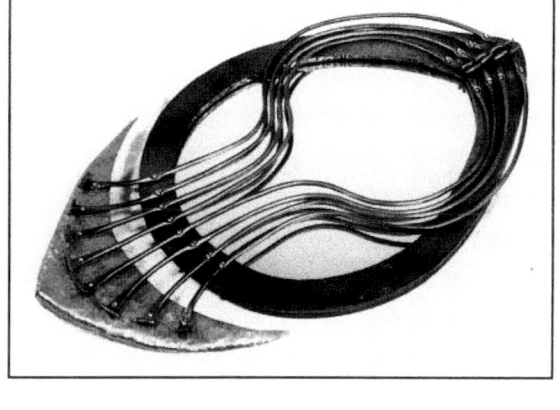

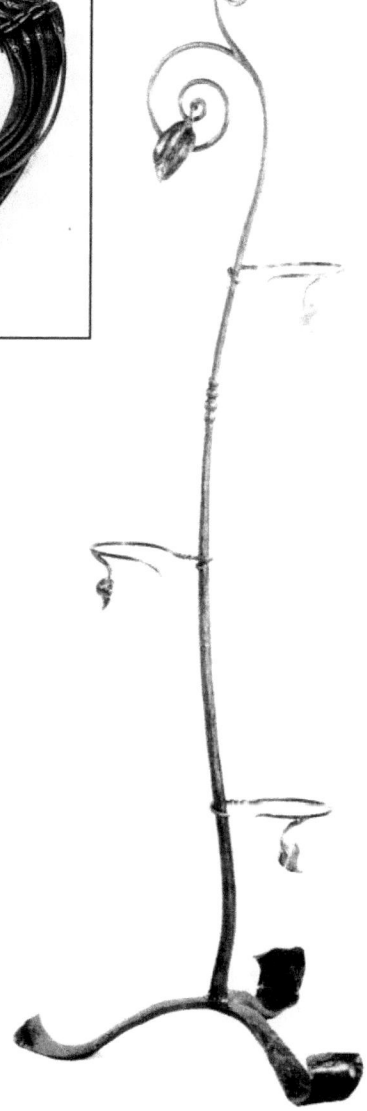

Top above: Chair forged and jointed with punched holes and tenons in mild steel, co-ordinating dark hide leather seat, by Lennox Kilner, awarded title of National Champion 1989 by the Worshipful Company of Blacksmiths.

Above: Torso, 100 x 85 cm, a wall sculpture by Susan May, made by gas flame cutting steel plate, smoothed on edges and the pieces built up one above the other. The centre part of each was cut out to lessen the weight so that all except the top piece are frames welded to each other. The relatively stylised pattern gives a great effect of strength and virility.

Top above: Table by Paul Wynne 70 x 35 cm. apprenticed to Alan Dawson. A pierced circular glass top is supported on a pedestal made entirely of an entwined mass of forged and beaten leaves, buds and flowerheads, with a dark-green finish.

Above: An eye-shaped Mirror by Cara Frost. Constructed in mild steel and copper. The delicate overlaid bars are pinned in place with copper rivets 24 x 15 in.

Right: One of a pair of Plant Stands by David Palmer.

All photographs on this page are by Glynn Clarkson.

David Hawkins

Capricorn Design

In the early 1980s, the vocabulary of most smiths working in the modern manner was very limited, but by the 1990s the field was wide open and creativity unlimited. The following pages, of mainly small pieces, show some of the great diversity of subject and style to be found today.

Far left: Gate inspired by Art Nouveau, made by Neil Hawkins and designed by David Hawkins, Devon.

Right: One of two gates for a modern bungalow, picking up one of the sparse design features of the building, slanted slats of garage doors linking with the nearby stream. By Capricorn Design, Hammersmith.

Below left: "Grandfather's Gate"—"Not too modern not too old" by Simon Robinson, Shropshire.
Photograph S. Robinson

Below right: "Art Deco" Stair balustrade. Wrought steel, polished after making, with chrome plated brass rectangular section handrail by Capricorn Design.
Photograph Capricorn Design.

Above: Gate by Bill Poirier, Somerset.

Above: Vase by Simon Robinson, in mild and stainless steel. Shropshire.

Below: Gates by Tim Fortune, Somerset. Tim has always had a strong feeling for natural forms. The gate on the left was inspired by icicles and snowdrifts, and the one on the right by dried earth and heat haze.

Tim Fortune married Jane Wilson. (See her drawing for Fire Basket on page 47). Tim now runs Riverside Blast Cleaning Services, next to his forge. Here he operates blast cleaning and hot zinc spraying, as well as decorative finishes with hot metal spray in brass, bronze or copper.

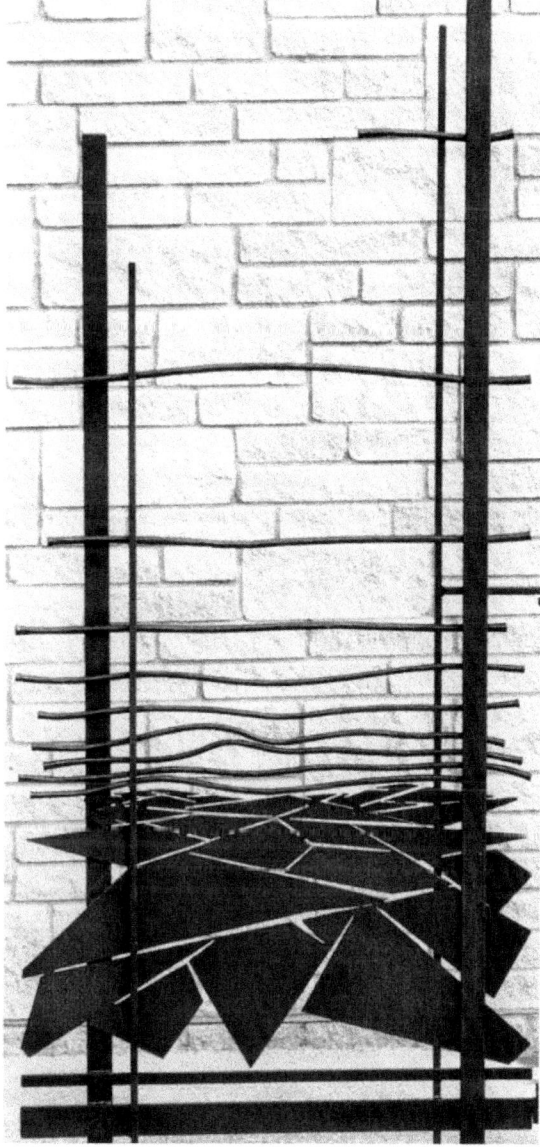

Left: Candlestick by Craig Knowles, Bristol. An impressive piece in which all parts interlock by passing through other parts.

Below right: Bollards in Gloucester by Matthew Feddon from the Forest of Dean. The "Needle" design aptly picks up with the famous "Taylor of Gloucester" story.

Bottom of page: Fence by Mike Crummy, Inverness-shire.

Photograph Mike Crummy.

Top: Wall Light for private West End Bar. 1993. Brass and aluminium copper smithing and forging, fabrication and sheet metal working, with patination. Capricorn Design, Hammersmith.

Photograph Capricorn Design.

Left centre: A Votive Candle Stand for York Minster by John Hill, Bridlington. Designed by Charles Brown, architect.

Photograph John Hill

Below left: Gate by Peter Crownshaw, Tenbury Wells.

Photographs Avril Wilson

Above left and right: Candelabra by Avril Wilson, Hove.

Below: Wall Sconce, Fire Grate and Candlesticks by Saraj Guha, Hampshire.

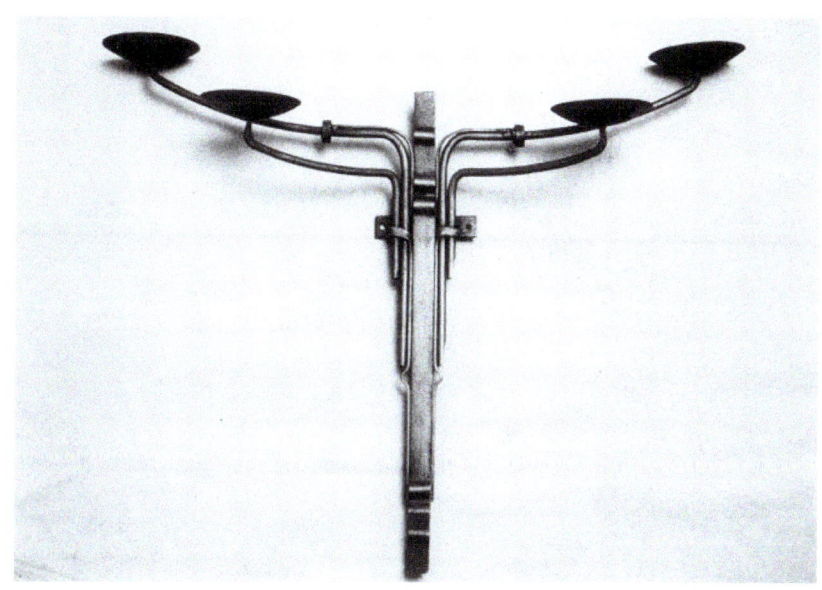

Photographs Saraj Guha

Above: Detail of "Cat" Balustrade 1994. "first cat too happy, the second too sad, third just right!"
David Townsend, Photograph Capricorn Design.

Below: "Fish" by Steve Payne, Glasgow.

Left: Sculpture by Mark Tilley "Liberty" after Aristide Maillol. 1992. 70 cm x 40 cm. Made of mild steel with all edges turned in. This is how Mark started doing sheet metal work. Solihull.

Mark Tilley

There are a number of smiths who, over the last few years, have begun to work seriously in the modern way; with results that auger well for the future.

They are grouped separately from the smiths in Part II because those have worked in a contemporary style over a far longer period.

RICHARD BENT	62
ADAM BOOTH	64
PHILIP JOHNSON	65
JOHN CREED	66
PAUL MARGETTS	68
PEAT OBERON	69
BRIAN RUSSELL	70
ANTHONY WOOTTON	72

Left: 'Smiths II'
Limited edition
Wood Engraving by
Rachel Reckitt.

RICHARD BENT

Richard Bent was born in 1948 and is a self-taught blacksmith. He tells me the only instruction he has ever had was for a single day when Laurence Love taught him to forge weld. Perhaps this is why he has always been determined to pursue relentlessly a path of excellence. Since 1982 it has brought him over 200 awards at major agricultural shows for both traditional and modern pieces of forged metalwork, entered in wrought iron competitions. In 1992 he was National Champion Blacksmith of the year and runner-up in the following year, and is now a Liveryman of the Worshipful Company of Blacksmiths.

His first forge was at Broadchalke in Wiltshire, but in 1982 he moved to larger premises in Braishfield near Romsey, Hampshire. He has been giving instruction to mature students on a part time basis since 1983, initially for evening classes at Sparsholt Agricultural College, and more recently at Braishfield at weekends. In late 1994 he was appointed an Associate Lecturer in Blacksmithing at Hereford College of Technology.

He has restored a number of fine old gates including a Bakewell screen in Oxfordshire. He first began to take an interest in modern ironwork design after contact with BABA in 1985. Today his commissions are extremely varied, some traditional and some contemporary. Ecclesiastic work includes a medieval tomb surround with sword shaped uprights and elegant spear corner standards, in St. Mary's Church, Slindon, West Sussex; a cross and candlestick in St. Mary's Church, Wookey; fonts at Birkenhead and Woking, and a candle stand in Sherbourne Abbey. One of his gates is at The Priory Church, Christchurch, and he has made a Cross and Reredos and a Paschal candle stand for Romsey Abbey. In a very different vein are his light-hearted gates for Cupernham Junior School, Romsey, and a Weathervane Tree all covered with little matchstick-men and painted in bright colours. Another unusual piece is a suspended Mobile at the Rivergate Centre, Peterborough.

In 1987 Richard exhibited at the "New Iron Age" exhibition in the Building Centre, London and was awarded a Diploma for outstanding Craftsmanship awarded by the Worshipful Company of Blacksmiths. His work was also shown in the "Heavy Metal" exhibition touring England and Scotland in 1988, organised by Northern Arts. The following year it was in "Wessex Iron" at Winchester and was shown at the Guildhall, London, to celebrate the 800th anniversary of the Lord Mayor of London. In 1992 he exhibited at the Barbican, in an exhibition co-ordinated by the Livery Companies of the City of London. In 1994 he showed at Basing House "Forging Contacts" organised by the Hampshire Sculpture Trust and also at the Guildhall in another Livery Company exhibition.

I first met Richard Bent at a Seminar at the Royal Welsh Agricultural Showground in Builth Wells in 1990, and this is just where one might expect to find him as it is a milieu that he has made particularly his own.

For many years wrought ironwork had formed a part of County Agricultural Shows, and in 1986 The National Blacksmiths Competition Committee was formed, (such committees already existed for other agricultural crafts such as sheep-shearing). Their aim was to encourage the highest standards of blacksmithing by the promotion of seminars, competitions, and exhibitions at shows throughout the British Isles.

Left: Detail of a school fence in Daisy Lane, Gosport for the Gosport Borough Council and Hampshire County Council.

Photograph Richard Bent.

They enlisted the help of the Worshipful Company of Blacksmiths and persuaded them to draw up an official panel of Judges for Wrought Iron competitions. In 1988 they introduced the National Blacksmith of the Year award, which is competed for at seven of the main Aricultural Shows throughout the United Kingdom.

As smiths began to enter modern designs, as well as traditional, in the competitions, certain problems began to arise. The Seminar at Builth Wells was one of a number the Committee had arranged in an effort to raise the standard of show judging for these pieces, and to encourage individual craftsmen to enter local and national shows; confident that their work would receive a fair and considered judgement.

The day took the form of well known smiths speaking on a given subject, first a smith working in a traditional way would speak on, say, "design and Construction", to be followed by a smith working in a modern style giving his views on the same subject. This went on throughout the day, not without some fairly heated discussions; Richard Bent spoke on modern techniques and quality, while to me fell the rather unenviable task of summing-up the days proceedings.

Richard had for some time felt quite passionately that show competitions needed a new system of allocating points if both traditional and contemporary works were to be judged in the same competition. In the past, for instance, very few marks had been given for design, which was fair enough if smiths were making, perhaps, a traditional bracket from a CoSIRA pattern. In modern pieces the creative design was vitally important, and had to come from the smith, so many more marks seemed applicable. In an effort towards resolving such problems he wrote a paper published in The Forge and The British Blacksmith, seeking to define the traditional and contemporary aspects of smithing largely on the basis of technique. In so doing he became largely instrumental in initiating a whole new, and far more satisfactory, system. His definitions were discussed by the NBCC and judges and now forms part of the "Handbook for Judges Stewards and Exhibitors in Wrought Iron Competitions"; though it is always under constant review.

Right: Storm Gate. Photograph Richard Bent

Today Richard Bent is a progressive blacksmith who promotes the hot forging of tradition with the creation of modern forms. He believes that, by a reflective appraisal of the work of earlier times, it is perfectly possible for the onward march of contemporary smithing to react to the past in a way that can link it with the future.

Richard makes some particularly interesting and unusual gates; he likes them, when possible, to be asymmetrical and for each leaf to have its own identity. Instead of dividing a car entry gate into equal halves in *Storm Gate* he has made one narrow part, easily swung open for pedestrian access, and the other large so that both leaves opened together can accommodate a car. The design runs through the whole gate and the integration of the frame into the pattern adds to its impact. These gates were made in 1987. More recently we see, in 1992, a garden gate with Fritillary flowers, again using the curved front

rails where the leaves of the gate come together. In this case thick flat plate has been bent backwards to give strength and to prevent the central front rails appearing too heavy and broad. The general lateral bending of the rails tends to *lose* them as they fade into the bending flower stems of the main design.

Left: Fritillary Gate.
Photograph Richard Bent.

ADAM BOOTH

Adam Booth was born in London in December 1963. He served a motor vehicle apprenticeship from 1980 to 85; and during 1985-86 attended a Blacksmithing course at Hereford Technical Training College. The following year he worked as a crew member on transatlantic yacht delivery. At the end of this time he started up "Pipers Forge" and was the winner of regional finals in the "Livewire" start up award; and three years later was a National Finalist in the Livewire "In Business Challenge". In 1988 he exhibited work at the Glasgow Garden Festival and was a winner in the craft guild competition.

Adam's work first came to my attention at the "First Festival of Iron" in Cardiff when I admired his unusual design for an interlaced *Log Basket*; which I understand proved a very saleable item. In the open air exhibition in the castle grounds he showed *Washing Line*, shirt and trousers hanging on a line, which won the Rachel Reckitt award for figurative iron sculpture. This arose from making iron *shirts* for a boutique; as he was anxious to test the possibilities and limitations of this form of work. He found no limitations and still enjoys making peculiar and unusual items.

In 1990 he was selected to represent the UK at the EEC crafts exhibition in Avignon, and the following year he was a winner of the "Forging Links" design competition.

Glynn Clarkson

He took an active part, with the official title of Treasurer, on the organising committee of the highly successful "Fireworks" exhibition in Scotland.

Past commissions include three ornamental fireplaces for the Lord Provost of Aberdeen's banqueting Hall; interior and exterior ironwork, including gates, for an "Arts and Crafts" mansion in Devon, and a balustrade for a mansion in Aberdeen. He made a Well Cover to an historic well in the Royal Mile, Edinburgh.

He has just completed a 4m screen for the Scottish Museum of Fisheries in Anstruther which was unveiled by Princess Anne at the beginning of July 1994.

Above: Washing Line. Hot forged and gas welded, acid etched and galvanised finish, 200 by 150 cm.

Below left: Log basket. 70 cm diam.

Below: Detail of a "fish" gate.

PHILIP JOHNSON

Philip Johnson was a signalman in Naval Communications. Just before leaving the navy he took a retraining course in welding and another in mechanical engineering at a Government re-training centre. This led to an interest in plant and construction equipment.

Blacksmithing was, as it were, in the family as his wife's father Jimmy Finnegan had been a foreman blacksmith at Charles Henshaws in Edinburgh; a firm that started in the 1920s and continued into the early 1970s.

In 1973 Phil started his own business in construction plant; repairing, operating and hiring out diggers and other machines. He gradually began to go over to blacksmithing though for a time he operated the two businesses side by side. He found out about BABA in 1980 and took courses at West Dean in 1983 and 84.

Today the plant has disappeared and blacksmithing has taken over. He began to be interested in modern smithing about five years ago, partly because he found the customers were beginning to ask for new designs.

Phil's daughter Shona is now a blacksmith, trained by her father, and working with the firm.

They recently completed interesting modern curving tree guards and rail outside the Play House Theatre, Edinburgh; and very exciting *Organic Sculptural Forms* for a Council Car Park in Cupar, Fife (see page 53). Also unusual a group of *Lily Flowers* on top of a pillar in Market Street, Edinburgh.

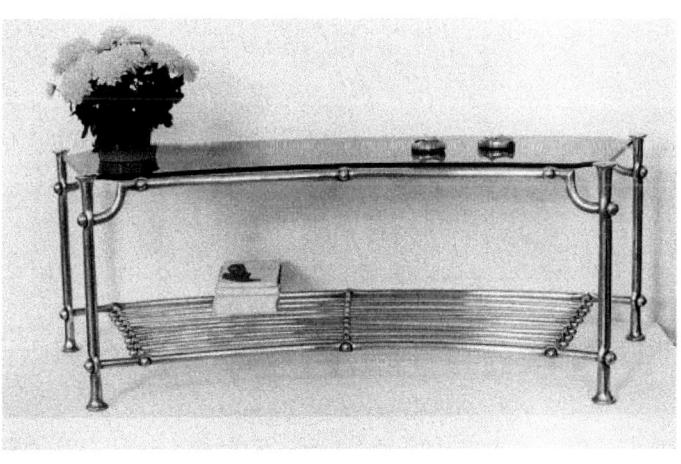

Above:
"Cockalorum"
forged stainless steel and copper, about 5ft high.

Far left: Table in forged brass.

Left: "Mustard and Cress" gate.

JOHN CREED

John Creed, born in 1938 in Cheshire, is a silversmith who has come late to ironwork. He studied silversmithing at Liverpool College of Art 1955-59, his National Diploma in Design being later augmented by an Art Teachers Diploma. He enjoyed forming silver under the hammer and the infinite choice of shape and surface finish that could be achieved. He feels that a turning point in his career was seeing a demonstration, in the early 1960s, by the last few remaining professional spoon-makers who were forging flatware in sterling and britannia silver bar. After that he was regularly hot forging spoons, ladles and table settings.

To use iron in the same way did not occur to him until he attended the International Conference on Forging Iron at Hereford in 1980, where he was excited by the demonstrations and the attitudes of those present. Yet the gestation period of his development as an ironsmith was a long one; it was not until eight years later after a career in industry and teaching silversmithing, at Liverpool and Leeds Colleges of Art and finally at Glasgow School of Art, that he began to think seriously of working in iron.

He attended the ABANA conference in Birmingham, Alabama, as part of a study tour of eastern U.S.A in 1988. Then for two weeks he joined the work force of Albert Paley in New York where he was impressed by Paley's philosophy on the unity of function and decoration. Later, taking a Sabbatical from teaching, he gained workshop experience with Alan Dawson in Cumbria and Denys Mitchell in Kelso.

A thing that he greatly enjoys is the difference in scale made possible by working in iron and no longer being bound by the constraints of the cost of silver. He feels that iron has created a new dimension for him; he likes the responsivness and plasticity of it when hot compared to its strength when cold. [1]

He now feels a greater fusion between the material, energy and the creative process. It is probably part of his Quaker upbringing that has led him to a paring down of design to an absolute minimum—clear simple sculptural forms mark his very distinctive personal style.

There is a very calligraphic quality to his work—his *Wind Sensitive Bird Bath* has aptly been called "a drawing in space".[2] He himself has written ". . . my work is created to express the linear quality of forged metal through the development of drawing in three dimensions." [3]

In 1989 he held a one-man exhibition of work in iron "Forging On" at Glasgow School of Art and since then has shown in a number of exhibitions; in 1994 The Scottish Gallery, Edinburgh, held a solo exhibition of his new work.

He has been recently moving into architectural ironwork; major commissions have been a pair of screens and gates in iron, brass and bronze for Scottish Metropolitan Properties Ltd., and sliding screens in stainless steel and alumunium for The new headquarters of Borders Regional Council.

He won the National Competition for Gates and Railings for the Usher Gallery, Lincoln in

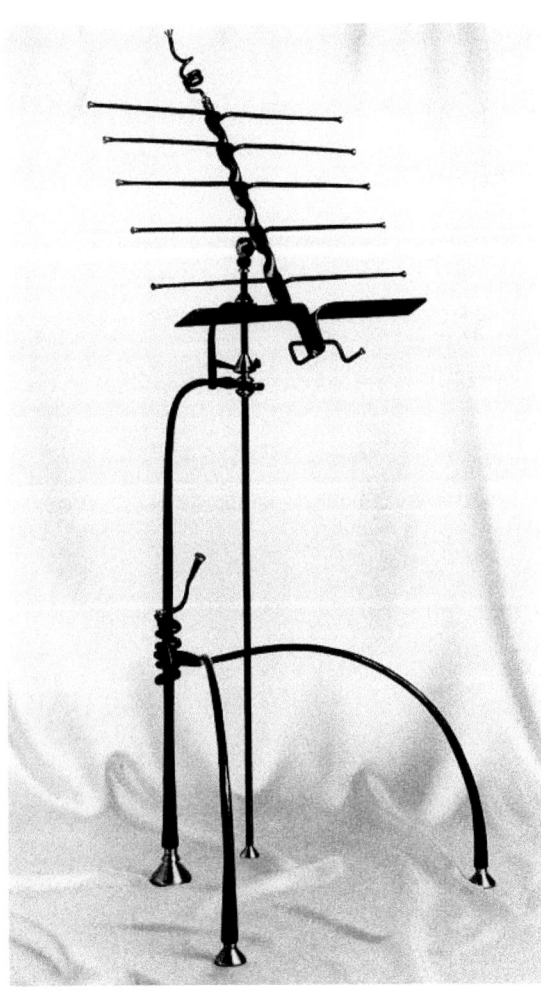

Below left: Music Stand 1989. Forged steel & brass. Adjustable.
Photograph John Tomlinson.

Opposite page: Wind Sensitive Birdbath.

Photograph John Creed.

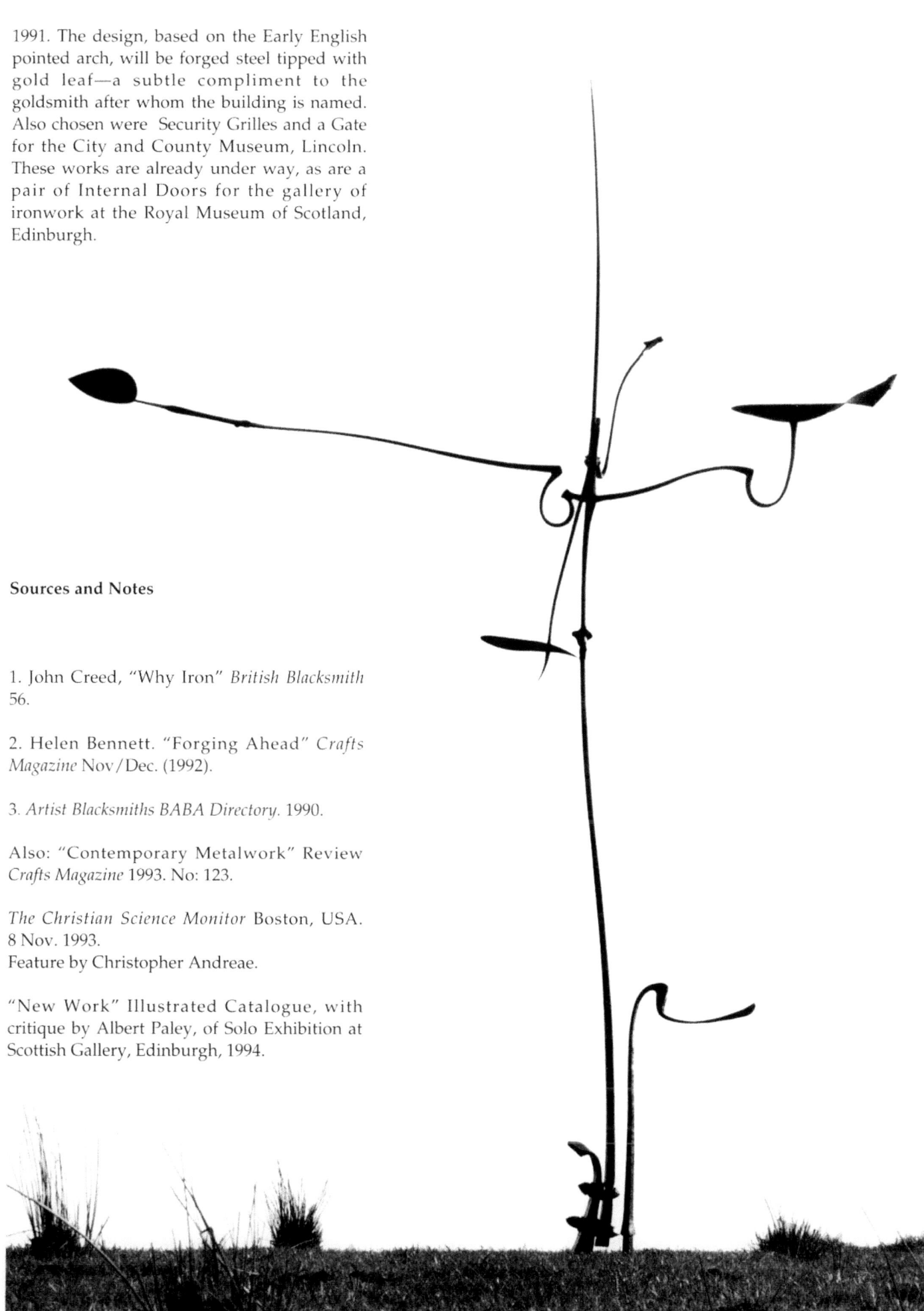

1991. The design, based on the Early English pointed arch, will be forged steel tipped with gold leaf—a subtle compliment to the goldsmith after whom the building is named. Also chosen were Security Grilles and a Gate for the City and County Museum, Lincoln. These works are already under way, as are a pair of Internal Doors for the gallery of ironwork at the Royal Museum of Scotland, Edinburgh.

Sources and Notes

1. John Creed, "Why Iron" *British Blacksmith* 56.

2. Helen Bennett. "Forging Ahead" *Crafts Magazine* Nov/Dec. (1992).

3. *Artist Blacksmiths BABA Directory.* 1990.

Also: "Contemporary Metalwork" Review *Crafts Magazine* 1993. No: 123.

The Christian Science Monitor Boston, USA. 8 Nov. 1993.
Feature by Christopher Andreae.

"New Work" Illustrated Catalogue, with critique by Albert Paley, of Solo Exhibition at Scottish Gallery, Edinburgh, 1994.

PAUL MARGETTS

After a traditional four-year apprenticeship in 1975-79 with Skinner's Forge at Drayton, Belbroughton, Worcs., Paul spent several years working in the U.S.A. and Israel.

In America he worked as a lumberjack cutting timber in the Redwood Forests and welding equipment. In Israel he was occupied with industrial fabrication and milking cows!

In 1986-88 he was in Zimbabwe with Voluntary Services Overseas, teaching blacksmithing to rural blacksmiths and developing low-tech equipment. He evolved a design for bellows, in the form of a displacement pump. It used scrap oil drums one 50 litre size with a top valve, inside another 200 litre drum containing water and an air pipe. This proved to be a highly efficient low cost way of getting air to the hearth; enabling a temperature high enough for welding which traditional goatskin bellows could not achieve. (See British Blacksmith No 48.) For this he received a prize from the United Nations.

In 1989 he studied Art and Design at Bournville Art College, before opening his own forge at Belbroughton, Worcestershire.

The 1990s saw him winning the BABA trophy (made by Antony Robinson which he prizes highly) at the Royal Show on three occasions. Then in 1992 he won the Championship Challenge Trophy, presented by the Worshipful Company of Blacksmiths, at the Bath and West show and again at the Three Counties Show in 1994.

Above left: Family Group.

Above: Door Handles.

Photographs
Paul Margetts.

Far left: Floral Sculpture of forged mild steel 3.5 m high, in Ashton-under-Lyne.

Left: detail of the Floral Sculpture.

Photographs
Paul Margetts.

PEAT OBERON

Operates a Victorian forge in the recreated "Period Street" of Preston Hall Museum, Stockton-on-Tees, Cleveland. This is no mere museum piece, however, but a real workshop where Peat and his three-man team make a living.

His early ambitions to work in metal and take up sculpture were unfulfilled. There were no metalworking classes at the Grammar School he attended, though he excelled at woodwork. Then, instead of his wish to attend an Art School he found himself a draughtsman with Dorman Long Steelworks. The break came when he enrolled at Bede College to train as a craft teacher and then had the opportunity to use a forge. [1]

After fifteen years as a school teacher he found he was spending most of his weekends and holidays in the forge, where he was doing something he really enjoyed and felt was useful. In 1980, at the age of 40, with his mortgage paid off, but with four children still in education, he took the plunge and became a self-employed blacksmith.

Peat Oberon is a traditional smith of great quality and his work is known for its fine finish—this he attributes to J.K. Powell, his instructor at Bede College who was a brilliant craftsman.

An ardent conservationist and restorer of ironwork, Peat today now finds himself more and more drawn towards modern creative design. A recent commission was for 13 panels between brick piers outside a new office block, occupied by the Inland Revenue, in Russell Street, Middlesbrough. Steel flats have been given a double twist in two places and assembled in each frame to create a Saint Andrew's cross; seen from many different viewpoints and in various lights they have a variety of textural effects.

Peat tells me that Saturday mornings are for pleasure when, by himself, he works "with one mind alone" and wholly concentrates on modern work. I particularly liked the Art Nouveau gate he made in 1988; and the painted urn gate with flowers and foliage displayed in the Sotheby's exhibition in 1991 was a crisp modern version of an old theme. Although the making of animal heads can be traced back into the very dawn of blacksmithing, his horses head forged from one piece of steel is so vibrant and vivid that it seems to have all the lively creativity needed to make it part of the 20th century.

Source Note

1. Keith Seacroft. "Peat Oberon a Profile" *British Blacksmith* 63.

Glynn Clarkson

Above: Art Nouveau Gate. Photograph Trevor Swan.

Far left: Gate with Flowers. Photograph Glynn Clarkson.

Below: Horse Head. Photograph Peat Oberon.

BRIAN RUSSELL

Studied Fine Art at Sunderland Polytechnic 1970-74 and established workshop at Little Newsham, Darlington, in 1976.

Brian, a lean 6' 4", is apt to pick up gates with one hand. His demonstrations, although almost silent, are much appreciated by blacksmiths. I have heard them say "His hands are magic", and "He simply goes like hell, and every shut is right first time !"

His work, until recently, has tended to have a fairly traditional appearance, which may be because he has a natural inclination towards symmetry. This can be seen in his gates for Bishop Auckland Town Hall, Co. Durham; though looked at closely the elements can be seen to be completely modern in concept.

An exceptionally beautiful gate, made as an entry for the Lincoln Design Competition in 1992, is a modern design suitable for a Gothic building. It was built up from the base with wholly traditional joins; spikes pass through drifted holes, lugs go into narrow openings in side uprights, and central collars (the last thing to be done) hold everything together. If it had not been made perfectly it would not have fitted together.

A gate, more freely made, perhaps because it is for his own drive, appears "roped" together, with flat leaf-like forms as the decorative element. The centre rises at the bottom because the road rises steeply and as the gates open they need clearance. It is a joyous design, perhaps because it was made with children in mind, being near where Brian's son and his friends play, it is to prevent them running out into the road.

Having access to a really good galvaniser, he galvanises his gates and paints them with Hi-build Vinyl paint, which is specially formulated to cover galvanised steel.

6 mm and 3 mm plate were used for his Heraldic Beasts.

Top above: Heraldic Beasts.

Above: Fish Weathervane. Made as a demonstration piece in 1994. Length 2 m, weight one hundredweight.

Below: 'Teazel' Gate.

Below right: One of a number of bollards in Stockton-on-Tees.

Photographs by Brian Russell.

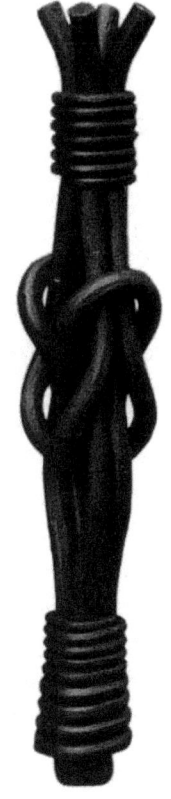

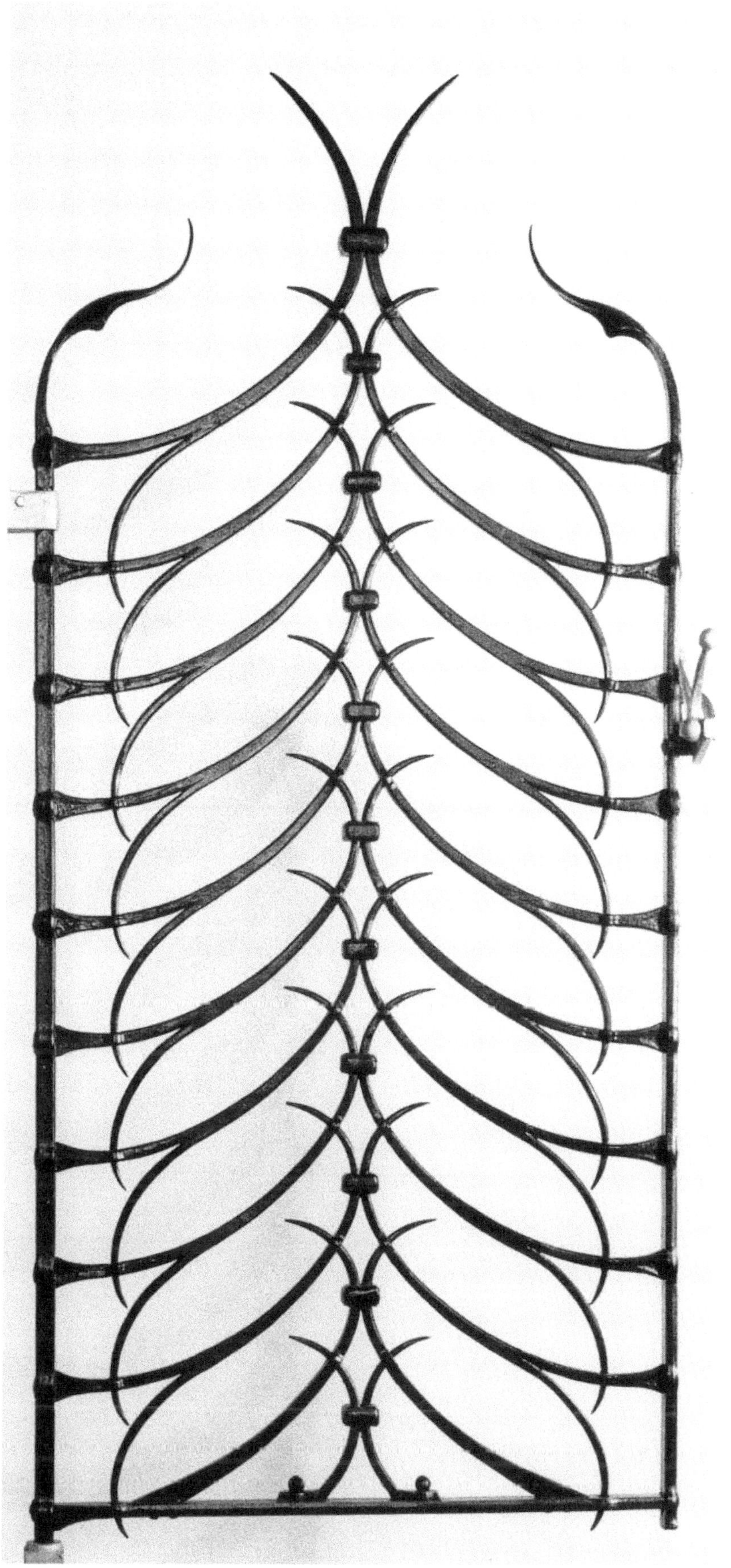

Left: Detail of the gates for Bishop Auckland Town Hall, Co. Durham.
Photograph Robert Elliot

Above: The 'Gothic Gate' made as an entry for the Lincoln Design Competition in 1992. A modern interpretation of a Gothic theme.
Photograph Studio 7 Lincoln

ANTHONY WOOTTON

Was born in Torquay in 1952. From 1974-76 he took a course in constructional design at St. Paul's College of Education, Cheltenham. He was then employed in general fabrication and smithing and studying part-time with Alan Knight in Worcestershire. He appears in this section, rather than in Part II, only because he has spent so much of his working life in Germany, and not in this country.

During 1979-80 he was an apprentice with Paul Zimmermann at Pliezshausen, Germany; then for the following two years with the firm of Manfred Bergmeister, Ebersberg, Germany. In 1981 he received a journeyman's certificate (Gesellenprufung - Schlosser - Handwerk) from Metall-Innung, Munich. (See also his work page 41.)

It was while studying in West Germany that he sent back to the British Blacksmith (No 9) a personal view of the Artist-Craftsman and his impressions of working in another environment. This included his belief that those—"Who would aspire to the title of 'artist craftsman' must satisfy the criteria implied by both terms. The obligation of an 'artist' is to produce, in response to the

stimuli of environment, personal observations which make coherent statements to the recipient. The responsibility of the craftsman is to create through the exercise of utmost skill and a precise understanding of the function of objects, work which transcends mere function."

He found in Germany specific focal points in social life that both needed, and provided themes for, ornamental ironwork. This was not only in the home, and the hanging signs in the streets, but above all in the life of the church. The traditional objects of the past were also being joined by modern wall sculptures for banks and municipal buildings, and with free standing sculptures, mobiles and fountains for new developments. Such ironwork he felt must stand "as a witness for generations to come of an attempt to create, in a given environment, a form that refreshes the eyes, the hands and the minds of all those who confront it."

At the Lindau Exhibition in 1980, Tony exhibited a finely wrought iron cross, a candlestick, a candle holder and a wall sculpture. In 1982 in the "Towards a New Iron Age" exhibition at the Victoria and Albert Museum he showed several pieces, all notable for a strong grace and economy of line.

He made a wall mounted "Chapel Cross" for St. John's Methodist church in Bloxwich; it is in stainless steel mounted on a gilded central cushion boss of squarish form. The cross was made by Tony while he was in Germany; to be placed in a modern part of the Chapel whose development was instigated by a minister, himself of German birth, who had been a prisoner of war in this country.

Far left: "The Master's Gate", High Street, Sevenoaks.

Photograph by Chris Fairclough.

In 1983 Tony was awarded a two year Fellowship at Sevenoaks School. This had become an established tradition; the intention being straight forward symbiosis — an arrangement designed to benefit both parties. In reality he found it a somewhat ambiguous position. Under the auspices of the Art Department a photographer, a lute-maker and a weaver had all preceded him in taking up temporary residence.

By-products of the fellowship included a one-man show in the School Library at the Sevenoaks Summer Festival in 1984, and an exhibition of work by students in a local bank the following Autumn. He carried out

Above: Sign with forged deer.

Photograph by Anthony Wootton.

further tradition by making "The Master's Gate" adjacent to the Almshouses, No 1, The High Street, Sevenoaks. In the adjoining wall a stone records that "Near here stood the 17th Century Master's Gate". This was instigated by the South-East Arts Craft Award (1983/4) and the making recorded on video. A balustrade adjoining the school Chemistry Laboratory was made as a group project in a design derived from test tubes or phials.

Tony felt that during his time there more significance was to be found in ". . . the unquantifiable effects of chance confrontations and the seeds thereby unknowingly sown . . . ." (*British Blacksmith* 34 p. 9)

Tony had married a German girl and continued to work in the Sevenoaks area for a further twelve months. They had the intention of setting up a forge at a Community Heritage Centre that was to be formed at Edenbridge. This project, however, failed to materialise and they decided to return to Germany. They have a twelve year-old son and for the past seven years they have been living in Bavaria.

WHAT *IS* MODERN IRONWORK ?

Obviously *time* is not the only criteria because ironwork can be made *now* but *in the style of the past.* Doubtless there have always been some smiths who were more conservative than others, and some of a more avant-garde nature who have sought to push back boundaries. It will undoubtedly be easier to describe it, with hindsight, in fifty or a hundred years time. Definition is difficult because we have not yet completed its creation. For those smiths at the beginning of the modern renaissance, whether abroad or in this country, it must have been very difficult to know in what direction to go, because they had little but their own creativity to guide them. Let no one think that to produce good modern work is the easy option. It is certainly not easy to evolve a shape that is simple, beautiful and *new*.

The Arts of any period of time have their own corporate identity. We can look at an antique and say *this is Medieval* or *this is 18th century* —because there is an almost indefinable wholeness about the arts and crafts of any time span, which usually tends, for the sake of convenience, to be roughly divided into centuries.

In times past ironwork did not stand alone it had quite definite stylistic similarities with other crafts. In that part of the middle ages known as the *Age of the Locksmith* when much of the iron was worked cold we see layers of sheet or plate pierced with patterns and built up one above the other; but compare this with the stone tracery of church windows or the old wooden pews in Jarrow church and one sees there is an obvious similarity between all the examples. Indeed the iron tracery at the top of the screen (1425-1431) to Henry V's Chapel in Westminster Abbey is derived straight from the architecture of the period.

It was probably no coincidence that 17th century furniture so often had *barley sugar*

legs and stair rails were usually made of turned wood in twisted forms, when the most commonly used decoration in ironwork was twisted bars. What we think of as typically 18th century iron scrollwork occurs in very similar designs in carved woodwork, or in stone memorials; as well as in jewellery and furniture mounts of the period.

Perhaps it would be helpful in defining what is *contemporary* ironwork, to look at the other arts and crafts of the 20th century. The ground swell of any movement is never easy to define but, as just suggested, there is a certain consistency across the arts or disciplines. One might therefore postulate that to be contemporary ironwork must have some similarities, as much of belief as in practice, with other 20th century arts.

The fine arts were the first to free themselves from the naturalistic restraints that had grown up with the *old masters*. It would have been far more consistent if modern ironwork in this country had indeed *taken off* with Mackintosh, at the time when Picasso was moving away from realism and opening up exciting possibilities of free expression; and as we have seen this did happen more on the continent than it did here.

Already in the later years of the 19th century the Impressionists had begun to question the

Above left: Balanced Sculpture of welded iron and composition with moveable iron parts, 1951. By Lynn Chadwick.

reality of the accepted naturalistic vision of, for instance, the Pre-Raphaelites. They began to paint only what they could *see*, not what they knew to be there; if half a face faded into shadow they depicted it in that way. They no longer necessarily placed their compositions formally in the centre of the canvas, they were not afraid to cut part of the body off by the frame if that was the way they wanted it to be. For the first time (if one excepts Turner), they tried to paint the reality of light, often by the way it changed the same object, at different times of the day.

Gertrude Stein observed **that people do not change it is only the way they see things that changes in each generation ". . . a creator then who creates is necessarily of his generation."** [1]

The painting of the Impressionists, that had seemed so fresh and new and light, began in the early years of the 20th century to be questioned, and changed by Picasso, Braque, and Matisse, because they were seeing things with new eyes and struggling to create a new art. They in their turn were not afraid to symbolise and to remove all but the essence of form. They were influenced not so much by the Classic as by the intense vitality of Primitive Art. To leave naturalism it was necessary to accept simplification, stylisation, and even the abstract. They experimented and changed and created; they introduced collage and invented cubism as the first stage of abstract art. It was all a great freeing from the realism of the past.

Even more relevant to ironwork than painting were sculpture and architecture. Sculpture evolved into the 20th century not much later than painting. By 1924 Henry Moore had begun his long struggle, and was endlessly observing nature and studying organic forms so that, in the end, his sculptured figures owed as much to the shape of pebbles, rocks and trees as they did to the human form. We have become used to his new way of seeing, we no longer feel shock that there is a hole through the middle of a figure; the massy female shapes no longer seem strange or ugly to us, but to have a monumental peacefulness, born of much strife and reality.

Moore believed that all art was to some extent an abstraction; and that in stone, and indeed the same might be said of iron, **that the material itself forces one away from pure representation towards the abstract.**

Picasso, as ever, was far ahead of everyone else, making in 1912 a sculptural still life out of flat metal sheet. The Spaniard Julio Gonzalez (1876-1942) was already producing abstract iron sculptures in the 1930s, such as *Danseuse a la Palette* 1933, a three dimensional piece but very much inspired by Picasso and Braque paintings. Although less avant-garde his life size female figure *La Montserrat* 1936-7 of wrought and welded iron, had the simplification and stylisation of modern sculpture, which gave it a monumental aspect and placed it firmly in the contemporary scene.

Gonzalez was later followed by his compatriot Eduardo Chillida, who works mainly in iron and steel in an abstract way, though he prefers to describe it as rejecting physical appearances. His pieces seek to open up and extend space rather than to define it.[2]

The advent of the Mobile, often made in metal, originated in America with the work of

Left: La Montserrat 1936/7. Forged iron, 165 x 47 cm. By Julio Gonzalez. In the Collection of the Stedelijk Museum, Amsterdam.

Alexander Calder. In this country Lynn Chadwick first began to make lightweight mobiles in 1946 but knew nothing of Calder at that time. By 1950 he began to make larger works and realised the necessity of learning to weld both copper and iron. So in some ways the mobile was bringing sculpture closer to the work of the smith. Indeed, who can say if John Creed's *Wind Sensitive Bird Bath* (1990) (p.67) is a mobile or simply an example of modern ironwork. Similarly the use of steel as a medium by sculptors abroad and by Reg Butler in England, from the late 1940s, further blurred the distinction between the two disciplines.

Reg Butler won "The Unknown Political Prisoner" competition in 1952 with a symbolic steel *Watchtower* and Lynn

Left above: Maquette for The Unknown Political Prisoner Competition, Welded iron, height 43cm. by Lynn Chadwick.

Left and left below: Detail of large Mobile in different positions. Made of iron and copper in 1951. Height 228cm. by Lynn Chadwick.

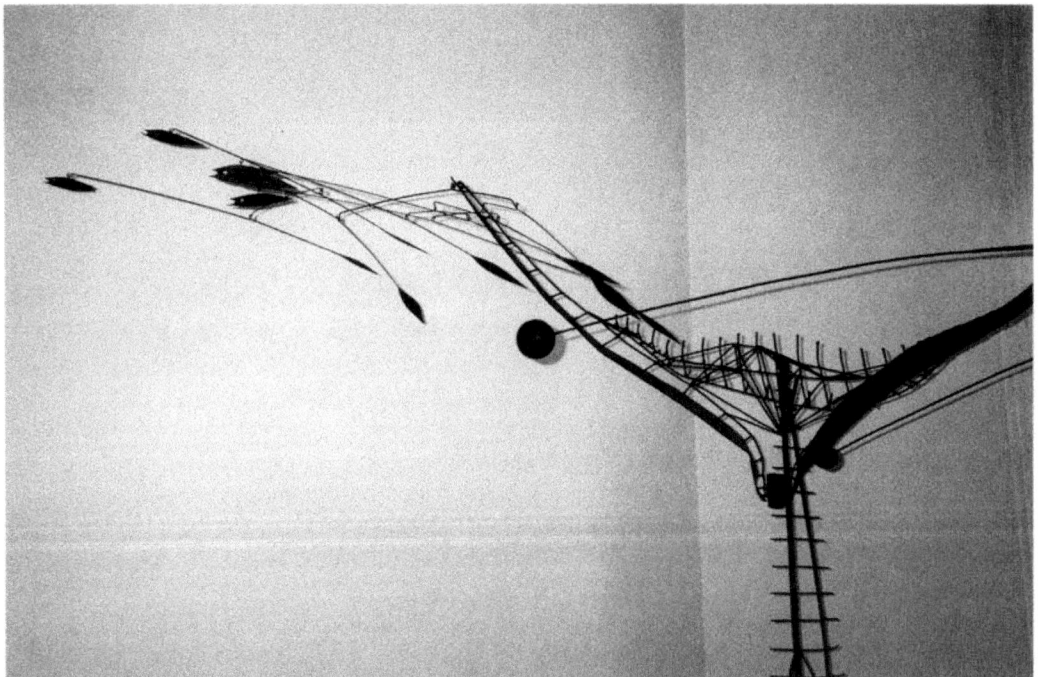

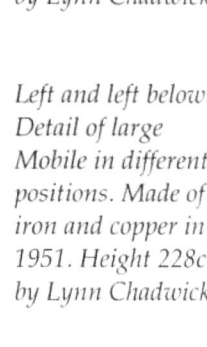

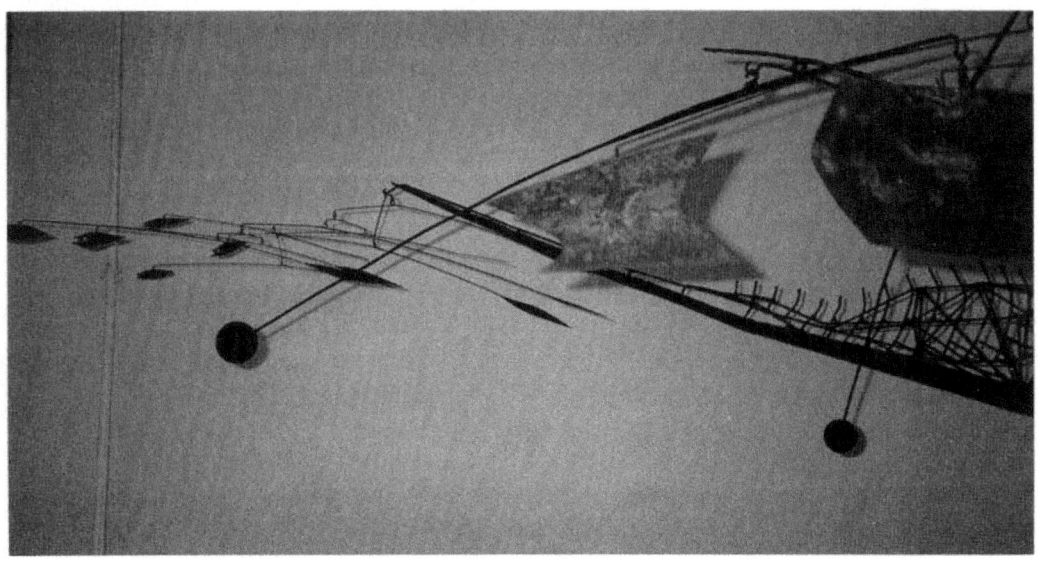

Chadwick achieved a lesser prize with a maquette in welded iron consisting of four lozenge-shaped spiky forms in which a fifth, at a higher level, seemed imprisoned by this hostile palisade. Later out of his work with mobiles Chadwick evolved some welded iron sculptures, in the 1950s, with balanced or moveable parts; and others that incorporated glass or crystals (page 74).

In the 1960s he produced a number of sculptures in welded iron only or incorporating *found objects* of metal such as chains, horse shoes, cast cogged wheels and worm gears. Using only welded plates and rods: Tower of Babel I & II, in 1963 (heights 51cm and 68cm respectively), were as impressive and important as many of his later bronze sculptures. These he makes today by welding an armature of steel rods and covering them with an industrial artificial compound of gypsum and iron powder called *Stolit*, applied over a base of polystyrene foam. They are then usually cast in bronze.

Today we have the modern work of Hamish Black and Peter Pay. You may ask why their work has not been featured in this book?—it has not been easy to decide where to draw lines between metal sculpture *per se* or sculptures in metal made by Artist Blacksmiths, Designer Metalsmiths, call them what you will. There are times when definitions are impossible to distinguish.

Equally there are some impressive works being made for welding and showground competitions, but many are realistic, and could not really be said to be contemporary in styling. Other works, sometimes even made from scrap, have all the life and originality that typifies modern work, but perhaps fall more into the art of sculpture. If lines are to be drawn it is difficult to know where.

Whereas the use of metal was gradually taking place in 20th century sculpture, by welding or fabrication as apart from the traditional bronze casting, it appears to have had little or no influence on the modern smithing movement. It is, however, an interesting facet that some of the first smiths to create modern ironwork are now turning full circle, so that their main preoccupation is that of the sculptor; but with a very much higher degree of expertise in metalworking. So that today sculpture is being greatly enriched by the skills of the blacksmith.

The Benettons had always been sculpture orientated and Achim Kühn was producing a number of important pieces; while Serge Marchal is now known as a *sculpteur fer*. As long ago as 1987 he had dreamed of creating four great sculptures on submerged bases on a lake near Montpellier, in the south of France. In this arid and deserted region the four pieces would represent, in an entirely symbolic way, the elements of earth, fire, water and air. They would be lit at night and have specially composed music playing around them; it would only be possible to hear the music by taking a boat or surfboarding out from the shore, or swimming or surfing in amongst the gigantic sculptures. Fire, painted blue, and eleven metres high, would have aluminium balls with solar cells giving occasional flashes, and a large gas jet flaming three times a day. The Water sculpture, 9m high, would jet great fountains of water into the air. Each sculpture would represent a door, carrying through the idea of entry into the elements. Alas so far it has not yet proved possible to raise the funds necessary for so grand a project.

In 1991, he made ten sculptures for an important open-air exhibition for Pézenas, Herault, for chosen locations in this historic town. One, shown here, recalls armour clad forces "that never joined in battle . . . suspended in memory . . . between past and future, in a symmetry too perfect to be measured in the disorder of reality".[4] Both basalt and wood are used in this sculpture as well as steel.

Albert Paley is in 1994 being referred to as the *jewellery-maker turned sculptor*; and he also has begun to explore the possibilities of

Below: A "Landscape Viewing Piece". Garden Sculpture by Peter R Pay. Fabricated stainless steel sheet, with a patinated finish, giving the impression of a split and twisted block of steel.

incorporating wood and stone, marble and slate into his works of steel. Some of his larger pieces, like the screen shown here, have become completely sculptural, while in his 1994 exhibition "Organic Logic" even works *called* candlestick, bookends or tables are each individual pieces of fine art sculpture.

Originally revelling in the physical transformation made possible by the malleability of hot iron, he has gradually come to design more by drawings—making a whole series of sketches on paper and even using cardboard cutouts to explore the manipulation of planes to be formed by the metal.[4]

Recently the Memorial Art Gallery of the University of Rochester organised an exhibition "Inspiration and Context: The drawings of Albert Paley", which will travel for three years. In the catalogue he is rightly credited with changing metalworking "from a utilitarian craft into a dynamic art form".

In Architecture Mackintosh's "designing from the inside outwards" was, by 1928, becoming recognised as Functionalism, namely that the function of a building determined its form.

Photograph Alain Surelle © Serge Marchal

"... Sculpture is now being greatly enriched by the skills of the blacksmith"

Above: "Champs clos" 1991, forged stainless steel, wood and basalt. Height 160cm, width 300cm, depth 280cm by Serge Marchal.

Below: Sculpture Screens 1993 for the Federal Courthouse, Camden, New Jersey. Formed and fabricated steel, polychromed. 107in x 67in x 12in. by Albert Paley.

Paley Studios

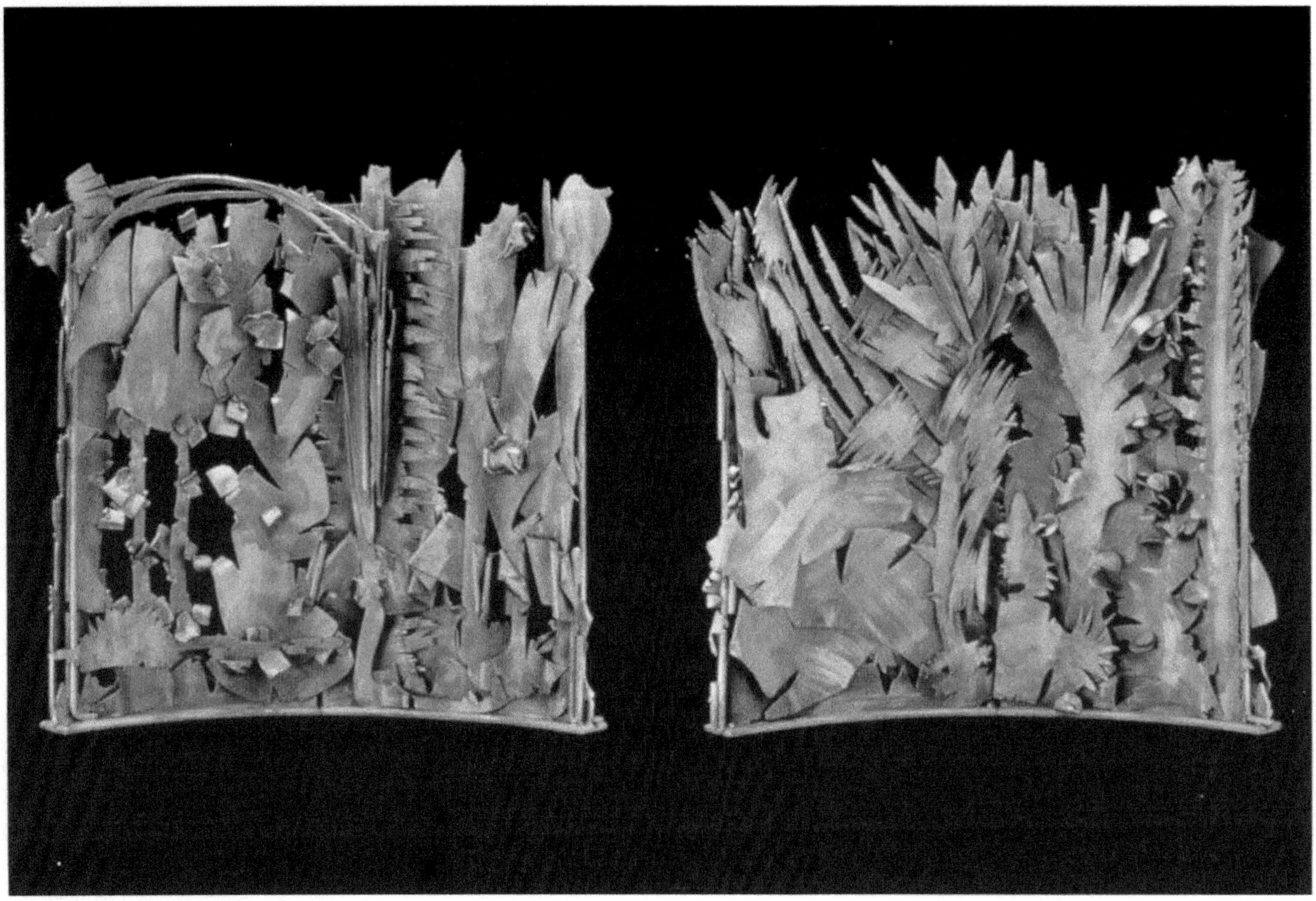

"The house shall be a machine in which to live." (Le Corbusier) Modern architecture was also making a complete break with the past in the sense of no longer copying past styles.

In both sculpture and architecture the concept of *Truth to Material* became a part of 20th century thinking. Another tenet of architectural belief, this time one that affected both sculpture and ironwork in a rather adverse way at the time, was the suppression or elimination of ornament of every feature not demanded by necessity. Architecture and ironwork are only at this time beginning to come together again in harmony now that domestic architecture is more humanised and ironwork is more abstract and less ornamented; that is in the sense of being no longer *decorated* but having its design as an elemental part of its structure.

On another plane—it could also be said that the Lloyds Building in the City of London has metalwork as an *elemental part of its structure*. Some modern architecture is almost becoming metal sculpture in itself. Interesting thought —is it too futuristic to suppose that in time to come, the blacksmith, the sculptor and the architect will be indivisible !

Modern blacksmiths will frequently take their cue from the design of the architecture, being influenced by both its shape and texture, as was Jim Horrobin at Crown Reach, and Alan Evans in the crypt of St. Paul's Cathedral.

It has been said of ironwork in architecture:

"When designing a railing or trellis my starting point is always its architectural context and above all its task of protecting, supporting, dividing, and affording a view through." Fritz Kühn (Decorative Work in Wrought Iron and Other Metals)

. . . "it must belong to the building and enhance it in some way. That is to say that without the ironwork, the building is diminished; but also without the building the ironwork is diminished." Peter Parkinson (BB 56 1990)

"I try to make pieces that reflect my emotional reaction to the space and yet physically respond to the adjacent architecture. I have discovered the possibility of provoking a response in the beholder equivalent to my response to the site." Alan Evans (1992)

Albert Paley has gone further and asks himself not only how his works will

Below: Coil Table 1992 and Desk A 1994, by Albert Paley. The Lloyds Building, London. R. Rogers Partners.

compliment and amplify the building and the landscape, but also how it will relate to pedestrians.[6]

The quotations above were written mainly with contemporary buildings in mind but modern ironwork is not necessarily incongruous on old buildings. This is exemplified by Achim Kühn's immensely successful work for the church of Mary in Berlin (1968) where iron doors are fitted into Gothic Arches, solid, but deeply grooved and textured, rather like the bark of a tree. Also successful, in this country, in a different way, are the modern hinges on a new door to replace one, with vestiges of iron remaining on the famous early door, at Stillingfleet, Yorkshire, dating from c 1145. Chris Topp has used straight modern patterns for the large decorative hinges—a brave and interesting solution; worked out in collaboration with the architect. (1990) The venerable old door, with its Norse iron dragons and boat, can now be conserved and is mounted inside the new door. There are, of course, a number of modern designs in ironwork to be seen inside churches today, and these are becoming well accepted. Many of them appear in the second section of this book.

Today the merging of modern smithing in its sculptural and architectural context, is becoming a very exciting addition to architecture and the space that surrounds it.

Jewellery has always been the handmaiden of the arts and has followed in the steps of Art Nouveau and Art Deco. It entered the modern epoch in this country somewhat before ironwork and by the 1960s was producing work based on natural forms and minerals. It is interesting to note that what may be the sole surviving jewel, c 1905-7, designed by Charles Rennie Mackintosh, and made by his wife, would not look out of place in this company (see page 15).

Perhaps enough has been said to point up that similar aims and beliefs are to be found across all the arts of the 20th century:

The necessity of a creative outlook.

The importance of the eye in concentrated observation.

An appreciation of the ultimate function of the object.

The desire to reduce design as far as possible to the elemental.

Undoubtedly the most difficult concept to describe in words is that of creating elemental forms in ironwork.

Consider the making of a gate inspired by grass—doubtless traditionally the smith would have looked at grass in a literal and naturalistic way and made a gate showing groups or tufts of grasses and it would have been very decorative. The contemporary smith, however, would be more likely to go and lie in a field of grass; and taking a piece between his fingers, he would note how a blade of grass comes from the ground, small and round in section, then becomes V shaped in section with a crease down the centre, then opens into a flat blade of grass, then from the sides gradually begins to taper to an elongated point—a beautiful form. A gate using such shapes would be based on the very true form of grass—the elemental form.

Below: New Hinges for Stillingfleet Church, Yorkshire, by Chris Topp.

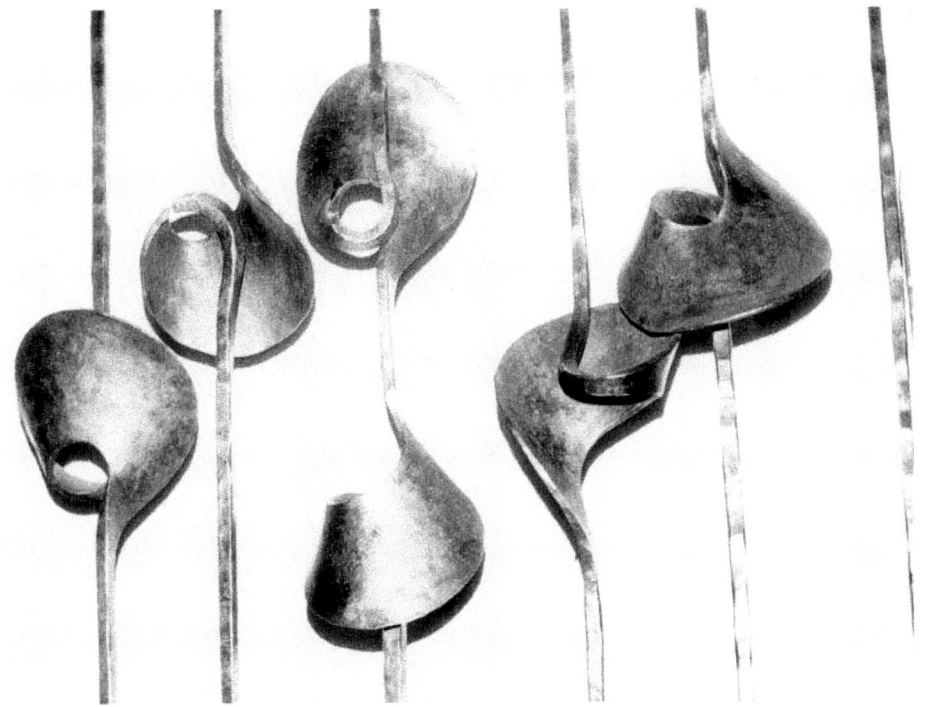

Even a smith working in a modern way has still to find his own identity, just as an artist has; so that we see in his work not only the general contemporary image, but also the more personal stamp of his own creativity. It was interesting, when Alan Evans, spoke about his grille for the Cheltenham Museum entrance, to hear him say at the unveiling, that he welcomed the commission because it was one with which he was in sympathy and one that could **take its place in his own design evolution.**

There are many grey areas in the way we consider contemporary ironwork. Is it legitimate on the *truth to material* theory to leave welds unsmoothed and to accept the welding beads as part of the design? Smiths have had to make their own choices on such matters as we can see in Part II. Modern machines and equipment are labour saving and an economic necessity. They can also be an advantage. They can produce strong and weatherproof joints [8] that give a much greater freedom in design than those previously used by the traditional smith. In this way smiths have been enabled to construct gates without framing if they so wish.

A very strong element in the creation of the modern style has been the utilisation of modern techniques. In many cases the forms have been dictated by, and evolved from, the processes of production. Whereas Fritz Kühn and Samuel Yellin experimented to produce new forms by traditional methods more recent smiths, like Albert Paley, have

produced a whole range of shapes by exploiting the new processes. The power hammer has made it far easier to draw out long lengths of bar, and the acceptance of

". . . to evolve a shape that is simple, beautiful and new."

Far left: Fern fronds. Natural forms have inspired smiths through the ages— never more than today when there is a search for the elemental and the organic.

Much new work has been achieved by simply following a line of investigation in the workshop, then evolving, and later exploiting, its potential; the work of Stuart Hill and his use of pressed tube being a prime example of this evolution. Other smiths have particularly explored the possibilities of cutting and opening out unconventional sections like angle iron or rolled steel joists.

While experimentation offers no automatic recipe for success it does help smiths to design for themselves, and to create forms that are very much their own. What they invent is likely to become far more a part of their own growth and individual style than any forms appropriated from others.

Surprisingly fabrication, which until recently has implied construction without the skill of the smith, is now being used to a considerable extent by Albert Paley. After his translation from jeweller to smith he produced, by forging, some of the most sinuously beautiful ironwork ever made up to that time. Today modern techniques have to some extent led him to different methods of working. Much of his ironwork is cut at other workshops by industrial methods. There computerised machines translate and enlarge his drawings to the metal where it is cut by heat or laser beam; thereby cutting out the long hours that would be needed to cut with a torch by hand. The elements then return to his studio for grinding, bending, forging and welding into his sculptural forms—he has lifted fabrication into an art form.[9]

Methods of heating are also changing. Whereas the small fire given by the traditional British back-blast forge is ideal for fire-welding and small forging it is not very adaptable for heating longer pieces of iron. This has led to many smiths changing to bottom-blast forges or using gas forges which enable longer lengths, greater masses of metal or larger areas of plate to be adequately heated. Neither is there so much fear of overheating as they are more controllable. So not only are many new techniques being used but even the traditional hearth is beginning to change.

The Art of Ironwork is very much an enigma. Having said how important modern techniques have been in creating contemporary work, one can equally say that it is all in the mind. Look at Jim Horrobin's *Hanging Irons* (p 131) or David Petersen's

welding has enabled drawn out bars to be joined into even longer lengths. The power hammer has also led to squashing bars into shapes not formerly used.

Partly through use of the power hammer contemporary work has become characterised by a more overall working of the iron, producing a richness of surface and frequent changing of section. This contrasts with much traditional work, where, after the introduction of stock bar it was often only the ends of the bar that were forged; leaving an expanse of unworked and singularly uninteresting plain bar in the middle. In this respect modern work has much of the liveliness of earlier work where the smith had little, or sometimes no, choice of bar size and had to forge his own lengths.

Smiths no longer necessarily try to hide the joins in their work, but take the attitude that many methods of forging joints actually enhance the structure and form the design. It will be seen in much of the work in Part II that hinges, latches and joints are no longer a necessary but subordinate part of the work, but form a very important part of the design.

Memorial to Graham Sutherland (p 172) they breathe the 20th century—but were made with nothing more than the hammer and anvil.

We are perhaps particularly fortunate to live when there is so great a variety of ironwork about us. Nothing changes overnight—we can still appreciate the best traditional ironwork of the past, while watching the exciting creative smithing that is taking place today, and forging the ironwork of the future. British smiths are no longer chained, they are creative, they are innovators. They are finding a new vocabulary and have entered into their own age.

Smiths with an interest in the contemporary outlook travel by many ways:

There are smiths who work in the modern way but are derivative rather than innovative.

There are smiths who work primarily in a traditional way but sometimes design and make modern work.

There are traditional smiths who have simplified and stylised form towards a contemporary interpretation.

All move along the same road but inevitably some have arrived further towards their destination than others.

Sources and notes.

1. Gertrude Stein *Picasso*. Batsford 1938.

2. Frederick Lloyd. *Chillida. British Blacksmith* 59.

3. Dennis Farr & Eva Chadwick. *Lynn Chadwick Sculptor* Clarendon Press 1990. Most of Lynn Chadwick's sculptures are cast in bronze at Pangolin Editions, Chalford, Gloucestershire.

4. *Cour barbare* catalogue. 1991.

5. Penelope Hunter-Stiebel. *Albert Paley: Organic Logic* Catalogue Peter Joseph Gallery, New York, 1994.

6. *Inspiration & Context: The drawings of Albert Paley*. Memorial Gallery of the University of Rochester. Page 3.

7. *Inspiration & Context* Mildred F. Schmertz. As above.

8. Richard Bent. *The Blacksmiths Craft. British Blacksmith* 55.

9. As note 5 above.

Left: Mouse Doorknocker. Forged by Robert Hobbs, Champion Blacksmith of the year 1988.

". . . traditional smiths who have simplified and stylised form towards a modern interpretation."

The smiths who feature in the last part of this book are those who have found, or are finding, their own identity, within the overall Modern Movement, and who have for some years, been consistently creating ironwork for our own time.

'Smiths Forging.' Limited edition Wood Engraving by Rachel Reckitt.

PART II

MODERN BRITISH BLACKSMITHS

TERRENCE CLARK	86
ALAN DAWSON	92
ALAN EVANS	104
THEO. GRUNEWALD	117
STUART HILL	119
JAMES HORROBIN	129
ALAN JACK	138
GIUSEPPE LUND	140
MICHAEL MALLESON	149
CHARLES NORMANDALE	155
PETER PARKINSON	162
DAVID PETERSEN	168
MELVIN PINNOCK and the Nailbourne Forge	174
WALENTY PYTEL	182
RICHARD QUINNELL and the Rowhurst Forge	187
RACHEL RECKITT	193
MICHAEL ROBERTS	197
ANTONY ROBINSON	202

TERRENCE CLARK

Was born at Walton-on-Thames, Surrey in 1946. He was apprenticed to a bookbinder and later worked for an engineering firm learning welding and fabrication skills.

He set up his own business welding and fabricating in steel for the commercial market in 1971, and three years later began to be involved in smithing.[1]

In 1981 he moved to his present forge at Wildfields Farm, Woodstreet Village, near Guildford. The first piece of ironwork that Terry designed in a contemporary style was a gate for a side entrance to a house where the opening was out of true, wider at the top than the bottom. He solved the problem in an astute manner, by confusing the eye. Only one of the horizontal bars went right across the gate, the remainder were attached on one side or the other but did not go the whole way across. Railings to the same house were given heads to correspond to the top of the gate verticals.

In the same year he made a Window Grille, clear cut in design, from mild steel, forged

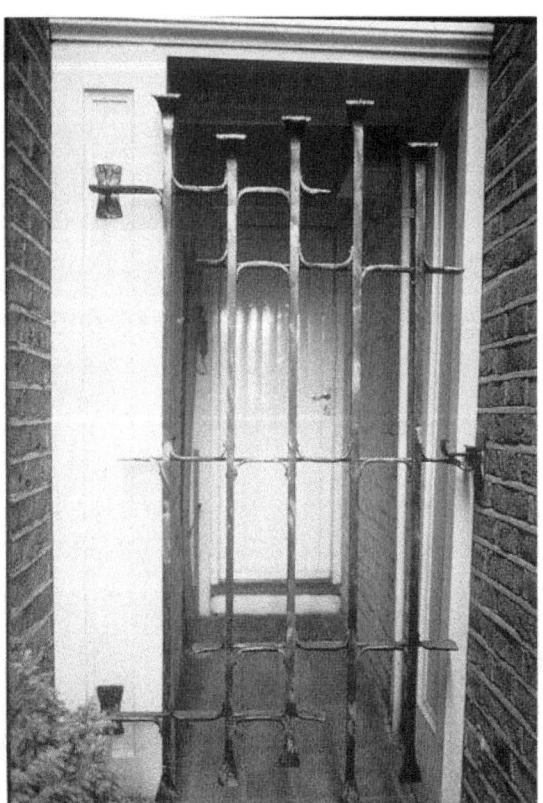

from solid section with the interlocking joints welded. 1.5m high x 1m wide. This was chosen to be exhibited in the V & A Museum in the "Towards a New Iron Age" exhibition in 1982.

A major commission at this time was a spiral staircase. Because the clients had a lot of carved oak furniture nearby Terry took its textures and oak peg fixings as his design theme. The rails, of 16mm and 25mm tapered to 16mm, were textured under the fullers of the power hammer and the fixings into the handrail gave the impression of circular wooden pegs. The rails curve outwards at the top then turn in to the handrail. A problem was to achieve the shaping without damaging the textured bar. A jig was constructed and the hot steel coaxed around it with wrenches and an occasional blow from a hide mallet. The central support was made out of two tubes one inside the other; the inner one was fixed to the base and the outer cut into

Above: Terry with a massive gate, width overall 5m, height over 4m, weight of each gate 1 ton. Completed in May 1994.

Photographs by Terrence Clark.

Far left: The first contemporary gate he made for the doorway that was out of true.

Photograph Terrence Clark.

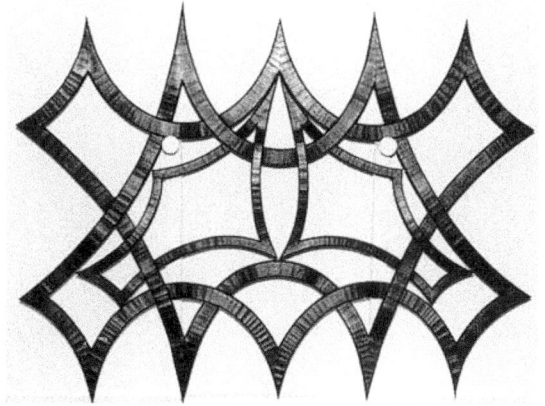

Left: Window grille exhibited in the "Towards a New Iron Age" Exhibition in 1982.

Far left: Spiral Staircase for a private commission.

Photographs by Terrence Clark.

"At last the stairs were complete and I could stand back and see all the forgings joined and fitted together. The handrail gave exactly the desired result. From the beginning it soared upwards to lift the entire stairs with it. From every different angle of viewing the profusion of vertical balusters and the swirling handrail produced an exciting different picture. The rail in places ceased to be a rail, more an anchorage for the soldier like balusters marching upwards." [2]

sections, each piece machined at one end to fit snugly into the next. These rotated and were held in position by the inner tube. The handrail was the greatest challenge; it was necessary to calculate stretching between the punching as well as working out the rivet points for each baluster. The handrail was cut out into three lengths and forged to shape on a specially made drum

In 1983 at the BABA Exhibition the Addy Taylor cup, presented by the "Worshipful Company of Blacksmiths" was awarded to Terry for his chess set and stand—a massive piece of power hammered tube with brass and bronze cast into the mild steel (see page 42).

An unusual commission was one for "The White Hart" just off the Wood Street Village Green. The owner wanted some ironwork put

Far left: Fireplace with flat cut-out trees, similar to those used on the Butterfield Gate and the "White Hart" frieze.

Below: Security grille with brightly painted flowers.

Photograph Terrence Clark.

on a low wall between part of the garden, where there were tables and chairs, and the car park. What Terry came up with was so unusual that it was a talking point for customers and indeed it is still. On an iron base he fixed cut out buildings that could be seen on a walk down the village street, the church, garage, school, the green, houses and trees. Tiny forged figures of children clamber in and out of the school and dance round the maypole.

These buildings cut out of steel had no background but seem to have led to his making a number of pieces in a narrative style forged out of plate. There was a gate at Priorsfield, Guildford, which included a monk, a sun, and a tree in fields; and another for a playground at Butterfield Green, in the borough of Hackney, where a cow took pride of place amongst fields and trees. A fireplace and hood shown at the BABA exhibition in 1985 was similarly decorated with trees.

A light-hearted work, that I have always enjoyed, was a security grille he made for an open cellar, commissioned by Whitfield Partners for the Crown Estate Commissioners. Brightly painted red flowers rise up as though in a window box, though really the stems are held by bands of iron at the base. It is a most decorative little piece; the idea for the design came from Terry's wife Sally (see page 85).

It must have been about 1984 that Terry first began to think about gates when they are open and appear uninteresting, because being flat they have no third dimension. When he received an enquiry for two pairs of double gates for Dalham Hall Stud, Newmarket, he decided to try and design a gate that would alter its appearance as it opened. He gave it depth by having the uprights shaped from front to back, rather like a horse's leg, instead of straight. The gates were massive, the horizontals were forged from 100mm x 15mm, the front and back stiles 50mm x 25mm, the uprights 20mm X 30mm. The main gates 5.5m wide were given confronting horses heads, at the top centre, and together with side panels weighed one ton. Some wall lamps were added to the commission which in total came to £52,000.

It was clear that Terry and his apprentice, Julian Coode, would not be able to do all the work themselves. Other blacksmiths, Tony Robinson and Charles Normandale agreed to

Photograph Terrence Clark

Above: One of the Dalham Stud gates. Newmarket.

Left: Detail of the gate showing depth to give interest when open.

Terrence Clark

join in making the gates. Some components they made in their own forges, then for several months they all worked together in Terry's forge at Wildfields. Fortunately the buildings are miles from anywhere, and all being interested in music they enjoyed the stimulus of working together to, mainly electronic, music. Although all are very

Left: The "Pavilion" gates 1990-91.

Below: Detail of the ironwork.

different characters they found an astonishing rapport grew up between them while they were working on this commission. When it was all completed, Terry wrote :

"It took me several weeks to wind down from the heady plateau that I had been on, and I felt very lost and alone in my forge."

The gates were for H.H. Sheik Mohammed Bin Rashid Al Maktoum and architects were the Hunter Price Partnership. They were followed by three similar gates in following years, and in 1990-91 by a pair of gates, grilles and railings, where a central arch in the gates echoes arched openings in two resplendent brick "pavilion" gate piers.

The idea of giving interest to gates when open continued to be a challenge. He made an experimental gate which was accepted for the Royal Academy Summer Exhibition in London in 1986—the first blacksmith to receive this honour. As you walk round it the appearance changes. It is a series of equally spaced uprights with a group of very attractive flaring forged forms extending forwards, and only seen at their best from the side. Also at this vantage point one is aware that beyond these forms the verticals become progressively broader as they near the hinge side. It was a gate that received considerable critical appreciation and was widely exhibited in this country and in Germany.

Far left: The experimental "flared" gate accepted for the Royal Academy Exhibition.

It was shown at the BABA exhibition at Coalbrookedale together with *Surrealist Gate* made of forged iron and handformed glass, clear and red, which appeared *thrown over* extended parts of the uprights. The back stile is normally the main structure giving strength to the gate, but in this case it was severed in the centre and the weight of the gate taken by one hinge at the top and a floor fixing at the bottom. Again from the side the upright bars were seen to widen and project forward at the base as they neared the hinge side.

Not long ago I visited Terry to hear about some of his more recent commissions. Wood Street is a long drawn out village the only one I have ever seen with a permanent May Pole on the Green. Wildfields Farm is aptly named, the unmade track from the village is very long, with Bracken, Ragwort and Willow Herb in the hedgerows. As I approach squirrels run across the road. There are goats and sheep in the fields near the house and fruit trees, one closely hung with enormously big red apples, like an illustration from a child's picture book. It is as unlikely a group of buildings as one is ever likely to meet—a listed country house, pale painted, verging on the gracious, a minute brick cottage next to a tumbledown wooden barn, both straight out of a fairy tale, and a fine modern brick workshop 100 ft in length. It is a country idyll hung about with the detritus of any forge or metalworks. Outside the workshop part of a large obelisk is in making for Westminster Council.

Terry Clark's work is very varied in character and I have been told that technically one of his strengths is in working to very close tolerances. He has produced some dramatic, but cost conscious, gates in bright blue, for a commercial enterprise; incorporating the firm's logo as part of the gate design. In complete contrast, in 1991, he was one of fourteen sculptors to create the only outside walk of Stations of the Cross in Europe at the Wintershall Estate in Bramley, Surrey. He chose to interpret the 5th station, *Simon of Cyrene helps Jesus carry his cross*, with a simple modern and very effective rendering.

On a more domestic scale a very successful gate and railings were designed to complete and enhance a 20th century black and white house. It is deceptively simple. The standards, with a slight mottled texture, flare out a little towards a domed top, and the horizontals appear like a rope that twists around them. It

Terrence Clark

Terrence Clark

Above: Railings for a private house.

Left: Detail of the "rope" railings.

was commissioned by architect Andy Hunter.

In 1991 Terry completed restoration work for the National Trust at Basildon Park. He has recently evolved simple modern punched and clipped Standard Railing 1.200m high, and Deer Railing 1.650m high, which has been used at Hatchlands Park and Clandon Park. He also has some very prestigious modern gates on the drawing board, some of them impressively large.

Terrence Clark

A new departure in his more recent work has been the use of round iron bar forged and twisted into shapes. The lattice sides of the Westminster Obelisk are rope-like and surprisingly intricate. Sometimes the ropes are forged into *roots*, and twisting round become a tree trunk, and then dividing move upwards to become branches—or in the case of a water garden feature to hold shell forms from which water overflows, falling into the next holder or down to pebbles on the ground.

Terry enjoys piloting aircraft and sometimes derives inspiration from his flying. The design of the votive candle stand he made for Guildford Cathedral grew out of an aerial view of the building with its two *arms* stretching out on either side of the West Door.

He has retained a schoolboy's addiction to big bangs. Whenever a function is to be closed by the firing of the anvil, setting a charge beneath an old anvil to blow it into the air (a blacksmith custom), he is always the one to organise the event. It seems perfectly consistent that he now has a sideline as a demonstrator of Pain's Fireworks.

Above left: Water feature.

Below Left: Stainless Steel Brooch.

Below Far Left: House Name.

Photographs Terrence Clark

Sources:

1. Catalogue *Towards a New Iron Age.*

2. Series of steps and risers ascending helically upon a vertical axis. Terry Clark. *British Blacksmith* 17.

ALAN
DAWSON

Left: Balnakeil Bay.

Timothy Porter

Alan Dawson was born in Whitehaven, Cumbria, in 1947.

He was craft orientated, was interested in woodwork at school and specialised in it, as part of a course in Creative Design, at Loughborough College.

In 1969 he left College qualified to teach crafts and secured a job, at Wellington Secondary Boys' School, Telford, Shropshire, as a teacher of metalwork and art. He soon realised that forging gave him more satisfaction than any other aspect of the craft, even making ring handled pokers, which was about the extent of his ability at this time. He also realised that teaching was not what he wanted to do. [1]

After three years he resigned and, with his wife, moved to the village of Durness, about as far north in Scotland as one can go. On the outskirts of this small village was a community of crafts people, living in an old army camp, of flat roofed concrete buildings. It was right on the edge of Balnakeil Bay, next to the ominous sounding Cape Wrath. Here they took their first tentative steps to self-employment. Alan still did not know very much about blacksmithing, so took up candle-making which, for some time, was to be the mainstay of their business.

Being so far north there were times when it never really became dark. After his work Alan would go onto the sea canoe-surfing. One night he had been out for some time and thought he would just surf in once more. As he neared the crest of the wave he saw three great dolphins bearing down on him. He was fearful that they would upset the canoe, but as they came to him they dived underneath the boat and came leaping up and away on the other side. He was so elated by this incident that he went on surfing and on every wave they did exactly the same thing as if, playing and joyful, they enjoyed his company —he found it an incredible experience and one he has never forgotten.

Three years later they returned to Cumbria

with their two children, sold the candlemaking side of the business, and began to rely solely on Alan's blacksmithing for support. [1]

Alan has written of those days:
"I was working in isolation in a collapsing cow shed, thinking that I was the only decorative blacksmith in the World when, in 1978, I heard through CoSIRA that a Mr Richard Quinnell was organising a gathering of blacksmiths. Scraping enough pennies together I managed to attend this inaugural meeting, which was soon to become the British Artist Blacksmiths Association, and my life changed."

He met others working alone like himself. He saw their work and the new techniques they were using. He watched Dick Quinnell using an electric welder with impunity:
"This was almost heretical for me at that time as I was then slavishly trying to emulate the great works of the past using traditional techniques, or trying to hide the fact that I had surrendered to the welder. [2]

In 1980 he attended the International Forging Iron Conference:
"I was humbled and at the same time inspired . . .
"The breadth of skill, expertise and technique evident at that gathering of the greatest smiths from around the World had the most profound effect on me and on British Blacksmithing too." [2]

Alan's contact with other smiths and their work gave him a much less restricted view of blacksmithing. He tried out new techniques and approaches to design. He increased in confidence and found that he could convincingly present his ideas to clients and architects.

"I was working in isolation in a collapsing cow shed, thinking that I was the only decorative blacksmith in the world . . ."

*Left: One of the front
panels to the bar—
"building up one
layer over another."*

He made a projecting sign for Bruno's Wine
Bar in Whitehaven, Cumbria, and this led to
one of his first large commissions. What the
proprietor called "a few more little jobs"
turned into large exterior lanterns, interior
lighting, wine racks, optic covers and a bar.
He was given a free hand in the design as
long as the result would be bold and striking
and the cost known in advance.

The bar was made of pine with three
decorative illuminated panels let into the
front. They were extraordinarily intricate and
effective, building up one layer over another,
as can be seen in the accompanying
illustration—practically building up three-
dimensional shapes. Above was a large
canopy of bold plant and flower forms,
almost sensuous in feeling. They were made
from 20swg mild steel sheet and thin walled
steel tubing of various diameter.

"These materials were chosen so a large, but
light, structure could be made and the whole
design was based on the tube—exploiting and
developing the shapes that were achieved by
cutting them in certain ways, juxtaposing
them and continuing and developing lines
and forms thus suggested using steel sheet
hammered and hollowed to shape. All the cut
edges of the tube and the sheet were finally
finished by gas welding on 6mm diameter

rod. I used hundreds of feet of the stuff, and a
great deal of gas and filler rod, but it *tied* the
whole job together by outlining and giving
weight to the convoluted and intersecting
surfaces. This technique also produced
rigidity in the structure and in addition, and
most importantly, made all the edges safe. I
also made two wall mounted wine racks
using the techniques developed on the bar
panels and canopy, and since have used the
same techniques to make table bases, lamps
etc" [1]

Before long Alan was asked to work for the
same client again—to design a wine bar in a
cellar below the Pasta House Restaurant.
After making some sketch proposals he
introduced an architect Tony Collier R.I.B.A.
to his client. They were then able to make
detailed plans and work out the completion
of the scheme. The idea was to give the
impression of a covered patio with an iron
tree in the centre, growing towards the
sunlight through a wooden trellis-work *roof*.
It was a bold and effective design.

Alan has described the making of the tree:
"The tree was forged under the Reiter power
hammer and is made from rather inferior
quality wrought iron, which worked well to
produce the *woody* texture that I wanted for
the tree. By fullering eight lengths of

approximately 75mm x 13mm flat iron strip until the iron started to split and open out on the convex back surface of the resulting *U* section, I was able to assemble them into a trunk which possessed the sort of quality I was looking for."

"The sharp edges formed by the splitting were made safe by heating them until molten with the oxyacetylene torch, and the bottom and top of the trunk were finished by welding in flared and hollowed fish tail ends.

"The foliage was forged from 38mm x 16mm flat iron strip under the power hammer, the whole foliage cover being approximately 2 metres square. The branches were fire welded up making two equal halves, which facilitated entry into the cellar.

"The whole thing was then shot blast and the trunk hot zinc sprayed before it was all sprayed eggshell black. Finally it was polished in parts with zebrite grate polish and highlighted in others with various coloured bronze powders mixed with lacquer.

"The three parts of the tree were assembled and welded together on site." [1]

There was also a wine rack let into a wall behind a pair of round topped gates of graceful forged flower, stem, and leaf forms, set in a fairly heavy frame. The archway was illuminated from behind "giving the wine bottles a beautiful soft green glow and silhouetting the gates".[1]

Alan found working with the architect on the project to be a great benefit, and a very valuable experience. The architect also felt he had gained, increasing his range of design, by adding the new option of ironwork.

It was around this time, at the BABA 1982 Summer Exhibition, that I first saw work by Alan Dawson. I wrote then, in glowing terms (see page 38), about his Floral or Lily lamp. I liked it then and my admiration for it has not dimmed over the years. It is particularly interesting that he also showed *Gate with Singing Birds*, somewhat CoSIRA and Fritz Kühn inspired, and belonging to his work before he entered into his own creative and personally distinctive style. The lamp was to give birth to a whole genus of Lily Lamps, both free standing and wall hanging.

With hindsight one can see that he had

Ivor Nicholas

already set the main elements that were to be a lasting contribution to the style of his work.

● The free forms of plant life, so full and luscious that they sometimes seemed like broad floating seaweed, which had been born on the thin sheet edged with rod technique.

● The forging of graceful flower, stem and leaf forms, as used in the wine rack gates and the tree. Still an important and ongoing part of his work, they are reminiscent of Art Nouveau, although he has always said that he was never, at that time, consciously inspired by this period.

● The use of glass and the use of colour. The Lily Lamps owed much of their beauty to the integration of the delicate fluted light shades that formed the flowers. Perhaps the illuminated glass bottles also remained in his mind, because coloured glass continues to be an element in his work even today. Colour

Above: Gates to the wine rack let into the wall. . . illuminated from behind, and silhouetting the ironwork.

used in many ways has very successfully enlivened his work throughout.

It would have been about the time that Alan Evans was making coloured Wind Vanes and *Pink Gate* that Alan Dawson made *Yellow Gate*—a narrow gate with three leaves, a few sinuous tendrils and one massive yellow flower with red stamens. It had a frame on three sides, but the top was open, with plant shoots rising upwards on each side. Everyone was kicking over the traces, trying to break new ground and shatter past conventions. Colour was coming in and the accepted practice of a strengthening frame on gates, was breaking down; modern techniques of joining by welding made it no longer absolutely necessary and it was becoming part of the greater freedom available to smiths.

At the BABA Coalbrookedale Exhibition of 1985, Alan showed a new departure, the use of brilliant coloured enamel laid into the iron. It was a double gate of two peacocks, again open at the top, just the pattern and *eyes* of the tails rising into cresting. The effect of green and blue enamel on the bodies of the peacocks, with gold and red on the tail feathers, made it a most jewel-like creation. Again, consciously or unconsciously, the peacock was a very typical Art Nouveau motif and was before long to recur in Alan's work with great effect.

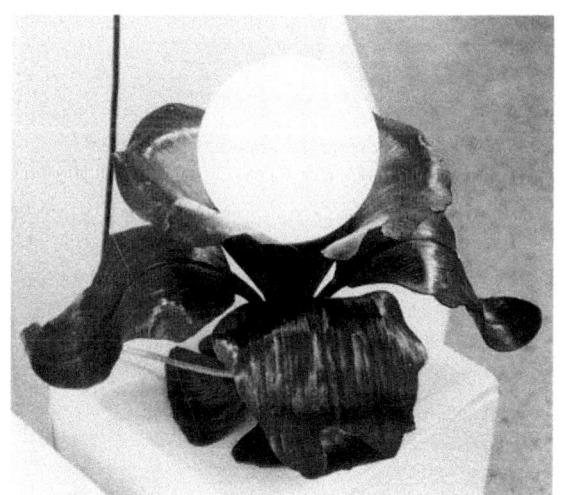

He had expanded in 1982 and transferred his business to Maryport; then expanded again in 1986 and moved to a workshop in Frizington. He had always been adding to his workforce and the number of his apprentices, but the commission for the ironwork for Prince's Square, Glasgow, was one that would quite change the direction of Alan's career.

It was a development, by The Guardian Royal Exchange and the Teesland Development Company, that made a considerable impact in both architectural and retail circles. For one thing it was unique. Shopping Malls were appearing all over the country; most of them were entirely predictable and one was very much like another. Prince's Square was different, for one thing it was created in an open square surrounded by the back

Ivor Nicholas

Above: The Tree in the Wine Bar of the Pasta House Restaurant.

Far left: The Lily Lamp (page 38) gave rise to a whole new genus of lily lamps.

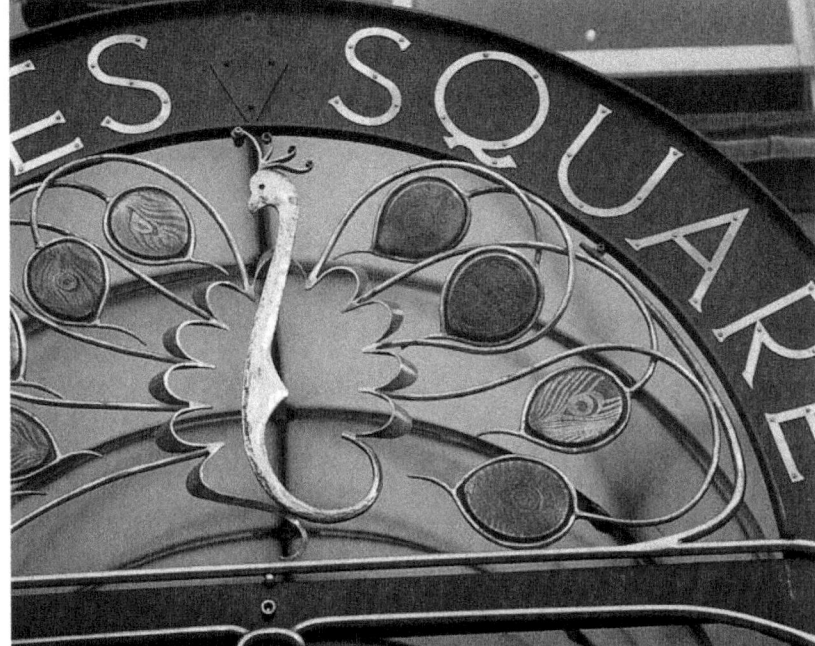

Above: Detail of Prince's Square ironwork with engraved glass panels and coloured glass lamps.

Above: Detail of the Prince's Square entrance canopies with peacocks—the eyes of the tail feathers filled with subtly coloured favrile glass.

Below: Peacock Gate 1985 with coloured enamel.

Below: Golden Apple Tree of steel and glass for the Churchill Hotel, London.

Alan Dawson

elevations of buildings, partly because of the developers policy of commissioning artist craftsmen for much of the work. One of its main attractions was the lively modern ironwork that literally linked the whole concept together. There was ironwork everywhere from the canopies outside, and a great peacock on the roof, through balcony panels on three floors, handrails on escalators and stairs, light fittings everywhere, and even benches and litter bins: all made by artist blacksmiths and most of it individually hand forged. It was opened with great acclaim by H.R.H. Prince Charles on 29th April 1988.

How did it come about that the work went to Alan and how did he set about coping with what turned out to be a commission in the region of £500,000.

Alan was in London on what has been called a *blind trawl* for work when he became aware of the development; keeping up pressure and supplying ideas, designs, and sample pieces, led to him being included, with two other firms, to produce final designs for tender.[3] The developers wanted all three firms to quote for making each others designs; since all three firms worked in completely different ways, some more automated than others, this was completely unacceptable, and anyway was not consistent with the law of copyright.

During the initial design stages Alan had joined forces with a friend Brian Dawes, who was managing director of Shepley Engineering Ltd., and combining the talents of blacksmith and structural engineer they formed Shepley Dawson Architectural Engineering Ltd.[3] In the end they won the commission prepared to a budget of £200,000. Their design was a fairly conventional one of scroll work and feathers, roughly based on some initial preliminary drawings by London consultants, The Design Solution. These designs were accepted until presented at a meeting to the chief concept architect who bluntly, and in no uncertain terms, refused them. In one way Alan was pleased, he no longer felt the necessity to produce a design that conformed to a popular notion of *Wrought Iron Work*. Within the next 15-20 minutes, at the meeting, Alan sketched out a whole new design based on the Art Nouveau style and applied to the age-old Tree of Life concept. In using this idea he was returning to one of his earliest works a *Tree of Life balcony* for a private house in Yorkshire, made around 1982. It is perfectly possible to see in

the sinuously, curling tendrils that climb the supporting *trunk* of the curved balcony the precursors for the Prince's Square plant-shoot balustrades.

By now the time scale was all important— only eight months remained to completion. Designs were often sketched out and sent between Alan and the Architects, Hugh Martin and Partners Edinburgh, by Fax machine, thus cutting down on the time involved. The principal architect was George Keith and the project architect Ian Prentice. Alan and his five assistants were augmented by Andrew Rowe (for five months) and various other blacksmiths. They were producing the decorative elements and Brian Dawes at Shepley's main works was co-ordinating the whole project.

The clients were worried that blacksmiths would not be sufficiently professional in outlook to complete the commission on time. However, on the contrary they were always well in advance of the programme and were eventually asked to construct 2½ times more work than originally planned. The commission grew from one of £200,000 to £500,000.

By the time of installation three wagon loads of materials were travelling to Glasgow every

Left: Tree of Life Balcony for private commission in 1982.

Alan Dawson

week, and thirty men were installing it into position. The skeletal framework of balconies were already in place when the decorative forgings of the balustrading were being brought in. A quick fix system, with tolerance, was devised to position these infill panels into the 50mm dia. upright posts.[3] Removable panels were installed above each light fitting to make it easy to replace light bulbs. The use of designer craftsmen who could successfully integrate with other building trades was found to be a financial advantage to the clients. A number of original ideas reduced costs and released more money for further metal ornamentation like litter bins. In the end there was even a shoe-shine stand in the form of a Roman Sandal.

Altogether 350 metres of balustrading worked out at a price of about £500/metre for the metal infill panels and £350/metre for the glazed balustrading. Approximately 220 lamps cost about £50,000, while the same amount went to the two sets of gates and three projecting canopies.

As one walks down Buchanan Street, lined with long established shops in buildings of conventional architecture, the first intimation of something different is an enormous stainless steel and aluminium peacock on the roof balustrade of one of the buildings. It is the central feature to the entrance of Prince's Square. Beneath, between shopfronts, three deep canopies project over the entrances. They are versions of the type of thing that tended to be used at the entrance to the larger hotels in the years between the wars, using metalwork, openwork lettering, and glass, often coloured. These serve as accents to the entrances, encouraging and leading pedestrians into the otherwise unseen square. They are saying quite clearly *this looks different* and from that follows peoples reaction *lets see what is inside*. The fronts of these semi-circular projections each contain a stainless steel peacock—the eyes of its tail filled with favrile glass which adds to its distinctly jewel-like quality. Each piece of glass is not only coloured in beautiful subtle shades but also individually patterned.

As you enter the building, pass not too quickly through these portals for they contain a vast amount of interesting ironwork. Above each entrance, as one progresses inwards, are two more semi-circular arches filled with simplified forged versions of the outer one—only the peacock is becoming more like a

Above: Entrance canopies to Prince's Square.

Left: First entrance security gate.

Left: Looking upwards to the top tier in Prince's Square.

Left: Top of main staircase in Prince's Square.

design of knotted plant tendrils. There are elaborate security gates of plant and tendril forms; these are integrated to the design of ironwork in the arch, by a long scrolling, rather naturalistic, leaf and tendril trail. There is a tremendous amount of work in these gates—they are heavy, protective, and very satisfying. At the top burgeoning shoots mass together, some as thick as a fist, like embryonic Triffids.

Central double doors to an escalator are wood with inset panels of graceful abstract ironwork—one of the loveliest parts of the whole scheme. The asymmetrical curving wooden frames, together with the ironwork they contain, are very much in the style of Guimard.

As one enters into the open expanse of the square itself one cannot help but feel an affinity with Art Nouveau; the use of both engraved and coloured glass seems redolent of the period. In many cases even the ironwork itself with its thin energetic lines is again very reminiscent of Hector Guimard's work.

There is a framework of simple white engineering ironwork which rises arching into the glassed roof space and includes long lift shafts with leaf and tendril covered tops. There are fan shaped semi-circular panels high at the top of the walls and spotlight cages like hanging baskets. Within this framework, all around the edges of the space, are three tiers of balconies. The two lower ones are walk ways and have been balustraded with ironwork panels, incorporating round ball lamps of coloured glass, and flat panels of engraved clear glass. Centrally at one end two double stairways lead to the second floor. Here there are three lamps, one on each side, on tall stands of growing plant forms. The stair balustrades have similar tendril and cotyledon, or primary leaf shoots, to the balustrades on the top tier, as do all the spiralling staircases hidden from first view. The top balcony ironwork incorporates green glass globes on the lights, the middle tier blue, and the lower one pink. The colours of the glass are never strident, always soft and subservient, supporting rather than overpowering the ironwork. Small rectangular favrile glass panels, all differently patterned, add a tremendous amount of detailed interest to the ironwork panels.

The balustrades with glass panels, very delicately engraved with plant forms, seem tranquil, compared with the hand forged

Left: Detail of the double doors to escalator.

Below: Balustrading detail.

Below left: Escalator hand rail.

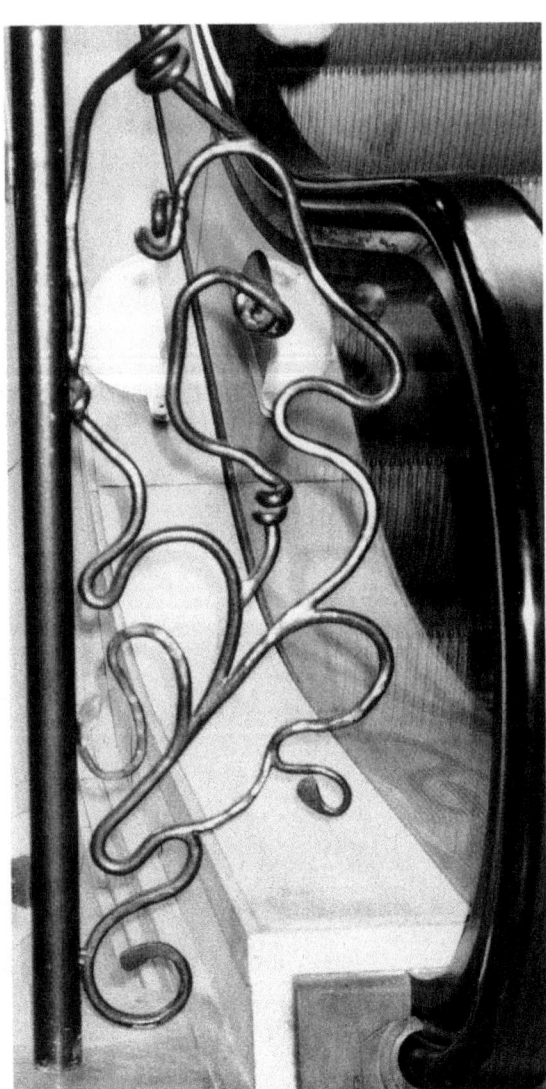

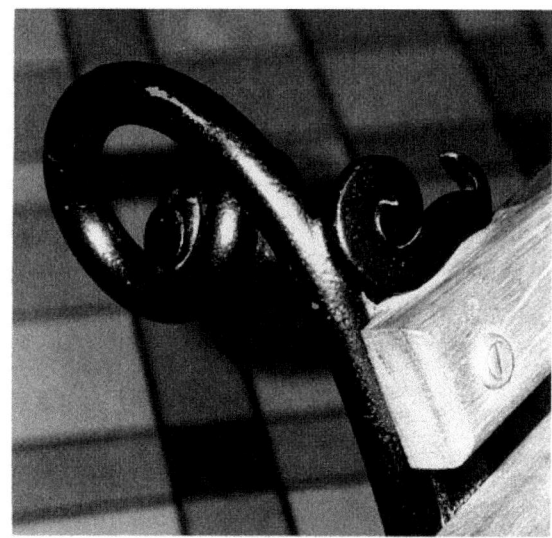

shoots. It seems as if they are everywhere, writhing beside the escalators and bursting into life up the stairs; what a good thing they only appear to be so lively, or the whole complex would be completely overgrown with an impenetrable jungle by now!

In 1990, through the *Fire and Iron Gallery*, Alan made an unusual activated sculpture for the foyer of the new Daily Express building, London. Taking his lead from how the newspaper used to be produced, he based the design on part of an old mechanical Olivetti typewriter. When any of the six massive keys are depressed their hammers, which rise towards the ceiling, are thrown back against against steel blocks set into the wall. The finished sculpture was approximately 750 kgs in weight and around 3.3 metres tall. The steel framework that supports the sculpture had to be erected on the far side of its background wall with arms projecting forwards to the back plates of the sculpture. It was no easy task to get the whole thing lined up and the moving parts to operate but it was accomplished working in the peace and quiet of a night. [4]

Today Alan still works with his right hand man, Graham Stephenson, who joined him as a school leaver fourteen years ago and they direct a team of nine highly skilled craftsmen in the forge, and a total work force of over one hundred. A far cry from Balnakeil Bay! They work in steel, brass, bronze, copper, vitreous enamels and glass and can undertake contracts from £500 to £3,000,000.

He has a large drawing office but is also happy to work to drawings from architects and designers, though he feels that the best

arrangement is to collaborate at the design stage. In this way a working relationship is established early on in a scheme; this is usually invaluable, and ensures the aesthetic and constructional integrity of the work. In the last five years, that is since 1988, the business has flourished, turning over some ten million pounds worth of architectural metalwork. The work is carried on all over the country and quite often a lot of the blacksmithing element in the projects is sub-contracted to other BABA smiths.

A major recent commission has been stainless steel balustrading with *wave* infill panels for the Foreshore Development in South Shields.

Another commission, very much in line with the tradition and development of Alan Dawson's style, has been a large steel and glass *Golden Apple Tree* for the Churchill Hotel, London, in collaboration with Theo Crosby of Pentagram Design.

Far left: Detail of bench seat in Prince's Square.

Below: Typewriter sculpture for the Daily Express Building.

Left: Palm Trees in the Royals Shopping Centre, Southend.

Another commission which had an ancestry in Alan's early work were seven painted brass and steel palm trees for the Royals shopping centre in Southend—they are remarkably like the copper and iron palm trees in the kitchen of the Brighton Pavilion, designed by Nash around 1820; though Alan had never seen or even heard about this early prototype!

Other architectural metalwork in speciality shopping or retail centres, often including telephone kiosks, seating, signage and street lighting, are to be found in Princes Quay Hull, St. Giles Centre Elgin, Swan Walk Horsham, Victoria Quarter Leeds, Camberley Shopping Centre, Lakeside West Thurrock, The Glades Bromley, and Vicarage Fields Barking.

Balustrades vary from traditional, in Stratton Street London, through bars and scrolls at Bethnal Green, to modern at Canary Wharf. There is bold Art Deco balustrading in the Caversham Hotel, Reading, and delightful tied and festooned balustrading and two large chandeliers for the classic interior of The Belfry Hotel, Wishaw, near Birmingham; the home of the Ryder Cup, one of golf's premier events.

There has been work for the Dorchester Hotel and three new canopies in cast bronze and brass, each about 2 tonnes in weight, for the Waldorf Hotel.

At the Sotheby exhibition in September 1991 Alan had entered *An unrestrained Gate* catalogued as "built of vertical shootlike forms bound together with tendrils and waterlily type leaves; the hinge is interesting being formed by coiling one of the shoots around the hinge post—the catch is simply a projecting tendril which springs onto the opposite post. 2.5m high by 1m wide."

I stood entranced in front of this gate—it seemed to me to epitomise Alan's work. I liked the asymmetrical top of gently *curling* tendrils, the firmer base of *curving* root-like forms; the *flaring* circles of the bright jade flowers or leaves—there are few smiths who can make iron *speak* to quite this extent. I liked too the bold step of altogether abandoning a frame. He had made it right at the last minute, it was almost hot from the hearth!

My mind went back ten years to the first Lily Lamp. Here was a man who could build up a business, adjust to administrative responsibility, take on massive commissions, and still turn happily to work at his anvil. The forms may have a new authority but, over the years, they have lost nothing of the first joyous creativity.

Glynn Clarkson

Sources and Notes

1. "Spotlight on Alan Dawson." *British Blacksmith* 18.

2. *British Blacksmith* 53.

3. Prince's Square, Glasgow by Mike Crummy *British Blacksmith* 50.

4. *British Blacksmith* 55.

ALAN
EVANS

Alan Evans, born in 1952, is the third generation of craftsmen to work from the family home at Whiteway, near Stroud, in the Cotswolds. His father designs and makes fine furniture, and his mother is a woodcarver. Her parents were leather workers and bookbinders who settled in Whiteway in 1922. The village had originally been formed as a colony living communally, with strong socialist views, in which craftwork had become increasingly important.

Although Alan felt drawn to craft he took a course in teacher-training, at Shoreditch College of Education, in case the need should arise to earn a living in a more conventional way. Then, in 1974 he joined Alan Knight, traditional blacksmith of Redditch, being allowed workshop space in exchange for help with the heavy work. He was making jewellery to support himself. He has said that the difference between making jewellery and ironwork was simply picking up a heavier hammer, but that he thinks of jewellery as his craft and blacksmithing as his art.[1]

In 1978 he set up his own workshop at Whiteway. At this time all his work was hand forged and fire welded. In fact on putting work into an exhibition, he was chagrined to find that his fire welds, on round loop tops and T welds, were not appreciated. They were so good that they could not be seen , and were therefore presumed not to exist. He bought a little Blacker Hammer and began to explore the possibilities of spreading and drawing out under power. He found that he could forge fire shovels out of a single piece of steel. After seeing Achim Kühn's work at the International Forging Iron Conference, he began to colour his fire-tools with brass copper flashing, using filings, or nibblings, fused into the iron with borax.

The first pair of commissioned gates he made were for the Quaker Meeting House in Painswick. It was necessary to make a few speculative gates, because he found that if prospective customers saw only fire-tools they did not think of commissioning anything else.

In 1980 the Higgins Ney Design Unit, London consultants, were designing part of the crypt of St. Paul's Cathedral to become the Treasury. Gates were needed to shut off the area and they decided to select five smiths, from information given by the Crafts Council, to take part in a design competition for the Commission. It was Alan's design that was chosen. What a happy continuation of tradition that the craftsman should be from the Cotswolds; for it was from the stone quarrying villages of Taynton and Burford that stonemasons had come to build the Cathedral.[2]

The time that Alan received the commission roughly coincided with his acquisition of a Reiter K23 pneumatic hammer, and the St. Paul's gates were only the second work he made with it.

When he descended into the crypt to see the place where the gates were to be positioned, it was being used as a store room and was filled shoulder high, so that little was visible but the curved arches of the ceiling. These curves, reflected in the gates, were to become the strongest element of his design. Although the actual iron shapes are clear cut and simple, the concept of the design is complicated and symbolic. He has depicted the Cross and the Trinity in the form of three great interwoven curved crosses. These integrate with three X shapes which we can

Below: Gates to the Treasury of St. Paul's Cathedral. Shown open.

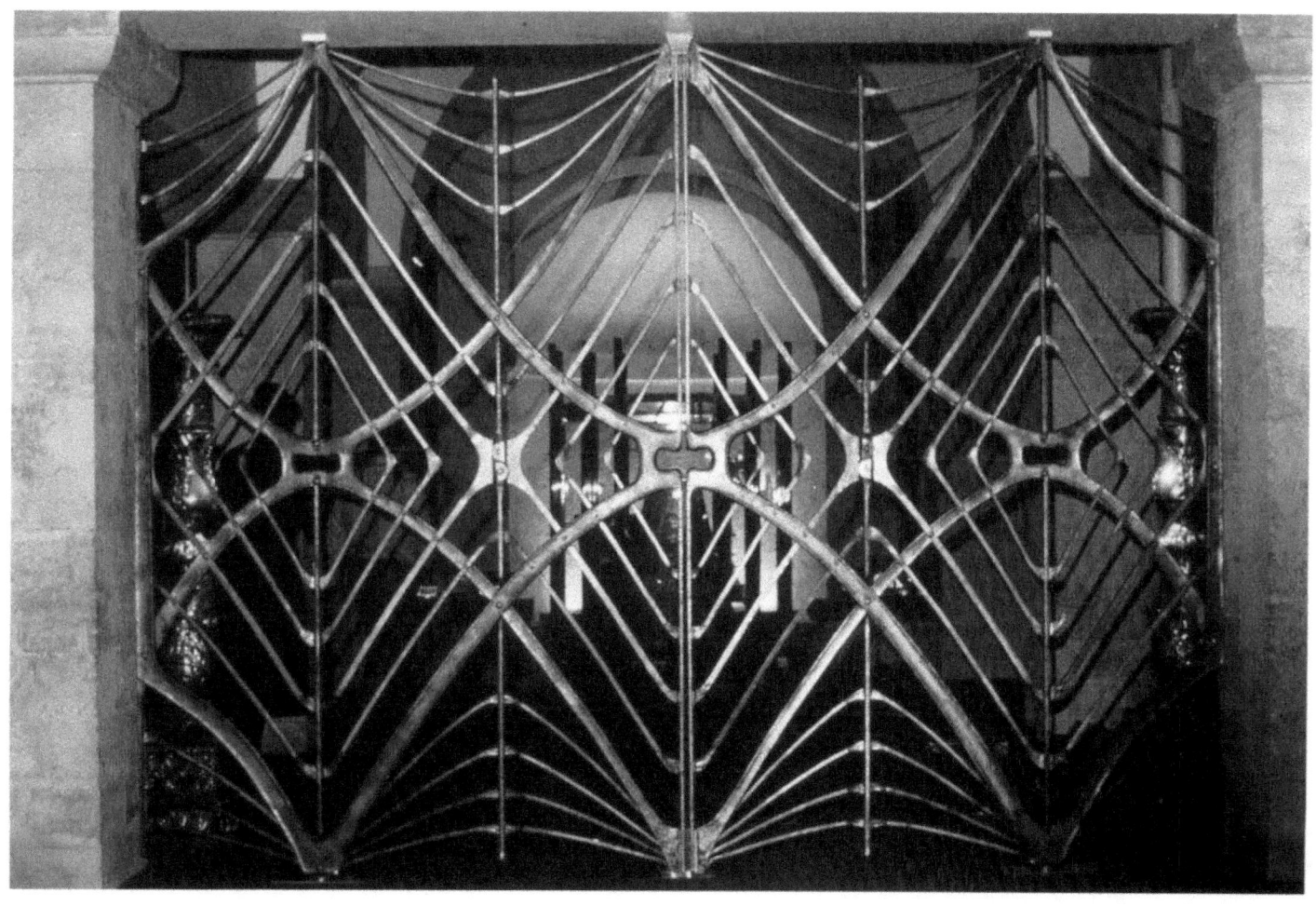

see as guarding forms, abstract arms raised and legs akimbo, joining the concept of spiritual and temporal. The tops of the curved crosses are like arrow heads pointing heavenwards, and when the gates are open, the curving sides of the crosses point towards the Treasury, leading and inviting people forwards.

It is a brilliantly conceived strong barrier, with all the natural grace of a web hung across a cave mouth. That the gates are not suspended from hinges, or in any way attached to the walls, but pivot each on its own single axis, from floor to ceiling, adds to the magical quality of the structure. The most important element in the inspiration of the design, the curves of the vaulted ceiling above find reflection in the arcing steel bars below. Made from mild steel plate and bar which has been cut, forged, welded and riveted; the surface was then shot blasted, wire brush burnished, sprayed with a two-pot lacquer and rubbed down with scotchbrite and wax. The surface produced is as softly mellow as old silver.[3]

When one looks at a great piece of ironwork of this nature, it is perfectly possible to admire the work that has gone into the design and the making; however, only by having the inside story of its creation can there be a real understanding of the problems involved.

For a start the brief was received on Oct. 14th 1980 and drawings, samples and maquettes had to be submitted by the 24th of November —a little less than six weeks! In December Alan was asked to make further drawings of joints and fittings and subsequently spent twenty days and about £70 drawing and discussing the project. Finally on March 12th 1981 the contract was officially confirmed.

The first step was to make two parts of the gates in the workshop of Terry Clark who kindly made his lathe available to machine the top hinge blocks. These were then fitted, by the Cathedral staff, to a rolled steel channel set between pillars just above a newly suspended ceiling.

Alan then faced a considerable problem. His workshop, at that time, consisted of a series of little wooden huts and nowhere was there a floor large enough to lay out the gates. Undaunted he laid a large slab of concrete outside the main workshop and built a

Above: The Treasury Gates — ". . . all the natural grace of a web hung across a cave mouth."

covering over it with timber and builders' polythene. This gave a level, stable base where the gates could be laid out, and later erected, with plenty of room to work around them. So it was that this 20th century craftsman began to make the gates for Wren's St. Pauls's in a kind of surrealist greenhouse.

As he could not be supplied either by the architects or the Clerk of Works with the dimensions of the site, Alan drew out the gates to an estimated minimum height. While he was working on this the architects contacted him and decided to specify his estimated size on their drawings. The new floor was set out in accordance with this measurement.

The main frames, in manageable sections, were transferred from the drawing to hardboard, cut to shape, and sent to Aljo Welding, a firm of profile cutters. At Whiteway work began on lighter bars of 12mm, 16mm, and 20mm.

The Reiter hammer was used to forge the curved lengths of the main frames, while the more complicated frame profiles, locks and hinges were forged by hand. Alan was anxious to produce a section with raised edges on the main frames, in order to give highlight and shadow, to relieve their visual weight. The main problem that arose in forging was distortion, as each blow was diagonally across the bar. As much as three quarters of the work on them had to be spent removing the twist and setting them true.

As work advanced it was fortunate that one of the architects advised checking the site dimensions before commencing welding. Calamity!—it turned out that the top hinge blocks, from which all subsequent height measurements had been taken, had not been correctly fitted. Not only were they out of plumb, in one case as much as six inches, but there was also a discrepancy in their heights. The new floor had been laid taking a measurement from the highest hinge block, and by the time they had been levelled, the floor to ceiling height was undersize by 20mm. Even worse, concrete under the floor was too high, shortening the gates, at the worst point, by as much as 30mm.

It became necessary to prepare a survey of the site and contact all the various parties involved. Alan, and his assistant Neil Spencer, revised the design and altered the work already done. In the end the height of the gates was reduced to fit, but the sub-floor metalwork had to be further let into the concrete by about 17mm.

After this set-back forging and fitting continued and bars were riveted in place with 240 rivets. A total of two hundred and two pieces of shaped steel went into the gates and sub-floor frame.

When complete, friends, relations and neighbours all helped to take down and load the gates, each leaf of which weighed over a quarter of a ton.

They were taken to Beaven and Sons, a firm of metal finishers in Gloucester. Each gate leaf was shot blasted for four hours in the morning, then Alan and Neil spent four hours burnishing them with wire brushes in the afternoon. Although Alan was wearing safety glasses a metal splinter got into one eye the first day and, in spite of treatment, meant that the remainder of the finishing and fixing was uncomfortable for him. Wearing an eye-patch did not help aiming a hammer at a 5mm rivet when fixing the locks!

The date for delivery was June 26th and after a 4.0 a.m. call they followed Beaven's lorry to St. Paul's and arrived at 7.30 a.m. One and a half hours later the gates had been unloaded

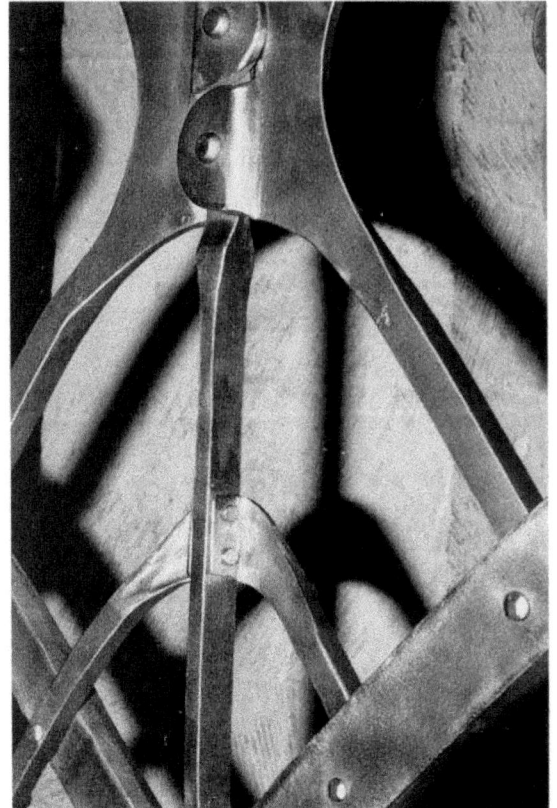

Left: Detail of the St Paul's Gates. Where the diagonal bars cross the shape of the join is the Yin-Yan sign of Buddhist and Hindu belief, representing "The two halves of the whole"— night/day, male/female, black/white etc.

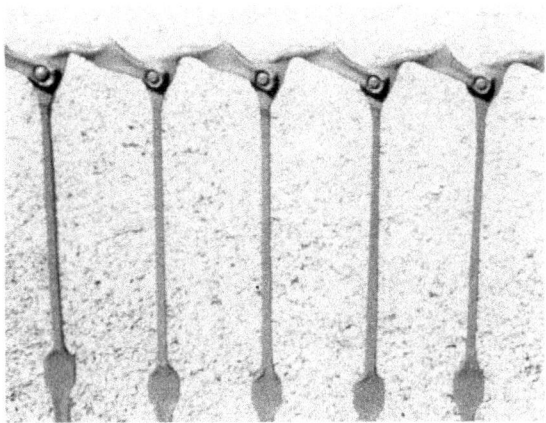

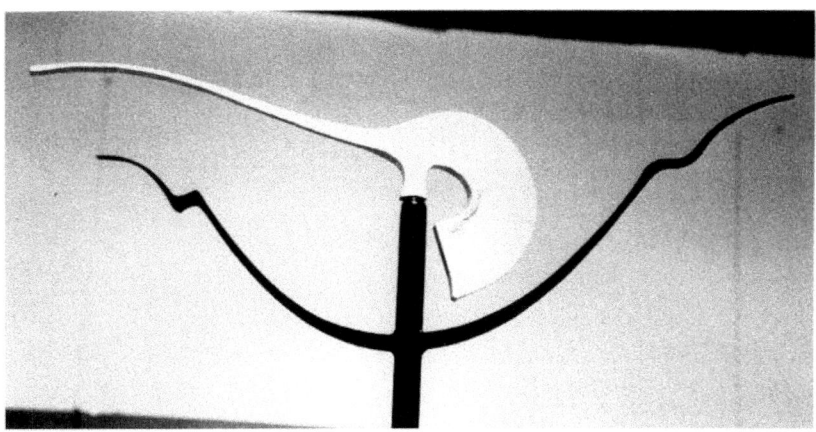

and were at the site. It was a tiring and frustrating day although officially they were simply overseeing the installation by the Cathedral staff. At last the offending concrete was cut out and the underfloor metalwork fitted, the gates erected and after some adjustments to the top hinges, they swung reasonably well. They finally riveted on the locks about 9.30 p.m. the hammer blows reverberating through the silence of the deserted Cathedral.[4]

This major commission firmly established Alan as one of the foremost smiths in the country. With this solidity behind him, and perhaps as a reaction to what must have been a period of intense intellectual and physical strain, he continued to work in a lighter vein, experimenting with bright colours and enjoying himself with squashing and drawing out metal.

In *Orange Gate* he followed a technique, used by Chillida, of chopping the bar almost in two at the top of the gate, and then bending over and forging the top of the vertical bar almost flat immediately below the *chop*. The bars are squashed together on the lower part producing a narrow bar grooved down the centre; the wider shape in the middle of the bar is the parent metal, while the upper part of the bar is thinned by drawing out in both directions. The latch is integrated into the design, and unlike traditional gates, it has no enclosing structural framework.

Pink Gate was a rather heavy, and expensive joke half inch plate cut into well designed chunky letters G A T E followed by an explanation mark. This pivots and the whole gate revolves on the G.

He also made a brightly coloured modern wind vane cut out of a straight piece of 25mm plate fullered on one side, under the power

hammer, to form a curve. As it turned out this was not well balanced, there was too much sail area above the pivot, and in Mark 2 he moved the pivot point up higher— beginning to realise why traditional cockerels were such a good shape for weather vanes. He concerned himself too with the balance of gate latches under the hand, sometimes fixing them directly into the wall instead of the gate.

Alan Evans made gates to a private house in Brimsfield, Glos., in two stages. In 1983 he was commissioned to make a single gate leading from the road through a wall into the garden. It needed to provide a certain amount of privacy yet allow light into a dark corner. The uprights were forged from 25mm round bar rippled under the fly press; the first of his designs that relied on undulating forms, like rippling water, for the main interest. The rippling bars arrest the eye and maintain privacy but the openings let in light. Wishing to relate the infill bars to the frame the top and bottom bars were pierced and opened into loops to produce a horizontal ripple through which the uprights passed.

A few months later the double drive gate and wicket were commissioned. These were not completed until 1985. There was a need to partly redesign the jointing details to meet the budget of the large work, and the frames were simplified to unworked bar. The uprights forged from 40 x 15mm and were again *wobbled* under the fly-press. Construction this time was entirely by continuous MIG welding, the uprights lapping the top and bottom bars alternately front and back, which countered weld distortion. These measures resulted in gates which maintained the same theme as the original, but proved to be aesthetically stronger for by removing unecessary detail the theme was emphasised. They were also physically stronger through the rigid

Far left: Detail of top of 'Orange Gate' showing the chopping and bending technique.

Above: Wind Vane.

construction, and by removing all crevices they were far less prone to corrosion. They also took about two thirds of the time relatively to construct, and almost met the budget. The altered design led to the question —when is detail appropriate and is it needed in a particular situation or not? The gates were zinc sprayed, finished with eggshell gloss and graphite polished.[5]

There were also ecclesiastical commissions; some hand rails in the crypt of St. Paul's Cathedral and a baptistery rail for the Church of the Holy Redeemer at Pershore, Worcestershire, in mild steel and copper. For St. Paul's Church Tupsley, on the outskirts of Hereford, a processional cross that would double as an altar cross was needed. As it was sometimes to be seen from all sides, the solution was to make a standing cross in mild steel into which the brass processional cross could be fitted at right angles when required; the whole being 6' 6" high. The cross is flanked by processional candlesticks with ashwood staves held in iron supports.

Between 1984 and 1986 there was a three-stage commission for Holy Trinity Church,

Brompton, of Gothic style window grilles, hand rail supports, grilles, glazed balustrades, and door handles. It was a commission on which he was assisted by several BABA members, especially with the fixing. Even his parents were called upon to help in cutting the window grille arcs.[6]

During the years 1983-7 Alan Evans was developing some interesting techniques, one of twisting, and the other of cutting into rolled steel joists. In 1983 he was commissioned by the Royal Society for the encouragement of the Arts Manufactures and Commerce to make six Pollution Abatement Technology Awards. It seemed to him fitting to make them of reused material, so each was forged from 6" x 6" of H shaped rolled steel joist. A logo was added in steel and phosphor bronze and an inscription engraved directly onto the forged steel. In a subsequent year, for the same award trophy, T shape joists were used cut and opened out into a scroll form.

By 1987 Alan had developed this technique into interesting sculptures which he showed at the BABA exhibition. One, fairly straight forward, was sliced through to one of the uprights and the *slices* opened out alternately. Another, more complex, had one side cut into waving curves before being opened out.

Twists made in straight bars have been used as a decorative feature for hundreds of years, but the twists that Alan was developing were different; they were put into a bar that had

Above: The Brimsfield Gates.

Far left: Detail of the top of the infill bars and the pierced and opened out top rail, of the first gate.

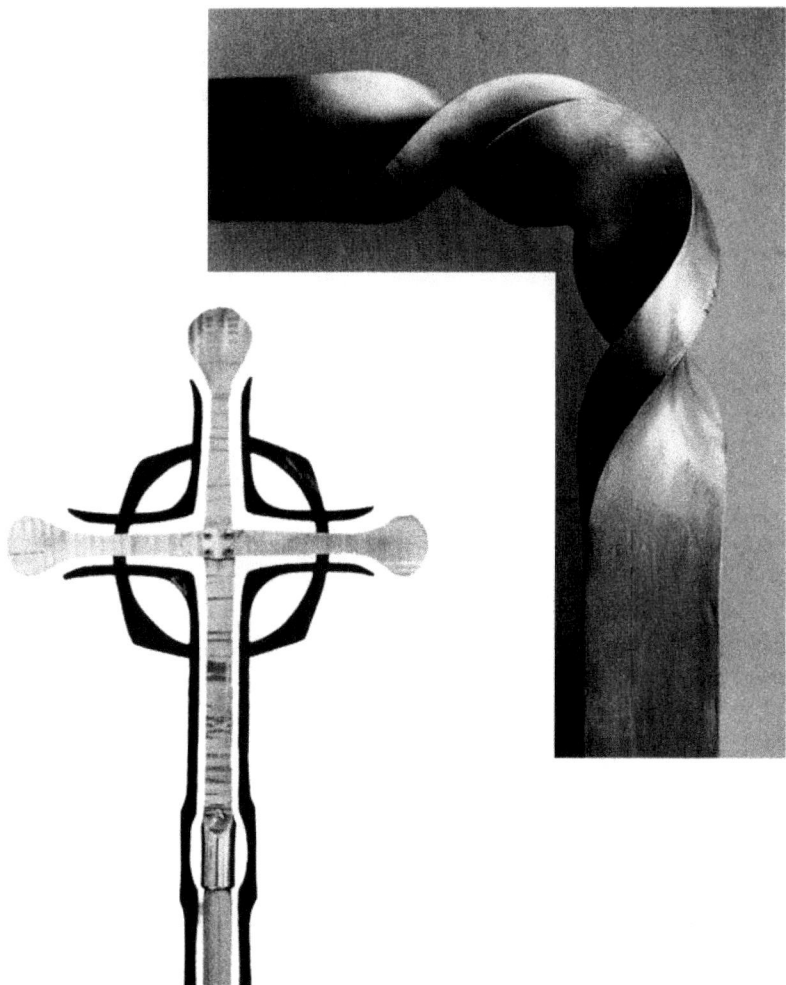

already been bent at right angles on the flat (the difficult part) by the use of a fly press. For a cross of steel, wall mounted, in the chapel of the Royal Surrey County Hospital, Guildford, four lengths of bar were bent at right angles and arranged flat to form a cross. Each piece was embellished by a single twist on each side of the right angle bend. The same system was used on a large aluminium door handle shown in the BABA exhibition in 1987. He sometimes took the concept further, flat bending a bar into a complete U bend and then twisting one leg of it, up or down, in to the same vertical plane.

He had used a chop and twist technique in 1983 when he designed a gate for Harrow Baptist Church. He forged each main upright element out of one piece (app. 80 x 15mm) twisting them up into a pointed cresting along the top. The construction work for this gate was done by Alan Puddick. This was during a short period when he was acting as a designer for Richard Quinnell Ltd.

Another work for which he shared responsibility was the tomb canopy in Lincoln Cathedral. 1986 was the eighth centenary of the enthronement of St. Hugh as Bishop of Lincoln and for the occasion a modern epithedron or tomb canopy was commissioned. It was designed by David Poston, who is primarily a jeweller. His

jewellery reduced to the simplest of forms follows his belief that "less is more" and the shrine cover is equally reduced to essentials. The tomb of medieval carved stone had been partly destroyed at the Reformation and remained incomplete until the modern sculpture was placed in position over it in July 1986.

The design aimed to highlight the area of the tomb, above the remains of the head shrine of St. Hugh, and although complete in itself, to enhance the prestige of the shrine by soaring gracefully upwards above it.

The canopy is made in mild and stainless steel, finished in pale honey-coloured aluminium-bronze, and from the side is like a great letter h. The incredibly fine spires at the top rise some 25' above the ground. The forging of the main work was done by Alan Evans, assisted by Stephen Lock, and Tony and Simon Robinson; structural joints and precision machining of the pointed stainless steel spires was undertaken by Richard Quinnell Ltd. The shrine is made of eight separate parts fitted together on site. Its serenely flowing lines rather belie the weeks of hard physical labour that went into its

Far left: I beam sculptures 1987.

Centre left: Processional Cross for St. Paul's Church, Tupsley, near Hereford.

Above: Twist put into bar already bent at right angles.

making. The total cost for the work was £13,970 and for this comparatively modest amount Lincoln Cathedral has been graced by a masterpiece of contemporary art.[7]

In the early 1990s the use of the ripple in Alan's designs seems to have been joined by the wave. He had made a small gate in which he had played with horizontal wave lines; then seeing it photographed in front of a Cotswold landscape he wondered if unconsciously he had assimilated the swelling curves of the fields and hedges across the Wolds into the design. Certainly wave forms were to play a part in several commissions. In 1991 an 8' x 15' screen, for John Innes, used a broad wave line at the base with straight uprights rising on each side of it, in three dimensional form, until in an undulating and uneven broken line the uprights came together and were held by a flat wave line near the top.

In gates for Southampton Railway Station Alan sought to provide a *soft and metally* texture to offset the adjacent shiny mosaic wall decoration. Here horizontal bars were set back and wavey ones forward.

Whether the Leicester screen can be said to belong to the *wave* period is more conjectural. He made a screen at the entrance to an underpass, to discourage mugging. It was set at two right angles so that as one passes it is seen with one part covering the other, so that the lattice type rails produce a moving moiré pattern such as seen in watered silk.

Above left: A small gate playing with wave lines.

Far left above: Gate with 'chop and twist' technique.

Below: The Leicester screen with 'moving' moiré pattern.

A major commission was the sculptural screen at the new Broadgate development in the City of London. Made of 24 forged steel panels it is set at the entrance to the broad pedestrian paving that leads from Sun Street towards the Broadgate circle, and was designed to deter delivery vans from going into the area.

Alan went to look at the site and felt he wanted soft undulating lines to humanise the overpoweringly angular buildings that surround the position. He then went to Australia for a holiday and believes that he was influenced in the final design by Aboriginal sculptural forms,

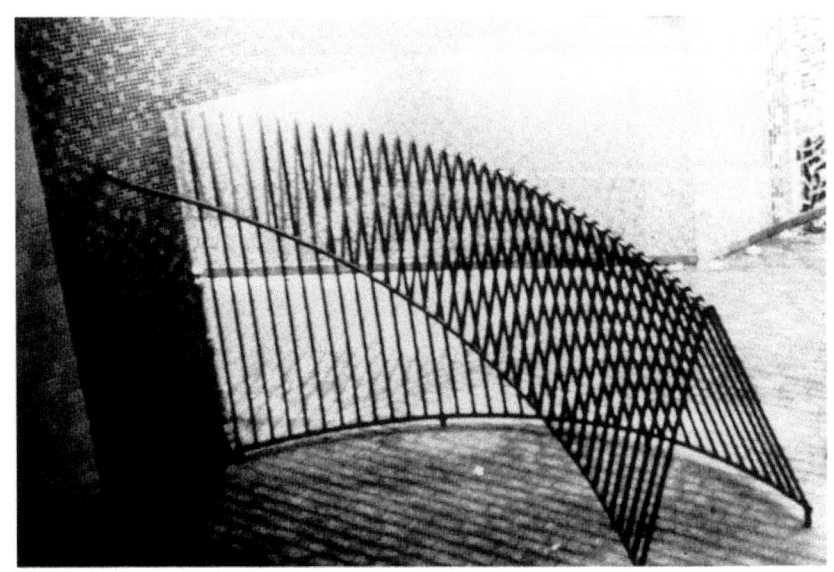

particularly in the *walking stick necks* that curve over at the top of the rails, and seem to have some affinity with exotic bird necks. Combine this with the waves and the last of the *ripples* and it is possible to see where this fits into his design development. The pairs of uprights, particularly strong at the base, relate to the geometric grid of the buildings and paving. The actual making of the work was an enormous task and began by spraying the design on to plywood sheets, set up round the walls of a nearby indoor riding school, and marking on the wave forms with masking tape.

Because of the time element involved Matthew Feddon and Stephen Lock assisted at the forge, and Charles Normandale punched holes in the top rail of the railings and made some of the light uprights, while Richard Lewis of Rotherham undertook the heavy forging. The screen was shot blasted, zinc sprayed, and finished with gloss paint followed by highlighting with graphite polishing.

Works seldom follow each other in neat chronological order and one that had been on the stocks for some time was a grille over the entrance to the new extension of the Cheltenham Art Gallery and Museum. Alan had been approached about the commission as early as 1987 but events conspired to delay its unveiling until July 28th 1991. Perhaps this is not so surprising when one realises that the making of this massive grille necessitated the installation of a three ton power hammer and the building of a new forge to put it in.

Since the 1930s the Museum has had a large collection of furniture of the Arts and Crafts Movement, mainly by Cotswold craftsmen, Ernest Gimson and Ernest and Sidney Barnsley. In recent years this had been added to, so that it is now of national interest. In view of this specialisation, it was natural that when the extension was built it should reflect the work of architects of that period. It was designed by the Borough Architects department in consultation with Sir Hugh Casson. The result is reminiscent of the work of Charles Rennie Mackintosh, and it seems safe to assume that the iron grille would have delighted him.

Alan's brief was to design a grille that would reflect in the facade the craftsmanship of the items within the museum, and be in keeping with the spirit of the Arts and Crafts

Movement. It was a commission with which he found himself in complete accord. His father being a maker of fine furniture, and Alan being a lifelong admirer of the Arts and Crafts Movement and its ideals.

The grille fills the upper part of an arched entrance. He has layered it three dimensionally back into the recess behind, so that it might be almost called a sculpture. In forming the design he has used the clean simple lines of the earlier craftsmen, while remembering the Arts and Crafts Movement and Post-Modernism; he has created a design for our own time, subtly asymmetrical, which takes its place in his own design evolution.

The front of the building was not strong enough to take the weight of the grille, about one and a half tons, so it is taken on the lintel below, with large counterbalancing bars cantilevered out into space behind, to balance

Below: Sculptural Screen for the Broadgate development, City of London.

the weight. Although the structural engineers had agreed some twelve months earlier that the disposition of the weight was absolutely safe, the letter confirming this did not arrive until the day it was due to be erected! Another problem was that the power hammer Alan was using during most of the making was really insufficient for finalising the work. He had therefore to build a new forge at the same time as making the grille. The building was specially designed for noise absorption, with walls one foot thick with a four inch cavity filled with acoustic wool, while the roof lights were quadruple glazed. A special rubber base was installed beneath the anvil above foundations four times the volume recommended by the manufacturers. The base was also isolated by an air gap from the rest of the floor. On June 18th the forge was opened with a *Hammer Warming*, and the three cwt hammer put into service. During the day about a hundred villagers and friends came to wish the enterprise well. His forge is no distance from my own town, but it was an unexpected pleasure to see Alan Dawson, Jim Horrobin, Terry Clark, Simon Robinson, and Dick Quinnell, so far from their homes.

The new power hammer was used in completing the grille, mainly to punch and open out large holes; a video was shown of the work in progress after the opening ceremony.

No doubt the people of Cheltenham will not find it easy to accept so modern a design, accustomed as they are to Regency scrolls and anthemion. Alan allowed himself one more obvious reference, affectionate and light-hearted, to the earlier craftsmen, and this will surely win them over. Within the entrance, over the heads of those who enter and leave the building, he has placed a flat copper squirrel in a roundel on the counterbalancing bars. It is taken from one that Ernest Gimson sometimes used in his own work, after he saw it in Winchester Cathedral. The aluminium-bronze nuts that hold the grille in place on the front wall are shaped like acorns. To Alan, while depicting the squirrel's treasures, they were functional necessities that were also an important part of the design, and as such continuing one of the basic principles of the Arts and Crafts Movement—the belief in honesty to function. The Curator of the Museum has taken the symbolism a step further, interpreting the squirrel as being surrounded by his treasures in the same way as the visitor is surrounded by the treasures within the Museum.[8]

The new addition is a powerful work and can hold its own with the Barbara Hepworth sculpture in the same street, only a few minutes walk away. Clarence Street has become the most important in town for art on architecture.

The cost for the grille was raised by The Friends of the Art Gallery and Museum. As the estimate of £15,000 which was thought to be low at the time, was given four years before installation, its worth is now thought to be in the region of £30,000.

The next major commission was for a newly built Ecumenical church in Milton Keynes. It was a cross or finial for the top of the dome. Alan first made a delightful maquette then translated it into the actual work, 5.8m high and weighing 1700 kilos, at a cost of £30,000. It symbolises the ecumenical concept of a universal world-wide church; the lower vanes, of textured 6mm plate, pointing in all directions welcome people in, while the central stems strive upwards towards the same goal reached by different paths. There are loose horizontal bindings, wave-like at the base, representing Christ the living water, and near the top reminiscent of a crown of thorns. There was some quite complicated engineering involved, and the fact that the whole piece was raised, not quietly, but with two thousand people below singing "Lift High the Cross", caused its maker some nerve-racking moments.

Below: Grille over the entrance of the new extension to the Cheltenham Art Gallery and Museum

Left: Detail of the
Cheltenham Art
Gallery and
Museum grille.

Far left : Detail of
the grille,inside,
showing the
'Gimson' squirrel.

During the Summer of 1992 Alan made a most ambitious demonstration piece at the ABANA conference at San Luis Obispo in California. It was something of a tour de force, and few smiths would have embarked on making it in front of an audience. It was a freestanding sculpture, some 3' high, which required very precise forging; no welds were used and the whole piece fitted together by spring tension. Called *Communication* it represents ears and tongues and symbolises "Mankind speaking with many tongues but bound together with similar aspirations".

By 1993 Alan was working on a fence for Castle Park in Bristol utilising some lengths of the original railings into the design, by bending them into flowing and circular lines, to be interspersed with heavier forged panels.

He has just designed railings and entrance gates for the Public Record Office at Kew. The gates 12.2m across and 6m high will weigh 7½ tons. The tall notched uprights that feature in the design are a reference to Exchequer tally sticks; these were usually made of hazel wood, each about 8in long, and by a complicated system of indenting and serrated cuts on their edges recorded the payment of taxes. Their use went back to medieval times and it is thought to have been the use of thousands of these old tinder-dry wooden tally sticks, in the heating system, that resulted in the burning down of the Houses of Parliament in 1834.

Alan believes that artists have certain things that they explore all their lives—in his case he feels it is finding what can be achieved by squashing metal about, by feeling its lively springiness and being aware of its malleability when hot. Every commission is an opportunity to explore his knowledge of the material and the effect a piece of metalwork can have in a given site—what is needed in that particular place? He sees himself not in competition with other smiths but with the space which will surround the work—how can he enhance the space and what effect will the space have on the work? Sometimes if he has an idea which is not wholly in line with his brief he may need to persuade either his client or the architect, or both, that he has developed skills that enable him to be more likely to have the necessary knowledge of his work and its placing than someone outside his personal development.

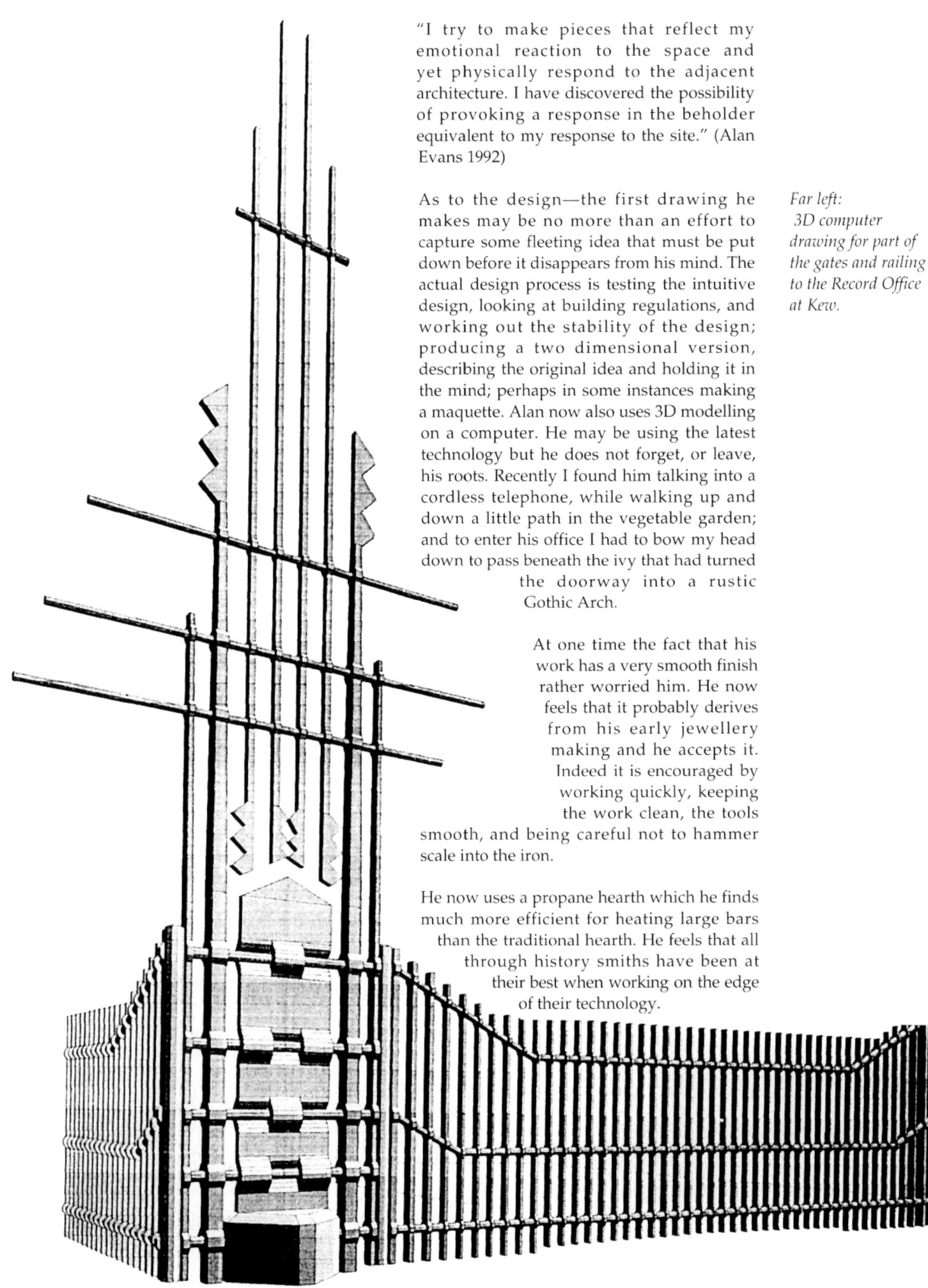

"I try to make pieces that reflect my emotional reaction to the space and yet physically respond to the adjacent architecture. I have discovered the possibility of provoking a response in the beholder equivalent to my response to the site." (Alan Evans 1992)

As to the design—the first drawing he makes may be no more than an effort to capture some fleeting idea that must be put down before it disappears from his mind. The actual design process is testing the intuitive design, looking at building regulations, and working out the stability of the design; producing a two dimensional version, describing the original idea and holding it in the mind; perhaps in some instances making a maquette. Alan now also uses 3D modelling on a computer. He may be using the latest technology but he does not forget, or leave, his roots. Recently I found him talking into a cordless telephone, while walking up and down a little path in the vegetable garden; and to enter his office I had to bow my head down to pass beneath the ivy that had turned the doorway into a rustic Gothic Arch.

Far left:
3D computer drawing for part of the gates and railing to the Record Office at Kew.

At one time the fact that his work has a very smooth finish rather worried him. He now feels that it probably derives from his early jewellery making and he accepts it. Indeed it is encouraged by working quickly, keeping the work clean, the tools smooth, and being careful not to hammer scale into the iron.

He now uses a propane hearth which he finds much more efficient for heating large bars than the traditional hearth. He feels that all through history smiths have been at their best when working on the edge of their technology.

Alan Evans

Alan Evans is very discriminating about the work he accepts. He always prefers to spend more time on a job, than may be justified by his renumeration, rather than complete the work in a manner which fails to please him.

His work has been extraordinarily consistent throughout, the assured clear cut style can be followed through all his work, from the early fire-dogs to the massive bulk of recent commissions.

Above all what stands out is his integrity to his work—the wholeness, soundness and upright honesty that makes his art.

Left: Ventilation grilles with architecton standards. The Standards increase in size and complexity towards the main entrance of the building. WCSHA building Cardiff Bay Development. 1993

Below: From left to right. Jim Horrobin, Gabrielle Ridler, Lesley Green and Alan Evans.

Sources and Notes.

1. Alan Evans lectured on his work at the British Artist Blacksmith Association at Redfield in November 1992. Much of the information is derived from that talk.

2. Janet Jarvis *Christopher Wren's Cotswold Masons* 1980. The Strong family of Taynton were concerned with the Cathedral over two generations, for 33 years, from the laying of the first stone to the ceremonial placing of the last stone at the top of the building. Christopher Kempster of Burford worked on both the Cathedral and the Dome; while William, probably his son, was promoted to be Master Mason at St. Paul's and built the spiral staircase, the Dean's door with its winged cherubs, and completed the south west tower.

3. Amina Chatwin."Work by British Smiths: Alan Evans and Hector Cole" *The Anvil's Ring* Vol 9 No 4. Winter 1981/2.

4. Alan Evans. "Gates for St. Paul's" *Crafts Magazine* Jan/Feb. 1982.

5. Alan Evans. "Brimpsfield Gates Commission 1983-85" *British Blacksmith* No 40.

6. Alan Evans. "Trinity Church Brompton 1984-6" *British Blacksmith* No 41.

7. Peter Wylde "Forging a Head-shrine. An Epithedron for St. Hugh" *British Blacksmith* No 46.

8. Amina Chatwin "Cheltenham Museum Grille" *British Blacksmith* No 60b.

Below: Cross being raised on the dome of the Ecumenical church, Milton Keynes.

Photograph Lesley Greene

THEO. GRUNEWALD

I first saw Theo. Grunewald's work at a BABA exhibition in 1987, when he showed a Paschal Candle Holder 4ft 6in. high with a figure of the risen Christ at the base. I was tremendously impressed by the forged head, I knew of few if any smiths in this country who were doing work of this kind and standard; it was a very powerful piece and was made for the Roman Catholic Church in Bridgend, South Wales.

He later showed work in the exhibition in St. John's Church, Cardiff, during the FIFI festival which included a repoussé copper head of Christ in a standing steel cross called "Christ in the Thorn Bush". Beautifully forged Madonna heads also appear in his ecclesiastical work.

Theo. Grunewald was born in Trier, Germany —so how does he come to be settled in a

Welsh village?—he left school in 1941 and started training in engineering, but after three years went into the German Air Force. So it was that in 1945, at the age of eighteen, he arrived in Britain as a Prisoner of War.

It was while he was at St. Mary Hill near Bridgend that he met the girl who would later become his wife. He returned to Germany after his release and continued his training, but kept in touch with the girl from Wales. They were married in 1953 and after he qualified as an engine driver, the following year, they returned to Llanharan, Glamorgan. This was partly because of family circumstances, his wife being an orphan with three brothers two of whom were younger than herself.

Theo. started his own business in General Engineering and Blacksmithing in 1957, in the same forge he still operates. Today his son and grandson are farriers in the same village.

His work encompasses a very wide range, from jolly traditional weathervanes to solemn, deeply thought pieces for churches —from light engineering to creative modern designs for gates, railings and balustrades; and his commissions have come from places

Above: Forged head of Christ.

Below left: A gate to give privacy, with floral forms at the centre and a bent-over top edge.

Photographs by Theo. Grunewald

as diverse as castles, cathedrals, mansions, marinas and garden centres. Two of his more unusual works have been a long cheval mirror, with a little round mirror to one side, for the wife of an architect; and a dress form with an abstract steel base and head and shoulders for a dress designer.

He began to work in a contemporary style from the beginning of 1970. Apart from his

figure forging, he seems to develop along two paths — the completely abstract full of strong and varied forms, and a modern version of floral ironwork. He says of the design of his pieces ". . . the style develops as I work at them in the workshop." His smithing has a straightforward honest quality wherein lies much of its appeal.

He tries to combine the artistic with the practical skills in working all metals, and feels that ". . . we must be able to create something new and not rest on that which history has given us."

Above and above left: Abstract gates.

Top of page right: An abstract gate of curves for a private house.

Right: Lamps and double gates for a modern house. A contemporary version of floral ironwork. Note the "hidden" edge where the gates come together in the centre, continuing the overall design. Note also how neatly the latch is incorporated into the whole pattern.

Photographs by Theo. Grunewald

118

STUART HILL

Was born in Bromley, Kent, in 1943.

From 1963-65 he was working with a welding firm in Kent.

Stuart himself dates his life as beginning from the age of 35. It was then, in 1977, that he happened to buy a forge and found himself to be creative. So it was that at Claydon Forge in Suffolk he set up his workshop: he did attend a CoSIRA course, but it was working alone in the forge that he began to produce a whole string of new techniques. His work is essentially cerebral; and his mind is incredibly inventive.

In 1980 an exhibition of his work, at the Minories Gallery, Colchester, was the first one-man exhibition of contemporary ironwork to be held in this country.

One of the things he had evolved was a method of forging frogs, from 1 inch square bar, and he had made the requisite tools to enable him to do this accurately and relatively quickly. In the same year his Frog Table called *Metamorphosis* won the Organizers' Award at the Lindau International Exhibition; it was later purchased for the Ironwork Collection of the V & A Museum. It is a rectangular table divided on the top into small squares. In the middle it is as if the water of a pond moves gently, and begins to undulate, as frogs move just below its surface. On each of the diagonal squares, from two points near the centre, frog shapes begin to form and move towards each corner. They become more apparent until a perfectly shaped small frog sits on top of each

Above: Stuart cutting plate for a sculpture at the ABANA conference in America in 1982.

table leg. The table is a work of art; and the making of a single frog could always be relied upon to hold onlookers spellbound at any demonstration. I have heard people say in tones of wonderment "I saw a man forge a frog once"—and I reply "I know who that was!"

He developed a system of plate cutting—he would make a series of concentric cuts, with an oxyacetylene torch into a flat steel plate, and ingeniously open it out into a three dimensional object, perhaps a fire basket or a fire screen. Whereas the Benettons used the technique for sculptures, Hill took the idea into a more technical and useful realm. He was able to visualise and produce patterns on the flat, that once cut, could be bent, twisted or folded into a form that had little resemblance to the original pattern. He even made an incredible portrait from one great plate of half inch steel by making a series of cuts and opening them out. This must have been very much more difficult than the finished work implies. It was preceded by making a long series of exploratory photographs, of straight lines thrown on to the head of a girl and becoming distorted by the forms of the face. The lines so discovered were the ones used to cut into the plate. This work is now outside a restaurant in Suffolk.

Stuart Hill began to work with deflected angle iron or flat bars squeezed in parts to a narrower section. He was first intrigued by patterns of rippling water. This led to his making experiments with a striped awning

Far left: One of Stuart's Frogs forged from a one inch bar.

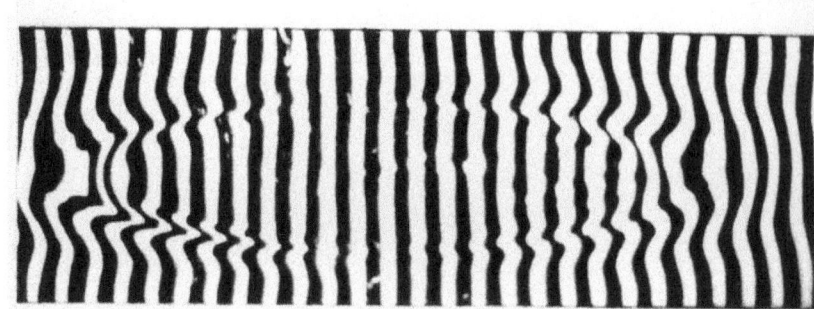

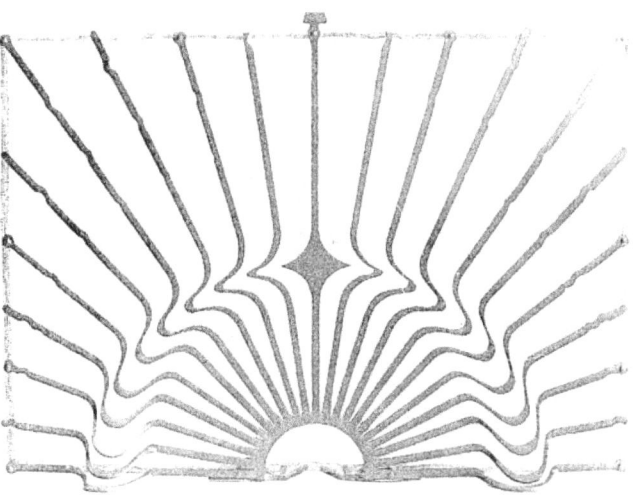

hung up at an angle beside a garden pool. He waited until the water was still, then threw in stones, and photographed the reflections of the striped cloth while the water was disturbed. The different ripple patterns produced design inspiration for grilles, gates and fences.

By using angle iron for railing panels, and altering the angle of parts of the bar, it became possible to produce various designs.

The distortion of the bars produced patterns of light and shade, and by using different colours of paint on each side, both patterns and colours appeared to change as pedestrians walked past.

It seems as if nothing ever happened in the workshop that Stuart's fertile brain did not turn to good use. Once, by mistake, a rod became irretrievably stuck in a pressed tube. From this grew a series of joints

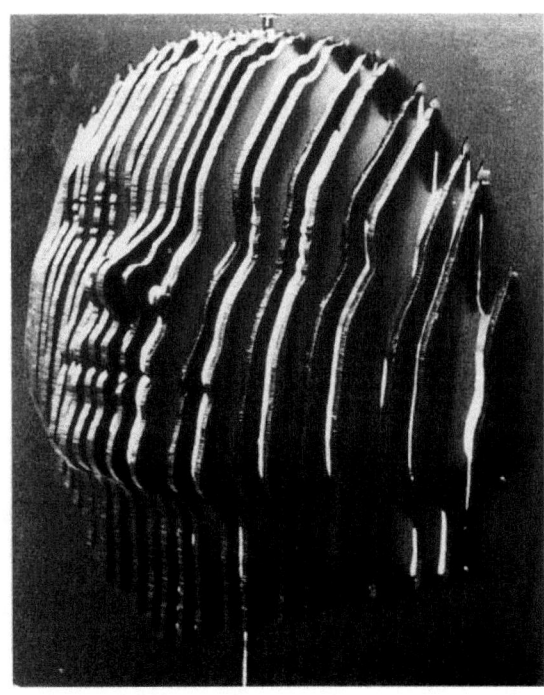

Above Far left: Drawing for cut plate fire screen.

Above: Plate cut as drawing and then opened out into screen.

Top right: Painting for design in ironwork; made by first photographing pattern in disturbed water.

Left and far left: Portrait cut from half inch steel plate.

120

Far left: Detail of
Distorted angle iron
fence.

Left: Grass fence of
cut plate. The
earliest simple form.

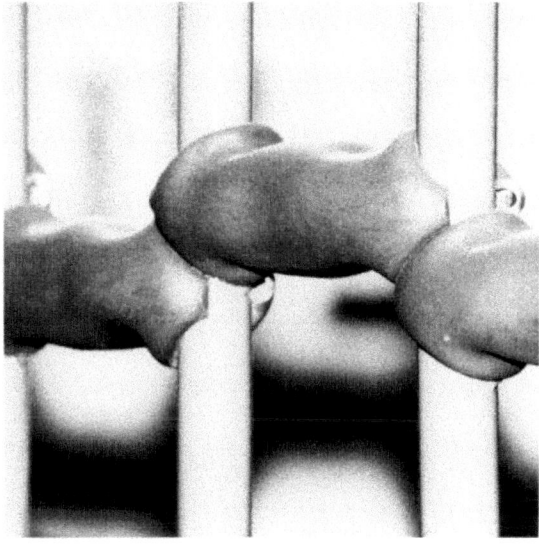

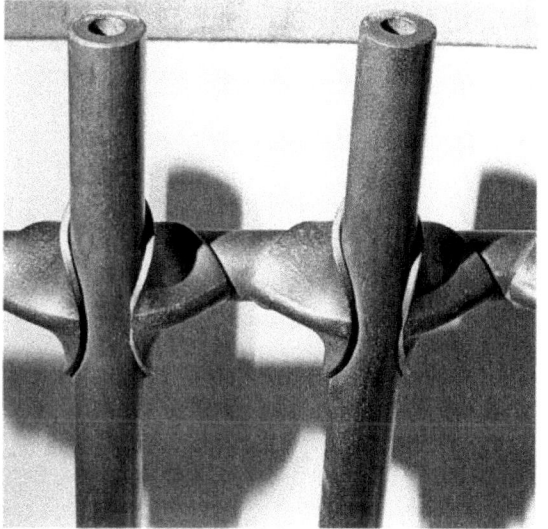

Far left: Detail of
Claydon Connection
joint.

Left: Detail of the
Claydon Clamp
joint. These joints
have now been
renamed, automated,
and patented.

—two of which were known as the Claydon Clamp, and the Claydon Connection. He was experimenting with these in 1982 and they have since been developed as a commercial operation patented under the name of Jointech. Basically these joints were an ingenious method of joining by squashing short pieces of hot tube around other tubes. The Claydon Connection joined two bars by a tube, either round or square in section, of twice their diameter. When the tube was hot the ends were nipped, pinching around the bar. The next joining had to be on a different level.

The Claydon Clamp joins a vertical and a horizontal bar, lapping around them in a pleasing cross shape. One bar is placed under the hot tube and the other at right angles on top of it then pressed under a hydraulic press, preferably of 50 to 100 tons weight. The speed of the operation allows him to produce interesting and practically vandal proof railings at a low price.

These joints have now been renamed and automated but still form an important part of his overall system, and can be seen on many London estates.

Stuart was also experimenting with squashing much larger tubes into various shapes, narrow, oval and figure of eight. In 1981 he was one of the short list to enter the competition for the gates in Winchester Great Hall. His entry was interesting as a design notable for using completely modern techniques in a way entirely suitable for an old building.

In 1982 he was awarded the Worshipful Company of Blacksmiths' Diploma for work of outstanding merit. He was also invited to demonstrate for the ABANA Conference at Ripley, West Virginia. He demonstrated his frog forging. He had taken a few frogs with him and was using them like currency bars; after the demonstration people were wild for them and could not get enough. He went on

Left: The banner inspired gates for St. Peter Mancroft Church, Norwich. Each gate "hanging" from a single central pole.

Left below: Detail of the gates.

to score a major triumph with an evening talk, with slides, on his work. His audience was amazed by the fertility of his mind; his experiments with reflections leading to the angle-iron patterns, and the squashed pipe joints—he even made the front page of the Charleston Gazette.

In the same year Stuart designed and made treasury gates for St. Peter Mancroft Church, Norwich. He based his design on ancient banners hanging in the church. In effect his gates are banners hanging, each from a single central pole, and making no contact with the masonry of the walls and floor. Fairly light straight verticals are crossed by two horizontal bands of heavier ironwork. The forms are very medieval in feeling, reminiscent of armour, and extraordinarily beautiful. Broad ridged verticals of 2" x 2" x 1⅛th" angle iron elongated out at top and bottom into shapes like a Bassinet Helm; while small lugs cut out of the verticals hold broad horizonal bands in position. These are pressed over ridges and take a diamond form between, which, more by accident than design, I understand, are exactly the shape of Cross-ridged Knee-defence armour of the 13th century. Typically Stuart was more interested by the production method than history and calls it the *tin plate technology* because the small lugs are the type of thing that used to hold the parts together in old model toys. There is, however, a concession to architecture as the holes are the same shape as

the arch above the gate.

Not all Stuart Hill's fences used the techniques that have been described. There was one with very solid square panels with a large cut out and raised chestnut leaf on each. These were divided by narrow box-shaped panels, with a continuous *skirting-board* drawing the whole fence together. Another had panels of *grass* shapes cut out of plate. This later became a *Watergrass* fence, integrated into one of the ripple patterns, so that the *grass* seemed to undulate gracefully, first one way and then the other.

He began to work on what he calls the "Christmas decoration technology" for railings, only opening up half inch cut steel plate instead of paper. It could be pulled apart with a tendency to twist, just like festive garlands; today it is done on a specially built stretching bed. Perhaps the ultimate in ingenuity is his public seating, where seven

seats are cut and opened out from one large tube and bent downwards so that the dish curve of the seat is part of the original inner curve of the tube; the back from the lower part of the tube curves upwards. The whole forms an elegant flower-like Lily shape, wholly functional and eminently vandal proof. When seat and back rest are folded into their original positions, the piece once more resembles a large tube.

In 1982 he began running courses for architects demonstrating the possibilities of modern ironwork and, within a couple of years, his work was beginning to attract considerable attention in the architectural field.[1]

He began to see that he could not expand while continuing to make everything himself. He most enjoyed the creative side of the work and began to seek out engineering and metalworking firms to make up to his designs. This, however, did not prove satisfactory. The processes were simple, mainly squeezing, crushing, and impressing, but to be successful they had to be done with extreme accuracy. The outside firms were not used to these techniques, and tended to think of them as bad workmanship, so they did not give them the care and attention needed. In the end he became more or less forced into acquiring larger premises, with a really large work space. In 1985 he formed Claydon Architectural Metalwork, and attracted by

what had been half a warehouse for processing chickens he moved into the premises, which are still his factory today. In this he was helped by the financial expertise of his wife Vi.

The foundation of his present industrial enterprise goes back to the time when he was working as a blacksmith. The creative use of metal is the same; the other two basic and necessary constituents are analytical analysis leading to low cost production. For instance in the early days he developed the Claydon Knot—he made a *rope* by winding strands of iron together then unravelling the end, then bending and tucking them in one behind the other to make it appear like a knot. This took about three days. By isolating the components of which it was made he found the knot was composed of Z shaped pieces linked together, as a kind of cage, with a *rope* round the middle—he was then able to make a Claydon Knot in about twenty minutes

This type of thought process is very similar to the work that is now going on in the factory. It all hinges on analysis and then finding quick and easy ways of production.

He believes it was a good thing that he did

Top above: Seven seats opened out from one large tube.

Above: the same seats viewed from above.

not have the ingrained training of a traditional blacksmith. For one thing it left him receptive to the use of plate and tube, not forms of iron much used or contemplated by most smiths. Neither was he so much interested in what his hands were doing, as in what the iron was doing. This he feels is the distinction between what he was doing and what his contemporaries were doing. It is a radical difference; now he no longer even feels that his own hands need to do the job, once the analysis is made and the problems solved, others can be trained in the simple techniques required.

Lack of early training too has left him with no preconceptions—his mind is open. So many of the shapes that can be made with iron are impossible to design on the drawing board; it is only by playing with the material that it is possible for the iron to achieve its potential. That is why, although all the design work today is done on computer, there is still experimentation on the shop floor. That is where a new process always starts because the edge of technology is there—not the other way.

Stuart believes that one of the most important and basic blocks on which he has built his success is in the fact that, in the early days, he could not afford to buy a power hammer. He had a fly-press and this allowed precise squeezing and crushing—the basis of all his innovation.

His early experiments with the striped awning and pressing patterns into angle iron for fencing has developed into the use of tube. Squeezing and crushing techniques have been used mainly on hollow sections, where, from the manufacturing point of view, there is significantly less work involved. When manipulating a solid bar vast distortions occur in the length, while when doing the same thing with tube the problem does not arise. One of his main fencing methods now is to sandwich a single line of vertical tubes between two pairs of horizontal thinner tubes. Much of his work takes a regular grid of tubular bars and distorts them into pattern; this may take the form of fencing or even sign boards. An example of the former is the semi-circular pattern impressed on a long fence for the Asda store at Roehampton; of the latter a 3' signboard of half inch square tubes distorted into lettering for Cleveland Gallery. Many letters have been incorporated into fencing, including a large repeated S for

Stuart Hill

Sainsburys. Variation in scale can be great.

It is even possible to so arrange the squeezing of tubes to give clear vision from certain angles, such as where cars are leaving car parks and entering a fenced road.

One of Stuart's most ambitious and effective uses of squashed tube, fill arches along the wall of a multi-storey car park. By squeezing the tubes in the centre of the arches, to an oval at 45 degrees to the panel, into the same shape as the brickwork between the arches, he has created the illusion, when seen from an angle, of a double colonnade. The top of the tubes are given a finial by crushing at 90 degrees. One of the arches was extra wide. Taking the basic arch shape and bringing it in half a bay from either side made more sense of the awkward arch and created the illusion of a colonnade in the rest of the facade, the pattern suggesting the shadows of brickwork in front and thereby giving apparent depth to the façade even though it is all in one plane.

More mundane perhaps, but equally interesting is the use of tube for making bollards—crushing and bending on a large scale can give a very powerful effect. A 168mm diameter round section tube, pinching a smaller tube at right angles at the top (a T joint formerly the Claydon connection), can be a most satisfying object. Soft detailing comes naturally to anyone who is used to working *hot* metal, but when it comes to tubes, as Stuart says "Nobody thinks of doing anything organic with them".

There are other bollards of square section tube. One design has long vertical grooves in the body; another, just a little crush at the top, which gives a subtle variation of form to the welded square top. A whole series of these line the taxi ramp at Liverpool Street Station. I particularly like the square bollard with the round collar; perhaps because I find it almost

Above left: Sign board with lettering defined by distorted tubes.

magical that a *square* tube can be pushed into a *round* collar. Experimenting, himself, Stuart heated the end red and pushed it down: result—a pleasant circular collar around the square form of the tube. Going into production to make 50, word came back to him that the operation was not possible. The tube was turning inwards and going all over the place. He had to sit down and think exactly what he had done when making the prototype; he then remembered that he had been interrupted and not pressed the tube until it had cooled from red heat. After this all was well, the operation could be as controlled or as manic as required according to the heat involved.

Car barriers are also made from large tube using a 160 ton press.

At school, in physics, Stuart was fascinated by physical phenomena and had become interested in interference patterns, normally seen in cell shapes under the microscope. It was this interest, coupled with the water ripple patterns that have given rise to one of his most intriguing techniques. He transfers a natural ripple pattern to a steel plate, cuts the pattern out, giving a negative and a positive, then sets the panels up with a six inch gap between them. As anyone walks past, the fence appears to move into true moiré patterns. Also if the fence is in an open situation there is a lot of shadow interest on

Stuart Hill

the pavement on a sunny day. Having seen such examples it comes as no surprise to find that Stuart admires, and is influenced by, Pop Art. It does not matter to him that such art is now felt to be out-dated—he just finds an empathy with the exciting patterns.

Some of his fences have equal length vertical bars set out to a mathematical relationship. Imagine spacing lines equally around a tube, when seen from the front they will, by the laws of perspective, appear to be closer together at the sides—just as unequally spaced lines on the flat will appear to give a three dimensional effect. Two such fences juxtaposed will generate a moiré pattern.

Above: Moiré fence showing shadow interest.

Left: Squashed tube giving the optical illusion of a double colonnade.

Stuart Hill

Other designs using straight tubes are *leaning bar* fences. Equal length, square section, narrow tubes incline in groups towards each other, which gives the optical illusion that some are shorter then others. The tubes being left open at each end allow zinc dipping without the expensive necessity of drilling and filling *escape* holes.

Cost is always in mind. One of the aims is to bring the firms more standard, but still creative and interesting, fences to be competitive in price with the ubiquitous chain-link.

One type of fencing that Stuart has evolved is *Stretched mesh* rather like the orange nets one sees holding fruit or peanuts. Steel mesh is pulled out so that 2 metres square becomes 3 metres long and develops a strong structural shape. He jokes that these come *pre-vandalised* and little further damage can be done. Some are so styled as to appear to be *Blowing in the wind*.

The basic economy comes from continual improving mechanisation and jigging of the machinery. *Barley Crush* is a tube which has been crushed to give rounded indents on four sides. At first these depressions were made individually, then a whole line at once, then the bar was turned at 90° and another set made. It is now done, orientated at 45°, with tools that interlock—from being a seven-stage operation it has become a single-stage operation. Sometimes used as a wave pattern *Barley Crush* catches the light, in a lively way, where it is deflected from the plain tube. Today Claydon Architectural Metalwork, CAM, is the only firm able to supply patterned guard rails to Department of Transport Specification.

One of the most recent fences to have been evolved is a design for a sloping site. Normally this is an expensive undertaking and results in an uneven stepped top. Using the usual tube between paired horizontals Stuart designed a short section of bridging bar welded to the upright and both horizontals, which gives enough movement in the joints to enable panels to be pulled out of square on site to follow the contours of the ground. This has been developed and patented.

Of smaller items there have been graceful small section handrails in red and yellow brass finishing in large open circles, for Terry

Left: *Maquette of the proposed gate that was entered for the Winchester Great Hall competition using squashed tube.*

Stuart Hill

Farrell at Tobacco Dock. There is the *Quiltcrush* bench with an upholstered look, and litter bins.[2]

I should not like to give the impression that Stuart today is concerned only with products for a mass market, on the contrary he gives a great deal of thought and time to individual commissions. Many have been the outcome of happy collaboration with architects. He feels the work is at its best when designer-producer can experiment from the beginning of the work with the architect and his building. That true harmony arises when he is exploring the plastic properties of his material and the architect is experimenting with modern structural techniques.

Richard Burton, architect, of Ahrends Burton and Kokalek designed for himself an exciting house in Kentish Town. One rarely finds a house that is so ingenious and so rich in ecological consciousness.[3] Stuart's deep blue gate is round, set into an otherwise blank wall of London stock bricks. The ripple pattern gate opens and shuts on a single pivot, and leads into an entrance court dominated by a great plane tree.

There are times when production methods discussed with an architect can help to reduce cost and add, rather than lessen, design interest. Railings for a building in Red Lion

Square near High Holborn were first visualised by the architect as flat. It was a stepped design with a lot of intersections, producing square shapes, costly to put together on the flat. By layering one group of rails with a top horizontal, over the next similar group the squares were easily achieved; while curving sections of this railing produced sufficient strength for them to act as *posts*.

Gates to a new shopping centre, formerly Kensington Palace Barracks, for the Building Design Partnership used crushing techniques to produce a more traditional pattern to evoke an idea of the site's historical past. Crushing techniques were also used on a balustrade to the New Court Building in Woodgreen. There was unfortunately insufficient funding to produce a forged balustrade for the circular stairway, but by jigging up to make an inverted L shape, with a design of varying horizontals attached, it was possible to make a series of units and link them together.

An especially fine gate, the main entrance for Queen Mary and Westfield College (London University), is situated on the Mile End Road. It leads to the Faculty of Arts and was designed in collaboration with a young Dutch architect Roeland Leenes for RMJM.[4]

The design of the double gates, five gently undulating lines, tenuously asymmetrical, run right across. More Surrealism here than Pop Art. The *dark lines* are really voids and one wonders what keeps these seemingly unsupported slices of gate in levitation—the answer of course, single pivots at the back of each gate. The surface is cast aluminium tiles, with a subtle blend of colour variation; cast by Stuart's *outcasting* technique, impressing the negative areas from the back.

Stuart has begun to enter the field of Industrial Sculpture, with two works for the Military Hospital in Utrecht. The most impressive is a group of five red tubes two floors high, about 8m; they lean together at the top and spread to a width of 12m at the base. They are held by a cantilevered arm on the upper floor and are not only decorative but serve a purpose in recirculating the warm air system downwards to the lower floor. Neon lighting is also incorporated into the sculpture. An ingenious, if unsettling, touch is that the floor has been relaid so that the pipes, supported on thin tubes, appear to be pulling out of the floor!

Stuart had felt for some time that design work would benefit from computerisation and in 1988 CAM invested in its first cad station—a 386 micro computer running Scribe 3D modeller. Once the system was mastered, producing drawings became a great deal quicker and the client could be presented with more alternatives. Also, of course, alterations could be made very quickly.

A unique and cost cutting method of presenting drawings has been evolved. A photograph of the site is photocopied and enlarged to A3 size. An acetate copy is also taken, to be used as a mask for the computer screen. The computer drawing is adjusted in perspective to fit the acetate and plotted out. Photocopying the computer drawing onto the site illustration brings the two together and handcolouring gives a high quality finish without the use of expensive printers or software.[5]

Below: Main entrance to Queen Mary and Westfield College by day and by night.

Photographs Stuart Hill

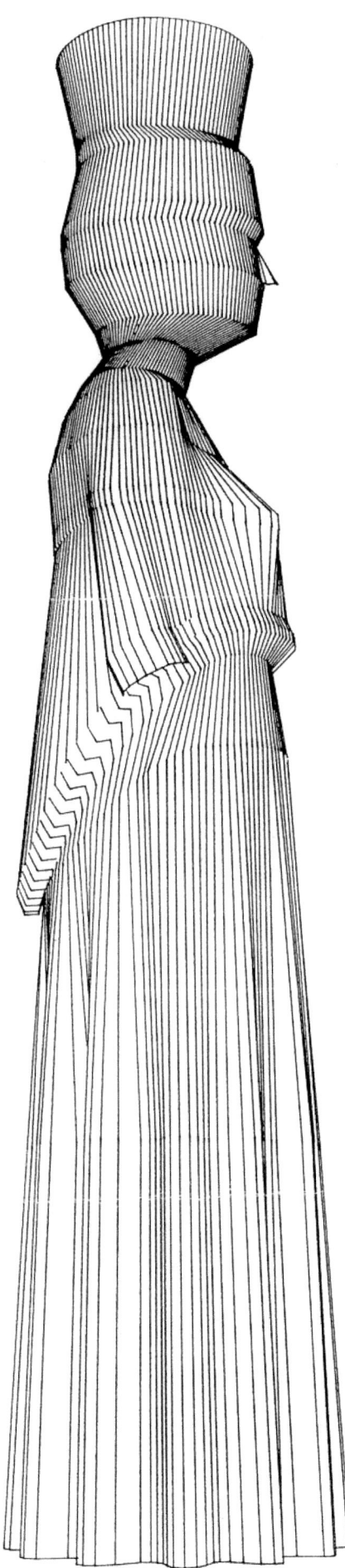

Computerisation is leading to all sorts of exciting developments; particularly impressive—drawings for 11m high caryatid figures designed for a motorway flyover on behalf of CZWG. (Campbell Zogolovich Wilkinson and Gough) See illustration left.

What of the future—Stuart looks towards his prototypes becoming standard available products for others to assemble in their own designs; this will of course be aided by the cad system. He showed me just two pages of components in his catalogue, different construction methods, patterns, bar types and heights capable of more than 7000 permutations. It is not surprising that the words Europe and America begin to creep into his conversation.

Stuart's blacksmithing days were almost entirely experimental. He exploited a niche that others left empty. His creativity and new techniques have given new life to low cost fencing and barriers. He has introduced undreamt of apparent *movement* to static ironwork with his ripple and moiré patterns. He never *applies* decoration, he simply takes and keeps the purity of line of tube and by slightly deflecting it breaks the monotony. When curves are introduced into his work they are of the very slightest, and never arbitrary, but subtly drawn from nature itself. By his introduction of new jointing methods; and by developing his creative craft techniques into industrial processes, he has achieved within his firm something of a new industrial revolution.

Stuart has now built himself a house in the Turkish part of Cyprus. He was his own architect and designed the building on computer. It is surrounded by the natural wild garden of the mountain and resembles nothing so much as a small Norman castle—the first castle to be built on the island since the Crusades!

This is not a man who spends much time sitting in the sun: at present there is no hot forge-work going on in the island, so he plans to take his blacksmithing tools over, so that he can teach blacksmithing skills to others—it will, he says, "give me something to do in the holidays!"

Sources and Notes

1. *Architectural Review* May 1984.
2. A J Focus June 1992.
3. *Architectural Review* Sept. 1990.
4. David Grindley. "Building. Economies of Scale: RMJM's Faculty of Arts" *Architecture Today* Sept. 31 1992.
5. Richard Twich "Metal Awe" *Building Design* Feb. 8th 1991.

Left: Computer drawing for 11m high caryatid figure, designed for a motorway flyover on bealf of CZWG.

JAMES
HORROBIN

Jim Horrobin was born in 1946 in Stafford. He was the son of an armourer, who becoming converted to the Peace Movement, decided to change to being a blacksmith. So it was that from 1961 Jim became apprenticed to his father, Harry, as a blacksmith. They had a forge at Bridgetown in Somerset, where they shod horses and repaired farm machinery. He also attended metalwork courses at Hereford Technical College and took advantage of the CoSIRA block release day scheme in which blacksmiths of the stature of Frank Day and Tommy Tucker would actually visit the forge and teach him on a one to one basis; something that he has always regarded as a great privilege.[1]

In 1965 they moved a few miles and set up a forge at Roadwater. Here they branched out more into decorative ironwork. Harry Horrobin had become something of a specialist in decorative pieces and Jim, by then 19, began to be known not only as a promising craftsman but as something of an artist in iron. They took their work to

Above left: Jim in America in 1982.

agricultural shows and it kept them in business. At the Bath and West Show in 1967 the Horrobin stand swept the board, winning first, second, and third prizes in the domestic ironwork competition.[2]

It was about this time that Harry Horrobin retired, Jim married and, in 1969, set up his own workshop at Torre near Washford.

All the work he was doing was of a traditional nature, ramshead doorknockers, an armorial sign for a Lombard bank in Exeter, sometimes a gate for a medieval church, and, more daring, firescreens with birds (during his Fritz Kühn phase). However, some designs were becoming less derivative than others.

Inside an ancient West Somerset chapelry, a simple whitewashed building, deep in mowing grass and buttercups, the theme that runs through the ironwork design is that of birds. They are to be found on the font cover, a flower stand, and soaring upwards on a beautiful candelabra; all early and fairly traditional Horrobin work.

Far Left: The Chandelier at Crowcombe.

Further east, near Bridgwater, Crowcombe Church houses an enormous iron chandelier, so large that it almost dwarfs the little church. This must surely be Jim's most ambitious project during his traditional period. It is a very fine piece modelled on the brass ones so popular in the 17th century but far beyond these in its ornate fantasy. The vicar of the church himself seems to have been a somewhat larger than life character, and rode around his parish on horseback in cowboy outfit with boots and stetson. Jim was paid £500 for the commission, which was made about 1973, when the going rate for the job was around £1 an hour.

129

Jim Horrobin's smithing development was never to be tranquil, and by 1976 he had arrived at something of a crisis. He had been working hard, isolated in one or another village forge for fifteen years. His day to day work was mainly in the style of the 18th century and he was using very little of his own creativity. He remembers thinking, when about to embark on making yet another fire screen, "well this time I am not going to put C scrolls in the corners—it is time for a change!". He felt he was using a smaller and smaller vocabulary—working mindlessly; he has even described himself as "mentally unemployed"[1] ". . . because I was isolated I had not broadened my outlook. I found myself using fewer and fewer design solutions to each job that came in, and I felt I could not go on doing the job in a mechanical way."[5]

He was not even sure that he wanted to continue being a blacksmith. There were obviously decisions to be made. What he did was to virtually take a year off, working only two days a week in someone else's shop, and spending most of his time wave-surfing in Woolacombe Bay. After the year was up he knew he did still have a personal commitment to work with iron.

It was not long after this that he became a founder member of BABA and it changed his life in a lot of ways. He has said that ". . . it allowed people to talk about techniques, instead of having a diminishing vocabulary there was an explosion of ideas".

By this time he was living, with his wife and two children, in Laurel Cottage, Carhampton near Minehead, on the road leading to the deer park. Attached to the 16th century house was a lovely old forge which had been worked by a succession of village blacksmiths since 1585. Now he was working on his own terms in his own way. He began to make forged bowls and small sculptural pieces which he photographed among the waving grasses of the nearby fields. He offered his customers his own original designs and was surprised how often they accepted them.

One commission was for a pair of gates for a garden owned by one of the County's oldest families. The customer became quite excited when it was explained that they could be made in a traditional way but using Jim's personal design solutions. The gates would reflect the shapes of the flowers beyond them, and relate to their environment."[5]

He began to experiment, to create, and to try and infuse his work with the movement he saw in the natural forms around him. He made a screen, slightly medieval in appearance, held together by collars (a typical joining method of the Middle Ages), and by something new, spirals inspired by the tendrils of bindweed. It stood on delicate pairs of tapered points, rather like inverted pitchfork heads. These slender coils and sharp tapered points were to be an important part of his new development.

The forms were hand forging at its best, drawing out and elongating bars in perfect graceful symmetry, or twisting them while hot and malleable round other bars of iron. His next major piece *Hanging Irons* was almost entirely composed of these new components. It was large and decorative though it had been inspired by simple traditional skewer holders. The two central forms were spread at the centre to a breadth

Above: Hanging Irons was the first important piece in Jim's development made in a modern style.

of almost four inches and pierced into round holes; both ends were then drawn out into fine rods, first rectangular in section, then round towards the graceful points. Each of the two horizontal members have been cut into and opened out to form hooks and the opposite end of the bar has been laced through the holes in the uprights. Six hanging irons each have fire welded loops at the top and four of them have been cut and opened out at the bottom to form double points. It has still one more innovation, that of fastening by iron *thongs*. The piece, which is 36" long, hangs from a wall fixture made of two flat plates of iron laced together with round section rod; rather like the front of a medieval garment might be laced together with fasteners. These appear to twist into a double loop and fall gracefully into a hook finished with the minutest scroll as small as a little flat baby snail.

Jim then accepted a private commission for a gate in a very beautiful garden which already had several good traditional gates; now a modern gate was needed to lead into the vegetable garden.

The gate continued the use of the new

techniques he had evolved in the screen and *Hanging Irons*. Seven uprights were broadened out in irregular shapes at intervals. Three horizontal broad flat bars were drifted into two more outer bars, which were only broadened into shapes at the top. The seven decorative uprights were knotted into the horizontals by round rods like leather thonging. A top cresting was formed by four horn-like features fastened to the uprights by spiral *thonging* which was sometimes allowed to tail off downwards in the manner of plant stems. A further Four *horn-shapes* were fixed, in the same way, on a more diagonal line around the centre of the gate.

About two years later the same client commissioned what was always known as the "Dog Gate". It was across the back doors which opened into the garden; its use was to allow air into the house (of which there was a great deal) while preventing the dogs from getting out. It was in two leaves fastening in the centre and the top dipped down in the middle.

The most decorative part was low down and this time horn-like shapes were vertical and the ends were forged out into discs. Where they were riveted into the upright the bar retained its square section but above and below was forged round. At the top of the gate the bars were upset then flattened, into a shape almost like the head of a duck, with a long spiral twist to join it to the next bar. This gate was made in collaboration with Stephen Lock.

Above: Detail of top of the gate to the vegetable garden. With thonging and "bindweed" spirals.

Far left: The gate to the vegetable garden.

The delight of all these works was the liveliness of the hand forging and the way bars swelled out where holes had been drifted through. In this they were more akin to work of the early Middle Ages than anything that had come between—yet they were new and wholly his own creation. The time had truly come when he could say ". . . Now I have entered into the spirit of blacksmithing using my own mind."[5]

So it was that by July 1980, even before the International Conference on Forging Iron, it was already being said that "Now he makes some of the most interesting experimental ironwork in Britain today."[5] Both the *Medieval Screen* and *Hanging Irons* featured in the travelling exhibition "Forged Iron" organised by the Ceolfrith Gallery, Sunderland Arts Centre, and shown at the Ironbridge Gorge Museum to coincide with the Conference. He also made a fire basket for a small exhibition, called "The British Grate", shown at the Conference, with horizontal flames spreading out sideways on the front and back (see page 33). One was later shown in the "Towards a New Iron Age" exhibition (1982) and is now in the Victoria and Albert Museum. After visiting America another design was influenced by the construction of a log cabin.

In 1981 Jim Horrobin was the winner of a select competition to make gates for the metalwork Gallery of the Victoria and Albert Museum, London. The gallery contains one of the world's largest and most important collections of wrought ironwork, and it was intended that these gates should be working exhibits, representing the best in modern design in wrought metal. They had, when required, to securely cut off the gallery from a flight of stairs leading to another section of the museum. We Have Jim's own notes on making the gates [4]:

The techniques used in making the gates were basically traditional, punching holes, riveting, stretching, bending and drawing down.

The horizontal bars 80 x 16mm and 100 x 20mm each had 5 tongues split out and shaped.

The splitting was achieved by using a hot set and assistant Ben Leach swinging a 16lb sledge hammer.

We were able to cut 12–15 tongues a day,

there being a total of 90.

The second stage involved making the vertical bars. We started with a stock bar of 120 x 12mm, first cutting the rough shape with the oxyacetylene torch. The bars were then drawn down and stretched under the power hammer. Care was needed to calculate the finished dimensions.

The four main frame verticals each with 9 slots drilled and punched out to receive the horizontal tenons, took a total of 150 heats in the fire to produce.

The curves in the centre of the hanging verticals were produced by hammering with a sledge hammer into a pre-shaped bottom tool.

The centre post was made from 150mm tube in 4 sections. The end of each section was belled out then welded and re-forged to form 200mm diameter spheres.

Assembly was a straight forward system of riveting, using Oxyacetylene as a heating agent.

Below:
The Dog Gate.

The finish is a combination of red oxide coated with wax then coated with black etch primer.

Jim Horrobin.

The decorative quality derives wholly from its integral form and methods of construction. He has said that, to some extent, when forming the design he was thinking of the way water ripples out from an object dropped into it.

The making of the V & A gates must have been mentally taxing in its inception, because it was so unlike anything he had done before, and physically demanding in the making. It was as brutalist as any modern piece produced in this country by that date.

No one looking at these gates, and then at the Crowcombe chandelier of eight years earlier, can doubt the self questioning that must have taken place in the mind of the craftsman to achieve such complete change of direction while still maintaining an integrity to his work. The gates were, in some ways, both a barrier and a bridge between two periods of his work—the hand forging that had come before (both in his traditional and modern development) and a series of large prestigious commissions that were to follow, and would inevitably involve the greater use of modern techniques.

By the time this stage in his working development arrived, life itself had opened up to a very much broader outlook. At the International Forging Iron Conference he had made contact with smiths from all over the world and in 1982 he went to the ABANA conference in West Virginia and demonstrated to the Blacksmiths Guild of the Potomac at Arlington. When he looks back on this period he says, with an engagingly honest smile ". . . I was just a country boy and it was the first time I had ever been abroad."

At home, he was often demonstrating and gave several short blacksmithing courses at Nettlecombe Court for the Arts Programme organised by the Wolsleys. The fine arts became more important to him and he began to sketch in the countryside, not only when designing his work. It was a skill that would be increasingly valuable in the years to come when he was sometimes designing ironwork that would be made by other craftsmen.

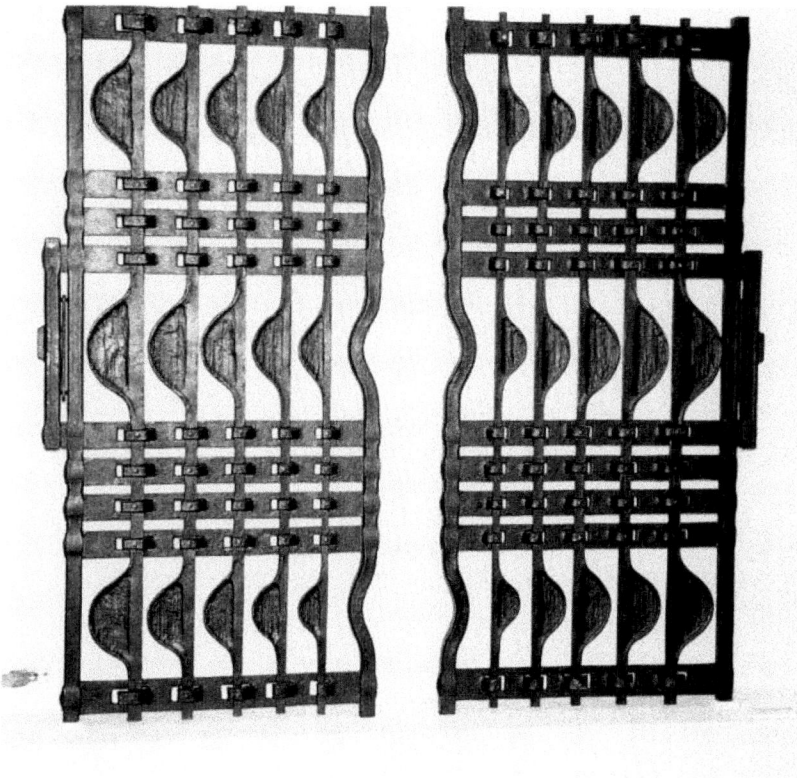

"Drawings can be changed easily and are a lot cheaper to work with than a whole load of metal. Besides you can send a drawing through a Fax machine." [3]

In a way the new commissions were a whole new ball game, and would range in price from £5 – £100,000. It would take some years to work out the ins and outs of the construction industry. Contracts were usually very complicated and seemed to have a different formula for each one. He had to grow wise to the pitfalls of penalty clauses and learn to work with architects and structural engineers.

"With the big architectural commissions I just respond to the building I am working with, I should say it is the complete difference between a sculptor and a craftsman. A sculptor putting a piece of work in a building need not necessarily relate his work to the architecture whereas a craftsman is constrained by rules and value judgments; a different set of values are in force for the craftsman."

His first big London job was for the Crown Reach prestige development of luxury flats, a most unusual modern building designed by Nicolas Lacy and built under the direction of Arno Jobst, on Millbank near Vauxhall bridge. Jim designed and made eleven gates of varying size and shape. According to

Above: Gate commissioned by the Victoria and Albert Museum to lead into the Ironwork Gallery.

which side one looked at the building, it presented two very different aspects. The curves and scallops of the front of the building were reflected in the top line of some of the gates, 3m high on one side and sweeping down in a single curve to a lower opposite post; the design is one of verticals and fairly dense to provide privacy. On the inner side of the building, square tubing was fixed to the vertical bars in different positions to reflect the cube-like architectural pattern.

As it was a large contract with a penalty clause if not completed on time, Jim was assisted by an ex-Farnham College student and two other helpers without previous blacksmithing experience. One had been a thatcher, and the other was a Yugoslavian, Jaques Horvath, with little English. It speaks much for Jim's philosophy, that rather than produce the gates on a factory system, he preferred individual helpers to produce whole gates and thereby derive job satisfaction. The design aided inexperienced assistants, since the components were simple to make, and to save time, the posts were cut out of rolled steel joists.

Next came two large gates for the Police administration centre at Rampayne Street, Pimlico, by the architect David Lyle of Whitfield Partners. Smith and architect formed a good working relationship and the next large commission was also under his auspices. This was for a 50m stretch of railings, lamps, and 5 infill grilles bordering Edgware Road, for Oriel House, Connaught Place. The same group who worked on the Crown Reach gates, Paul Jobst and Stephen Lock, were now partners in the new project.

The railings, like the building, are uncompromisingly linear. Two bands at the top of the rails and three at the base were derived from the design in the glass of the building. These rails were designed roughly in 2m sections, weighing 2 hundredweight, so that transport should not be too difficult.

It was a £50,000 job on a penalty basis, and halfway through Jim felt that his firm could possibly face certain financial problems. At a large management meeting for the development Jim discovered that he was one of the few people present who was not employed by someone else. He set out his problems honestly and was agreeably surprised to find that they were smoothed out. All was completed on time in 1984.

Photograph Chris Fairclough

Also designed at this time, 1983-4, for David Lyle and Whitfield Partners, was a screen and grille for Richmond House, 79 Whitehall, opposite the Cenotaph. A strikingly beautiful building of yellow brick banded in white, it has a strong sense of history. Inside the metalwork is by Starkie Gardner Ltd.

On the left of the main entrance (right if you are looking at the building) is a heavy portcullis-like grille. This uses square linking tubes in the style of the Crown Reach gates, while the verticals pick up strongly with the window bars and vertical stonework above.

The screen, some 5m high and 13m long, is round the corner in Derby Gate. It is a linking device entirely subservient to the architecture. A good deal lighter in

Above: One of the gates at the back of Crown Reach.

construction, it again picks up the forms in the buildings by which it is surrounded, and the arrow head rail tops re-stress an awareness of history. It was finished before the building was complete but when installed fitted perfectly. There were complications with the contract and, in the end, Jim nominated Richard Quinnell Ltd to make the ironwork; he did, however, assist with the work as at the time only an elevation drawing existed.

There were also design commissions for Arup Associates and Derek Latham Associates, the latter for a Leeds County Arcade.

A light hearted commission, with far more freedom, were clothes rack systems for two shops in London and New York. The architects were Munkembeck and Marshall and the Japanese client Yohji Yamamoto. The ironwork consisted of about twenty shaped brackets and adjustable rails ". . . pretty wild not a C scroll in there!". The American shop was successful, but the one in Sloane Street was not. In the way of the fashion trade all its fittings were swept away within six months, and the shop given a completely new image. Jim was not upset by this—the job was finished and he had passed on.

Above left: Richmond House, Whitehall with portcullis-like grille.

Far left: Detail of grille.

Left: the screen round the corner in Derby Gate.

In 1988 Jim moved to Porlock and set up a forge and craft gallery, the Doverhay Studios, right in the middle of the village by the car park. He is in partnership with Gabrielle Ridler a glass engraver. The premises had long been a forge and now Jim's design office looks into a showroom displaying not only ironwork but also carefully selected engraved glass, ceramics, prints and stainless steel jewellery. Perhaps this change marks a fourth stage in his design evolution.

Jim has always been at his happiest hand forging at the anvil. Machines have never interested him and he still only has three in his workshop. Preferring, as he does, to forge or design he rather resents long periods spent installing large architectural commissions. It now seems as if his style has finally come home and such problems have been resolved.

He has been designing and making a screen in an angular Art Deco design for the side of the Savoy Theatre, but it will be fitted up by Dorothea Restoration Engineers Limited. He is now at work on a wrought iron figure of *The Lord High Executioner* from the Mikado, for the Upper Circle Bar.

He no longer minds going back to scrolls and fire welds and has recently made a wrought iron ceiling rose for one of the rooms in Sir John Soanes Museum, Lincoln's Inn. An interesting design and fabrication job in 1992 has been on a building in Cheapside for Sun Alliance which includes fanlight grilles with gilded leaves and a mythical Coat of Arms. This, Jim has devised from Mantling a cloth worn by crusaders at the back of the neck, to protect it from the sun, and usually in ribbons by the time they came home. Inside a grille on the right almost Art Deco in feeling. Here he has been paid on a different system, monthly, throughout the job.

Perhaps the most significant, and certainly one of the largest recent commissions has been a stair case, handrail and balustrade in a private house, for Charles Saatchi. In thinking of the design it may have been a visit to the Picasso Museum which led Jim to want something of a curvy nature rather than geometric. Though perhaps one can see here the crest of a wave—Jim still enjoys surfing and is out on moonlit nights when the waves

Andrew Priddy

are high. It was decided that the whole 23m should have no repeat pattern. It runs, without interruption, up several floors; it is decidedly modern but has all the elegance of a French 18th century stair balustrade. It was all forged by Jim who started the design at the bottom, then went to the top and started again there. The shaped forged pieces were put together by Dominic Hess; though altogether about seven people were involved in the work for at least three months.

It seems as if the skill of Jim's early traditional forging, followed by the modern forging, which then gave way to the experience and expertise of the power hammer and modern techniques for large architectural

Above: Figure of Koko for the Upper Circle Bar of the Savoy Theatre. 1993.

136

commissions, has now all come together in another, and new, stage of his development.

There has always been something special about his forging. Any blacksmith can make a coat hook—but I always remember one he made at Nettlecombe. I cannot recall exactly the shape it took but the form was wholly organic, it made one think of fungii rising from some woodland floor, it was a small thing of incredible beauty. The sensitivity of his hand forging has always been his greatest strength. More than any other British smith he has harnessed his traditional hand forging skills and kept them as the very heart of his modern work.

Sources: and Notes

1. James Horrobin lectured on his work to the British Artist Blacksmiths Association at Redfield in November 1992. Much of the information is derived from that talk.

2. *British Blacksmith* "Profile " Nos 6 & 7.

3. *British Blacksmith* "Profile" by Peter Pay. No 51.

4. *British Blacksmith* "The V & A Gates" No. 22.

5. Interview with Lesley Adamson *The Guardian* July 19th 1980.

Andrew Priddy

Above: Maquette for the Saatchi stair rail. Now in the National Ornamental Metal Museum, Memphis, Tennessee.

Left: Fanlight Grille in Cheapside, City of London, for Sun Alliance.

ALAN JACK

Alan Jack lives in a perfectly ordinary suburban house but when paper boys enter through the front gate they tend to go goggle eyed. Large and vicious looking birds stalk the grass, enormous insects crouch under the bushes and a witch flies a broomstick up through the trees.

Alan's wife and son are computer wizards but what motivates him is iron. He has been with it all his life—he was apprenticed as a toolmaker and later became an aircraft engineer. The iron sculptures that crowd both his front and his back garden he makes for the pure enjoyment of the material. He cannot bear to see any carefully crafted piece of blacksmiths' work, skilled pieces of ironwork, thrown away. He thinks it is a crime and he would much prefer to recycle it into a new life.

He believes that we are going into a plastic age and that in a few years all the unconsidered trifles of iron that are at present to be found will have disappeared. That is why his small workshop is hung round with chains of varying sizes, bits of bicycles and motor-cycle parts, odd pieces of wrought

ironwork, and bevel gears some of which are, in themselves, quite exquisite forms. Tools and implements no longer capable of use or repair, spades, forks, trowels, files, rasps, spanners, all will find a place, perhaps as the crest of some exotic bird or the plumage of a fowl. Sometimes he will take the tools left by a craftsman, whose family can no longer put them to use, and turn them into a 'memory' sculpture; because these particular pieces of iron will have more meaning to the family

Left: Tractor

Below left: Fiddler Crab.

members than other less personal metal objects.

Who knows where it all began, as a youngster he used to make push-bikes out of scrap, mostly because he couldn't afford to buy a new one. Sometimes he makes thick-set tractor models, mainly from gearing, but for the most part it is birds and insects that inspire a use for the strange objects among which he works. When he turns to figure sculpture the scale is large, a Samurai warrior about life size, and menacing monsters, surely from outer space, larger than life. Some of the birds are immediately recognisable others weird and wonderful inventions. Their

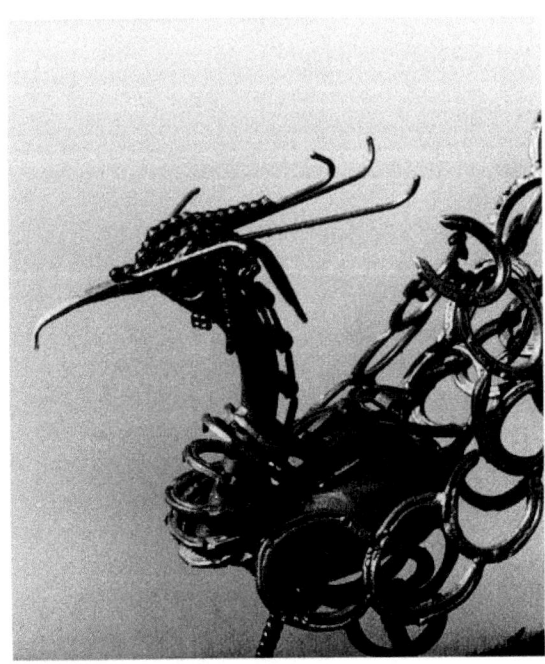

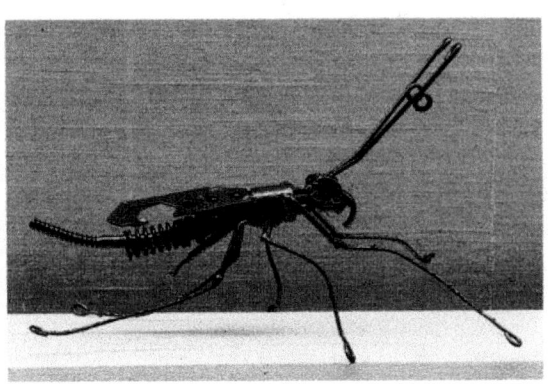

Far Left: Exotic Horseshoe bird.

Left: Damsel Fly.

Left and below:
Welded sheet metal
Owls, and below left
Tiger.

long necks are often formed of welding chain links together into a fixed position—the chain neck of a Flamingo is topped with a simple old and beautifully forged hook for a head. Other necks are made from springs whose use was to hold railway rails in position—obsolete now so already something from the past that is being preserved. Insects are another perennial interest; he tells me solemnly that there are nine hundred thousand different kinds of insects in the world, and—"I love stag-beetles!"

Give Alan a pile of scrap and in a few minutes he will know what he wants to do with it; but there is never time to make everything, the work is painstaking and time consuming, inevitably there will always be some piles of scrap waiting for attention.

One marvels at the ingenuity with which he selects exactly the right piece for the job. This is not any old lump of junk joined together to look like something else. Alan has an awareness of texture, an eye for form, and an appreciation of the integral nature of a piece of metal that enables him to select a length of motorcycle chain, for its soft flexibility, so that it perfectly becomes the wattles hanging from the head of a bird; or a handful of tools that become the stiff plumage of a Prairie Chicken. When all this is considered it has to be said that there are times when the ingenuity obtrudes itself between the art and the observer;

though to some this is the interest and humour of his work. Perhaps to a certain extent he is aware of this himself, when a piece is completed he hates to see the original colours of the parts, their provenance is too obvious and the wholeness of the figure is destroyed. This is why he prefers to paint them all over with one colour of Hammerite paint, usually rusty red, buff, or peacock blue.

Although he does not so much enjoy working with sheet metal, to me, some of his finest work is carried out in this material. His eagles soar on great wings with the noblest of heads, while a small "Little Owl" alights with every appearance of the wind ruffling his fluffy feathers.

Exhibitions of Alan Jack's work have been held at Wallsworth Hall Nature in Art, The International Centre for Wildlife Art, Gloucester; Slimbridge Wild Fowl Trust and Martin Meere.

GIUSEPPE LUND

Giuseppe Lund was born in London in 1951.[1] Between 1969 and 1973 he studied philosophy at Southampton and Bristol Universities, and music at the Royal College of Music.

In 1974 he attended a CoSIRA course and spent eight months training as a blacksmith with Antony Robinson.

He set up his own workshop in Brockenhurst, Hampshire, in 1976,[2] and as Lesley Adamson has said ". . . did what amounted to a do-it-yourself course getting ideas from photographs and setting himself challenges. At the time it was technique and not innovation he was after."

"I was doing really classical work and stopping myself having ideas because they broke the rules. My first public appearance was at the Chelsea Flower Show with a gate in the mood of the Davies Brothers' work. Someone said it was the work of a man of 50. After that my restraint went. It had to, if I was ever to do anything myself." [3]

By 1977 Lund had aquired an apprentice and took him to Europe.

"I just worked out a route through Germany finding famous bits of work and eminent people. That is how I walked into the forge of Herman Gradinger at Mainz-Gonsenheim and realised a whole new world existed.

"The strangest thing was that I saw shapes I recognised as my own half-formed ideas which I had pushed aside because they didn't fit with the rules of the game." [3]

Lund learnt that he could use modern techniques with impunity and became aware of the possibilities of cutting steel plate with oxy-acetylene gas. He was impressed by the use of heavy power hammers, giving the ability to work any size of metal, and by the concept of taking the heat to the metal rather than having to take the iron to the fire.

By 1980 he was working the forge at Rose Cottage, Coalbrookedale, assisted by Gino Rickard, under the auspices of the Craft Council and the Ironbridge Gorge Museum, whose director was making an effort to revitalise the skills that had once existed in the area. However, the use of power hammers and welding equipment disturbed local residents and the experiment was not long lasting. He continued for some years to operate in Shropshire, living, for a while, in a rock-cut cliff house in Wem.

He was at the International Forging Iron Conference, an exuberant golden boy with a parrot on his shoulder: and had pieces featured in the Ceolfrith Gallery Touring Exhibition, organised to coincide with the conference, and showing at Coalbrookdale. Much of his work at this time was chunky almost to the point of clumsiness, but this exhibition showed an interesting experimental grille where chunks of irregularly shaped steel were welded together and held within a frame. An experiment that he would later bring into use in gate designs. On the other hand a lattice gate shown at the Lindau exhibition in the same year, was completely different, giving an impression of tenuous agitation. Perhaps his attitude at this time can best be summed up by his own words, quoted in the Ceolfrith Exhibition leaflet ". . . Iron is a liquid solidified—I am a child playing in the wilderness."

The following year he used the idea of an infill of irregular steel chunks in a security gate to flats near Hyde Park, London. The chunks welded together filled a simple lattice framework to form the leaf of a gate 1m x 2m which opened within a surround of straight

Left: Experimental piece with chunks of steel welded together within a frame.

bars broken by short pieces of steel pointed at each end. The whole forming a singularly impenetrable barrier, giving considerable interest and great feeling of strength.

He used a similar design for an entrance to a block of flats in Shrewsbury. Nine Dogpole, where a gate, again of 1m x 2m made of a framework of 20mm square steel was filled with an infill of irregular fragments forged flat, almost like leaves.

He made other gates in Shrewsbury and Shifnal of vertical steel strips 75/12 mm and 60/10 mm (rather as one might make wooden gates or fences), but with the edges of the steel strips structured by hammer-peening giving a certain amount of patterning between the uprights and the openings. Similar double gates in Shrewsbury 4 x 3m were oxidised to give various colours. [4]

In 1984 Giuseppe Lund made five pairs of massive gates, contained within arches, for the entrance to the Victoria Plaza in Buckingham Palace Road by Victoria Station. Architects Elsom, Pack and Roberts. It was an extraordinarily successful work of uncompromising strength using traditional

smithing techniques. The design was softened only by the arches in which the gates stood, their angularities picking up the grid pattern of the higher modern building showing above the arched and balustraded older façade of the entrance.

Each gate measures 4.m x 6.m. Made of

Left and above: The Gates for the Victoria Plaza in Buckingham Palace Road.

heavy steel they were forged under the power hammer, giving them a texture that was largely part of the design. Basically the elements are L shaped with many of the horizontals drifted through the verticals. The base of each upright bar is irregularly stepped into a heavy foot of near square section.

He had used a very similar design, of lighter and more open construction, for an office staircase screen in Bournemouth. The heavy hoof-like bases developed for these pieces he also used in grilles and gates for Chelmsford Cathedral. It was a base form that had first been introduced by Albert Paley in the 1970s, though he upset from a round bar, and rarely used it without forging and polishing the form into a well defined shape, rather than

leaving it as Giuseppe does as it comes from the power hammer. He uses a heavy square bar and feels it derives from medieval work— certainly one can see a possible antecedent in Medieval heavy based standards of tomb railings with their *weathering* forms which copied exterior stone work, where the stone was shaped into downward slopes to throw off rain water. The Chelmsford gate with side grilles measures 4m across. There are no joinings above the base plate and no horizontal bars in the design. Forged from 150mm square steel the bars are gradually and irregularly drawn out into points and seek to reflect the ascending spirit of Gothic Architecture.[4] It was the first time Giuseppe had used large section stainless steel.

Above: Window grilles for the Ruskin Gallery, Sheffield.

In 1985 he made four Interior Window Grilles of forged steel, each 2.00m x 5.00m for the John Ruskin Gallery in Sheffield. These took a very similar basic form to the Chelmsford Cathedral Gates. Ruskin collected many disparate objects but he felt there was some kind of unity about them just as there is in nature. He wanted to place the collection in a *metal casket*—in a way this is symbolised by the grilles. Guiseppe chose to start the bars at the base with an angular form, almost that of crystals, in a heavy inanimate state. Then as the eye travels up the bar the organic nature takes over until at the top they become graceful waving fronds—consistent with Ruskin's belief in the wholeness of nature. Giuseppe Lund feels that this is one of his most satisfying works.

Just as the square heavy bases of the Victoria Plaza gates were further developed in the Chelmsford and Ruskin Gallery works, so also the L shapes were used again, in 1984, for archways and gates at Carillon Court, Ealing. In this instance the angularities were enriched with flower or leaf-like forms. He used a much more refined version of these *flowers*, with wavy stems, in 1985, for a very attractive hanging chandelier for the church of St. Mary the Virgin in Silchester.

In 1986 Giuseppe made railings for Dorset Rise, in Blackfriars, architects Renton and Howard. In the front courtyard, which has as its centre piece a sculpture of St. George and the Dragon by Michael Sandle (cast by the Morris Singer foundry), the railings follow a low rise along shallow steps on one side, and are used on each side of the entrance steps. There is a much longer run at the back of the building along Bridewell Place, which is a turning off Tudor Street leading from New Bridge Road near the Unilever Building.

These railings in stainless steel stand about 1m high and each upright has an irregularly shaped square or rectangular head impressed with the power hammer into different patterns. Some of the centres are highly polished so that the heads appear to contain *nuggets* of some precious metal. This is highly effective especially now that the unpolished stainless steel has mellowed providing a considerable contrast. In the long straight run at the back of the building groups of three rails at intervals have heavier bases which prevents monotony, and there is a subtle stem-like bifurcation of occasional rails at the front entrance. Altogether these are noble railings, unusual, forceful and beautifully detailed.

Above : Railings along Bridewell Place, and above left, at the entrance of the building Dorset Rise, in Blackfriars.

Left: Chandelier over the font in the church of St. Mary the Virgin, Silchester.

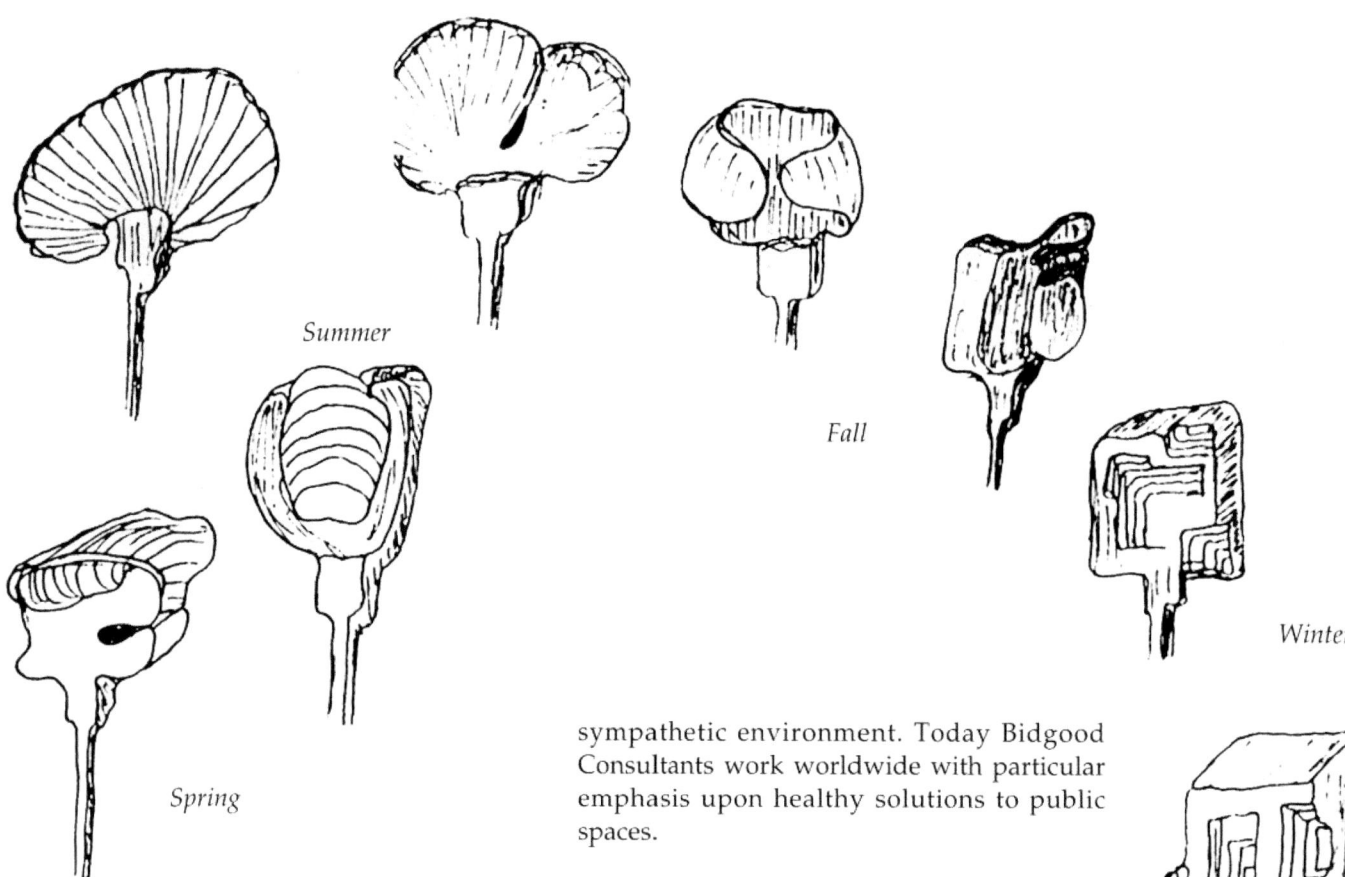

Summer

Fall

Spring

Winter

In 1986 Giuseppe Lund went into partnership with Jane Bidgood to form companies both in Britain and North America. With hindsight he feels this has led to the most fruitful time of his life. Jane has had a tremendous influence in design and the approach to the business. They re-employed Giuseppe's first apprentice David Waight and took on a new trainee Ryan Barber, which is the team today. They now have a workshop in Ontario as well as in Britain.

The many commissions Giuseppe Lund had worked on over the years gave him an excellent opportunity to explore solutions to a wide variety of problems that were architectural, environmental, technical and even philosophical. He came to recognise particular thematic solutions which led to the development of these ideas independently of specific commissions. From 1987 he began deliberately to minimise the number of his commissions in order to give himself time to explore the expressive aspects of his work and to share his view of life with others.

After studying in a College of Health Care, the Anglo European College of Chiropractice, he began to feel that many of the themes in his work could be more closely related to the well being of people, expressing the cyclical changes in life, or simply to create a

sympathetic environment. Today Bidgood Consultants work worldwide with particular emphasis upon healthy solutions to public spaces.

He designed a *Tree of Life* as a work for the Health Institute in Ottawa. It was a competition and in the event a mural was chosen for the site, but as a semi-finalist, he was able to create a design sufficiently complete, not only to be realised in its full form should the need arise, but to have entered into his vocabulary in a way that seems to have influenced his future work.

He also began to work in transparent forged acrylic, which could be lit with halogen, and had an exhibition in Ottawa based on two themes—peoples' spirits and concentrations of energy in space and/or in time. Another exhibition in 1989 in Ottawa City Hall took the theme *Breaking Free*. He created sculptures using simple forms breaking out of metal and acrylic plates mirroring the achievement of independence, the gaining of confidence or development of spirituality, paralleled in life.

Until that time his principal patron for expressive work had been the church but he now felt drawn to create for people in their places of business, institutions for health and physical well being, and educational establishments.

It was these philosophies that led to the creation of *The Four Seasons and the Tree of Life* as gates for Westferry Circus, Canary Wharf, for architects Olympia and York.

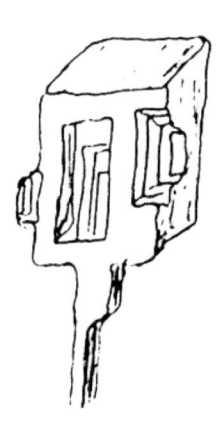

Above: Designs for foliage, indicating the cyclical nature of the seasons, for the Ottawa 'The Tree of Life'. Now in a private house in Washington.

To reach Westferry Gardens (Westferry Circus), unless arriving by river, one must take the Docklands Light Railway to Westferry then walk towards the river, into the breeze, keeping to the upper road level. Perhaps Canary Wharf will never again be as exciting as it is today. A strange Ozymandias land [5]—pink granite curbstones that one feels no foot has trodden;and encircled with a wide road, between the river and the glass skyscrapers, a beautifully laid out and completely deserted garden. It is girdled with Giuseppe Lund railings, the heads forged into scores of different leaf shapes, and two gates one on each side that each pivot on a single central support. The background pattern of the gates is similar to those of the Victoria Plaza—an angular grid and L shapes, but they are almost completely covered by a robust tree of life. Innumerable fine rods rise upwards forming the trunk and the tree blooms and blossoms into luxuriant flowers and leaves. The main form is oval and almost covers the gate. The tops of the railings and highlights on the flowers have been heat coloured into a soft gilded bronze.

The Queen Elizabeth Gates opened in July 1993 at Hyde Park Corner, South Carriage Drive, made in honour of the Queen Mother are undoubtedly Giuseppe Lund's most important commission to date. However few public works can have attracted so much controversy and received such a staggeringly bad press.

They are made up of several elements—a central panel with double carriage gates on each side flanked by single pedestrian gates, upheld by heavy angular stone piers topped by round lamps. There is an unfortunate disparity between these various elements, presumably because different artists have been responsible for the design.

The central panel between the two piers, designed by sculptor David Wynne, depicts a lion and a unicorn underneath a tree covered with roses. They give the impression of coarse flat metal cut-outs like a child's drawing, finished in bright garish colours. The gates are conceived in a completely different vein. Giuseppe Lund and Jane Bidgood have tried to convey a feeling of fairy-like femininity using polished stainless steel coloured only by the subtle use of heat and natural oxides— so immediately from the point of view of colour alone there is a clash between the two main elements. They destroy rather than enhance each other. Neither is there any cohesion of time; the gates with their unrestrained design and free techniques belong to the late 20th century, but the stone piers and lamps could have been designed a hundred years ago and the centrepiece may have looked modern in the 1930s.

"I met a traveller from an antique land
Who said two vast and trunkless legs of stone
stand in the desert . . .
And on the pedestal these words appear:
'My name is Ozymandias, king of kings: Look on my works ye mighty and despair!'
Nothing beside remains. Round the decay
Of that colossal wreck, boundless and bare,
The lone and level sands stretch far away"

Shelley.

Left below: The Gates at Westferry Park, Canary Wharf.

Below: Detail showing the Tree of Life.

I understand that there was no collaboration between the artists except in the very early stages when the designs had advanced no further than drawings. Giuseppe, who was trying for a three dimensional effect in the gates was, in fact, surprised to find the finished centre panel so flat in concept.

It is unfortunate that the gates are open all day. It is almost impossible to see one leaf of the gate without other leaves behind confusing an already complicated design. The long view is the most unsatisfying; from a distance one sees nothing but a tangle of monochrome steel overwhelmed by a bright red lion. Come in close and, especially if the sun shines, the metal sparkles and the flowers and leaves can be exceedingly pretty.

The workmanship has been much criticised, by blacksmiths particularly, for the welds which are often lumpy, mis-matched for colour and not ground down smoothly. Lund has never been against accepting welds and allowing them to show, on the basis of artistry overcoming convention. It was a very

acceptable feature in the heavy sections and patterning of the Victoria Plaza gates. It seems, however, more intrusive on these graceful Hyde Park gates which are far less aggressively *modern* in concept. The fine rods of stainless steel, the relatively small scale of the metal and the resulting delicacy of the work only serves to show up the rough welds and the strangely loose *wrappings* of the *collars*, whose dark colour also makes them obtrusive. But then Giuseppe nailed his colours to the mast a long time ago, when in 1980 he is reported as saying that his involvement with iron was all to do with ". . . that bubbling enthusiasm that runs me along. I do not have any great purpose to save the world from badly made gates!" [3]

Above: and far left: The Hyde Park Gates.

There must have been many problems in the production of the gate not least having the width between the piers changed by 250mm at the insistence of the Fire Service. Fortunately thanks to designing on computer it took only ten minutes to recalculate all the measurements! First sketched with Corel Draw the design was then imported to Drafix CAD where a dimensional database could be created. Since each of the large gates are cantilevered over 4.5m accurate structural analysis was necessary. The potential stresses were calculated, and the base and hinge bar developed, using Design View.

There was a need to lighten the frame because of the considerable span; therefore the main curves are two bars linked together so that the empty space between provides strength.

Left and far left: Details of the Hyde Park Gates.

Although the textures and details of the main curves were forged hot, the final bending was done cold with hydraulic presses which serves to stiffen the steel.

Giuseppe Lund and Jane Bidgood wanted to create gates that would celebrate the life of the Queen Mother in a form that was light and feminine. They wanted to welcome people into the park in a joyous and lighthearted way. For this reason they avoided straight lines and rectangularity. They used stainless steel to be light in colour and strong enough to be light in weight. They used sweeping lines for the frame itself, around which and through which floral forms could grow as they might in an English garden. Giuseppe washed from his mind the rigid framework of classical gates, and thought of the more curving lines of early Italian ironwork and of rustic Sicilian gates tied and woven out of branches from the surrounding countryside. He sees the loosely wrapped *collars* as the way gipsies wrap a piece of grass round little bunches of flowers to hold them together.

For twelve months the team, Giuseppe Lund, Jane Bidgood, David Waight, and Ryan Barber worked in isolation, leaves, flowers, branches and frame bars were forged, curved, and electro-polished before being assembled. Giuseppe has written ". . . Every space was filled with movement and growth. I wouldn't be surprised if the gods themselves slipped a few extra flowers in when we weren't looking!"[6]

After the gates were erected the team spent a month on site heat-colouring parts of the metal. They had never had so much feedback from the general public and it strengthened Giuseppe's determination ". . . to continue creating public spaces that celebrate the happy joyful child in us all."

At the new Broadway Centre, Hammersmith, the impressive 18th c. facade of Bradmore House has been retained and restored to form a focal point of a small square laid out with tables and chairs. Architects Elsom, Pack and Roberts. The building has had a chequered history, originally a manor house, it was demolished early this century and rebuilt to form the front of Hammersmith Bus Station. I remember wringing my hands on seeing it, many years ago, very dilapidated and, incredible as it may seem, with London Transport Buses driving in and out of the façade![7] It is a delight today to see it rehabilitated to its old glory and having on each side Giuseppe Lund gates of gracefully swaying reeds.

It is no easy task to design modern gates for such a building. Here the weight seems

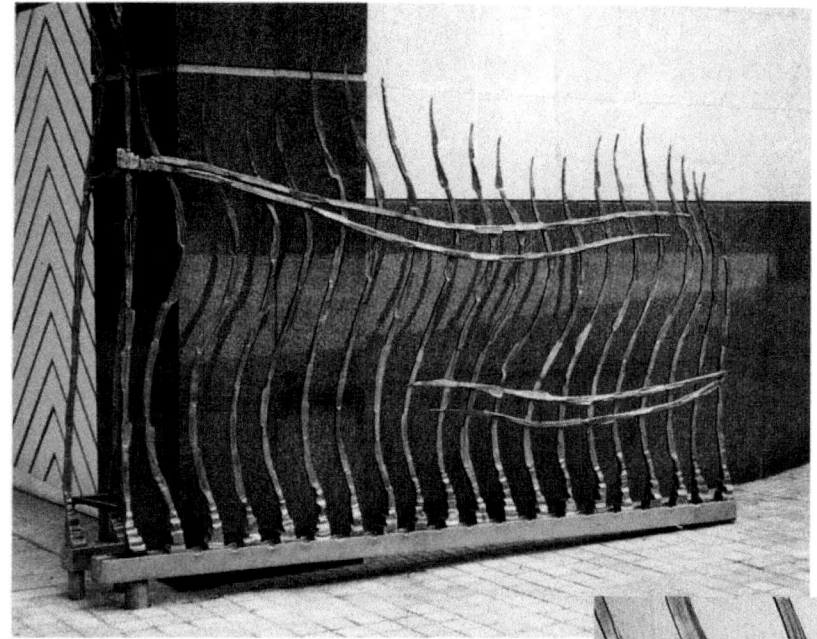

Sources and Notes

1. Gretl Hoffman. *Kunst aus dem Feuer* Julius Hoffman, Stuttgart, 1987.
2. Catalogue of *Towards a New Iron Age* exhibition at the V&A Museum.
3. Lesley Adamson*Forging links between men of iron. The Guardian* July 19th 1980.
4. Illustrated in *Schmiedearbeiten von heute* Julius Hoffman, Stuttgart 1986.
5. Reference to the poem *Ozymandias of Egypt* by Shelley.
6. *Crafts* Magazine Nov/Dec 1993.
7. For a photograph of the building as it was then, see *London: the Art of Georgian Building* by Cruickshank and Wyld. The Architectural Press, London 1975.

absolutely right, building and ironwork in harmony. Heat coloured steel giving an ancient gleam to ironwork at home with the past and with the 20th c. life that flows so actively about it. There is a more uncompromisingly modern wall sculpture by Lund on a building behind the left hand gate.

1994 saw him still pursuing the floral theme with a balcony railing above shop fronts, mainly Marks and Spencers, at number 81 to 95 King's Road, Chelsea. Again using stainless steel coloured by heat; simple uprights are wrought at the top into leaves and a bunch of flowers and eucalyptus foliage emphasise the building number 81.

The firm's most recent exhibition has been in Geneva and consisted of a collection of trees and birds. The sculptures are freely forged in the round, one of the rose trees some 1m high.

It was working, early in his career, with Manfred Bergmeister in Germany, Antoni Benetton in Italy and Antony Robinson in England, that gave Giuseppe Lund the confidence to explore and develop his own ideas.

He has always worked towards a greater understanding of the relationship between metal and architecture. A strong dislike of the use of standardised rolled bar in 18th and 19th c ironwork led him to appreciate the far more lively forging in primitive and medieval pieces—a trait that has influenced his work throughout. He believes that the texture of the metal serves to soften the visual line.

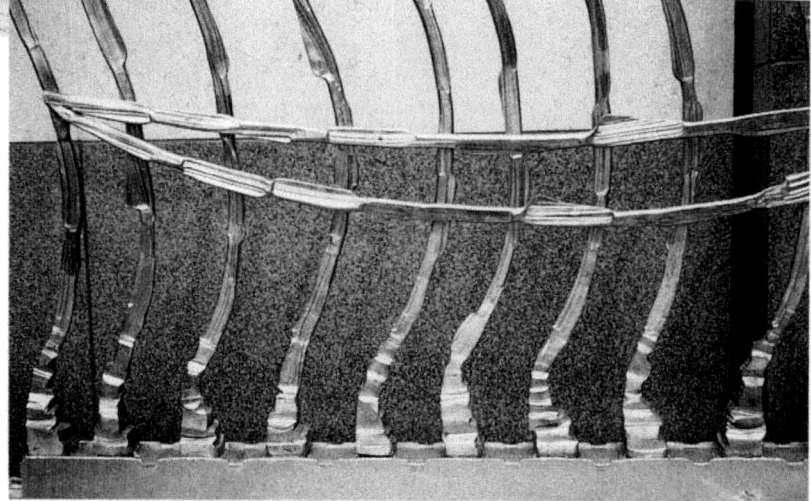

Above: The Bradmore House Gates.

Another influence has been Gaudi, not so much in the design of his ironwork as in his thinking. The architect was looking for organic precedents to help him form his structures; for organic clues to design —the twists in bones—the shell-like interior forms to the towers of the Sagrada Familia; the cliff-like shapes of the Casa Mila; the leaning pillars to the Guell Chapel. Giuseppe Lund is interested by the organic and the inorganic in parallel. There are times, as in the Ruskin Gallery grilles, where his ironwork depicts both aspects; in other instances as at Westferry the organic forms of his gates and railings are placed within the inorganic shapes of architecture.

He finds that a growing interest in crafted details among architects is allowing him to develop a closer relationship to their work. He feels that forging can be rationalised into a cost effective production, making good design available to a wide range of sites.

The other influence has already been mentioned—his meeting and business partnership with Jane Bidgood in 1986. They have since married and have two daughters. The forge is situated at a butterfly farm and they live close to the ocean—in a house at the sea on the edge of a forest.

MICHAEL
MALLESON

Was born in London in 1945.

When he was twenty-three, having obtained his teacher's certificate, he married and began a career teaching in primary, secondary and middle schools, first in Dorset and later he moved to Abingdon. When he was young his father had taken him on holidays in Wales and he had spent a lot of time with a blacksmith there who worked on agricultural machinery, and this remembered interest began to emerge. After seven years he gave up teaching and in 1977 began to forge. By the foundation weekend of BABA he was a typically isolated metal worker whose only contact with other smiths was through the Master Farriers Association and CoSIRA. He says that he and BABA have grown and developed together.

He knew already that there was more to ironwork than scrolls and water leaves, because he had been fortunate enough to have attended a course at West Dean under Sean Black from Pyecombe in Sussex. Sean was one of the earliest British smiths to have made modern forged sculptural works and to have been described in print at that time as an *artist in metal*.

Michael has described his first two forges; the first was at East Hendred and the second at Bishop's Caundle, near Sherborne.

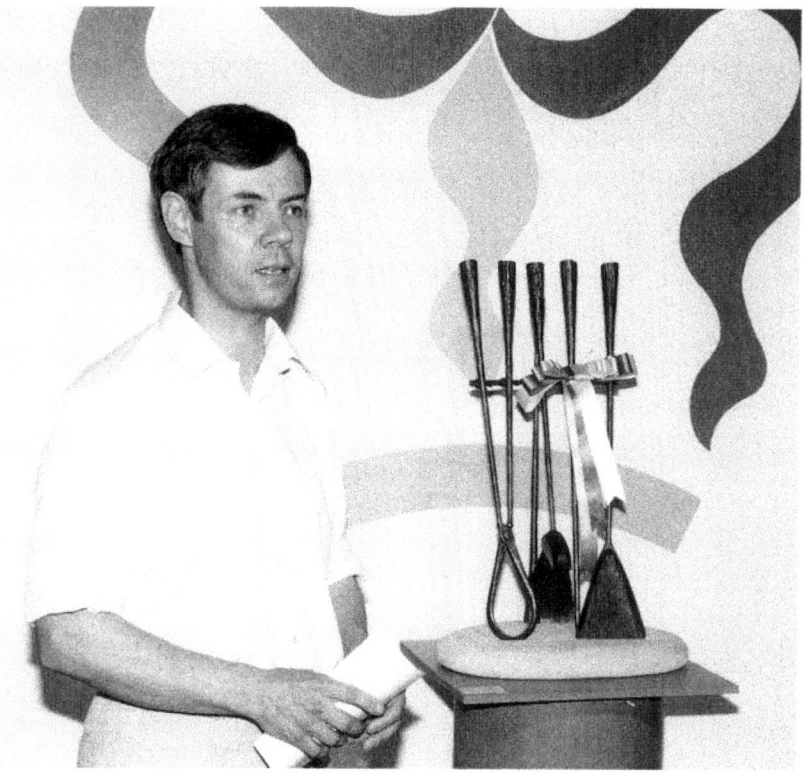

"The first was in south Oxfordshire, with a dangerously leaning flue, a set of bellows and a piece of gas pipe stuck into the burnt-out tue iron to get air blowing in the right direction—it needed replacing after half a dozen fire-welds! But it was a start, and I paid no rent. Then to Dorset, and another village smithy, this one with an old ducks-nest grate which only survived up to the first visit from a CoSIRA instructor. There, I maintained my quest for quality, now broadened into the beginnings of doing some design work. Two CoSIRA courses at Wimbledon with Tony West gave me a real insight into the forms and construction of traditional work, and what constitutes fine wrought ironwork . . ."[1] These courses also wakened his desire for a

Michael with the prize winning Royal Anniversary Fireirons at the Fire and Iron Gallery.
Photograph Fire and Iron Gallery.

Below left: Flame Fire Grate.
Photograph by Michael Malleson.

Below right: Table with plate glass top.

power hammer; a propensity for acquiring equipment that continues to this day.

He attended the International Forging Iron Conference in 1980, and the following year was elected a full member of the Dorset Craft Guild.

By 1982 he felt he had outgrown the forge at Bishop's Caundle. For one thing he was tired of the noise of his neighbour's parrots and the ever increasing volume of heavy traffic passing his front door. He moved with his wife Anne, and their two children, to their present forge at Trent where the fine old stone built house and barn had plenty of room to expand the workshop, and provided them all with the space and quieter environment they needed. Anne does the books for the forge and is a constant help and support.

In May of 1982 he received a rather amazing commission. He was asked to replace a dead cherry tree with a work in iron. His client came to his workshop and showed him a cutting from a newspaper of Alan Dawson's

Above and right: The Iron Tree Sculpture that replaced a Cherry Tree, where it was impossible to grow another natural tree.

Photograph by Michael Malleson.

Lily Lamp (see page 39). It had given him the idea of commissioning a forged iron tree and would Michael be interested in designing and making such a tree.

He accepted the invitation at once, since his leaning had been increasingly towards sculptural work, and he felt it was both a challenge and his first opportunity to produce a piece of sculpture. The site was a wholly enclosed back garden, and honey fungus made growing a new tree impossible. The derelict tree was still standing, some branches snapped off short and the bark fractured and peeling from the trunk. Mike made a three dimensional *drawing* in copper wire and sheet, and after discussion with the client, followed this with a forged maquette for the replacement. The trunk and branches of the finished piece were made of 4in. and 3in. diameter tube which were welded together. The large radius curves in the branches were bent hot, and the short radius curves were formed by cutting out a series of wedges, bending, welding and grinding clean. A piece of ¼ in. plate was used for the bark, wrapping round the lower part of the trunk. As the steel had a high carbon content, it began to crack as the edges were forged out thinly; this problem, however, proved to be controllable and produced the desired effect. Oxy-acetylene cutting produced some characteristic lace-like *wear* in the bark.

No doubt other blacksmiths would like to find equally eccentric clients — one wonders if this is the first metal tree to be produced for a garden in this country since the willow tree at Chatsworth from whose branches used to spurt jets of water. [2 & 3]

This comission led to another of considerable interest, by a client who had seen and admired the tree. In the Spring of 1984 Michael was approached to make a garden archway to span a gap in a low wall dividing a garden from a parking area at the back of an 18th century house. What he finally designed was sculptural and conical rising into the 'A'-form that resembled a crown roast of lamb.

Each bar was forged its whole length to give wedge-shaped cross section; they were forged in two halves for easier handling and then welded together to set the curves. There were two U shaped base plates that sat on the wall, one each side of the gap: from each of these fifteen curving bars rose upwards to an oval ring near the top then turned outwards to give the *crown* shape. A temporary suspension bar was attached to the oval and it was suspended from a beam in the workshop at the correct height from the ground. He then temporarily fixed the U shaped bases on site so that the mounting for the work was correctly established. Back in the workshop the U plates were accurately located below

the top ring, and fixed into the floor. Then came the most difficult part of the job. All but two of the bars had to be shaped in two planes and some had a twist. All thirty bars curved in a slightly different way. Some curved more on the flat others more on edge. It was a long and tedious procedure to relate each bar properly to its neighbours. Michael has written: "Frequently I thought I had a bar true but for one small correction: this completed would create a need for correction in two more places, and sometimes this went on until I couldn't see for looking, since I had to consider the relationships of all the shapes and spaces from several different viewpoints." Finally the arch was split in two and sent off for shot-blast and zinc-spray treatment, before being reassembled, spray-painted, and fixed into position with a tractor foreloader. In spite of the difficulties he found the atmosphere of the job was one of interest and excitement on both sides, and altogether a very pleasurable commission.[4]

Below: Detail of the Crown Garden Arch.

Left: Garden archway for private Garden in Sherborne, Dorset. 1984. 2.50m high x 2.5m wide x 800mm deep.

Michael Malleson

I have sometimes wondered why, blacksmiths design such difficult jobs for themselves; but when I mentioned this to Michael he said, "If I don't set myself challenges I'll never move forward. Sean Black told me 'never turn down a job because you don't know how to do it—accept the job and then find out!'"

In 1985 through the generosity of a Churchill Travelling Fellowship Mike Malleson was able to travel to Germany to work for six weeks with Paul Zimmerman. He admires Paul's work above all others for its depth and strength and the mastery of the medium it displays. On his return he realised that he faced the daunting task of finding how he could give his own work a greater depth and quality. It is on-going and he is still drawing on the experience:

"Qualities which are startling and exciting when observed in the work of others, are elusive beyond measure when seeking comparable qualities for one's own work." [1]

He keeps his work simple and believes that if it is to have a distinctive style it will probably emerge in its own time. He has always admired good traditional blacksmithing and believes, quite passionately, that modern smithing must have equally good craftsmanship and never hide behind impoverished aesthetics and lack of skill under the guise of *Art*.

In 1986 he made a replica Iron Age cauldron chain for the Museum of the Iron Age in Andover, Hampshire. He was given drawings and photographs of two Iron Age chains from which to work; one of them was the same great chain from the Museum of Archaeology in Cambridge that had so impressed me years before. The overall length was 12ft and used 30lbs of old wrought iron railing to make. He took the design elements from both chains and used the pattern of the reef knot and suspension hooks from the Cambridge example but in reverse, putting the scrolls on the top of the hoops instead of below. (See page ...). The links were made as separate pieces and simply passed through each other and folded over to assemble. Working in the wrought iron was rather frustrating as it was not of very good quality—but doubtless Iron Age smiths suffered from the same problem.

Commissions he made in stainless steel were processional candle lanterns for Sherborne Abbey. Candles were also part of a very unusual commission for a Shooting Lodge, where he made an enormous hanging chandelier, and two floor standing candelabra about 5ft tall.

The hanging chandelier had a central cone of six mild steel bars with a ring top and bottom on which were mounted six sets of Red Deer antlers and three Sika Deer antlers, with a coronet of small Roe Deer horns at the top. The standing candelabras were of iron, of a fairly traditional type, but with graceful upturning bars taking their curve from the horns. The candle holders for both the chandelier and the candelabras were of forged bronze.

Horns of a different type feature in his jolly weather vane of a Dorset Horn Ram made of 3mm sheet with 6mm bar bent up into horns and welded in.

Photograph by Michael Malleson.

Above: Steel, bronze and antler chandelier for candles. The Shooting Lodge, Dorset. 2.5m circle holds 42 candles.

Obviously he does more down to earth jobs like railings and gates. One recent commission was for Kingdons Yard in Winchester. He feels that of all the commissions he has completed since working with Paul Zimmerman, this one most clearly shows Paul's influence.

He had attended the First World Congress of Artist Blacksmiths in Aachen in 1986 and exhibited work at the International Exhibition of Ironwork in Friedrichschafen the following year. He was an official demonstrator at "Hefaiston '90" at Helfstyn, Czechoslovakia in 1990. The next year he travelled, with a bursary award from the Jinny Quinnell Memorial Trust, to see ironwork and meet blacksmiths in the former Soviet Union.

1992 was the 40th anniversary of Her Majesty the Queen's accession to the throne and a competition was organised, in conjunction with The Royal Anniversary Trust, to find a set of fire irons to present to her Majesty. There were some wonderful entries and the judging was extremely difficult. Finally the choice was made, and it was Mike Malleson's simple set with trumpet-like handles. It has no specific symbolism but could perhaps be interpreted as a five trumpet fanfare to celebrate the anniversary. It was chosen for its excellent functional qualities. The fire irons were beautifully balanced and a joy to handle and use; they stood on a slab of Ham stone from Duchy of Cornwall land. Above all it was felt that it was the only set that could not have been designed in the last century.[6] Michael and his family were able to go to St. James's Palace and meet Her Majesty the Queen and the Duke of Edinburgh for the presentation.

Michael Malleson is begining to feel that he might like to join the skills of his earlier career with those of the modern artist-blacksmith and teach ironsmithing to others, perhaps in a school or College.

Sources and Notes.

1. Profile. Michael Malleson. *British Blacksmith* No 54.

2. Mike Malleson "A Garden Sculpture". *British Blacksmith* No 33.

3. Amina Chatwin "Design and the Blacksmith". *The Anvil's Ring* Vol 12 No 4.

4. Mike Malleson "A Garden Archway". *British Blacksmith* No 39.

5. Mike Malleson "A Replica Iron Age Cauldron Chain". *British Blacksmith* No 48.

6. Lucy Quinnell "The Royal Anniversary Fire-Irons Competition". *British Blacksmith* No 66.

Michael Malleson

Michael Malleson

Above: Detail of railings and gates in Kingdons Yard, Winchester.

Far left: Forged sculpture 'Seedling' detail.

"Qualities which are startling and exciting when observed in the work of others, are elusive beyond measure when seeking comparable qualities for one's own work."

154

CHARLES NORMANDALE

Left: Group of candle holders.

Was born in Yeovil, Somerset, in 1951.

After he left school be became a power boat salesman at Chertsey. After two Earl's Court boat shows he decided the job was not for him, although boats and cars have remained an abiding interest. He thought of going to Europe but being short of cash was looking round for a job to make money for the trip. It was at this time that he heard Beethoven, at a high rate of decibels, issuing from a workshop in Elstead, Surrey. Inside he found Roland Ross a blacksmith who had worked with Werner Holzbacher a renowned German iron smith. From this chance meeting it came about that Charles became apprenticed to Ross; he started by saying he would work there six weeks and stayed six years.

He then became head blacksmith to a large commercial firm, The Elstead Forge, at Alton, Hampshire; where there were fourteen welders and two cutters. He was responsible for design, line development, tooling-up, and production from 1976 to 1983; mainly working on commercial lighting and fine furniture.

Charles attended the "foundation of BABA" week-end in 1978 taking with him an impressive pair of church door hinges he had made, loosely based on a 13th c. design.

He was also at the International Forging Iron Conference in 1980. Unlike most British smiths he did not find himself *bowled over* by the techniques that were demonstrated. From an early stage in his apprenticeship he had been familiar with the work of German smiths and the modern designs they were creating. He was, however, impressed with much of the ironwork from abroad from the standpoint of Art. He met David Petersen there, who was equally appreciative, and they struck up a lasting friendship. Later David's son Toby assisted Charles for over a year.

While Charles had been working at Elstead Forge he had been self-employed and already by December 1982 had begun to set up his own forge at Warnford, near Winchester.

In September 1983 he exhibited a very innovative gate at the BABA Conference Exhibition (see page 41). It has no frame and only one hinge. Thick and thin verticals are held by one broad horizontal in which large headed rivets form part of the pattern, and call attention to the gently tapering shape as the horizontal band narrows from the hinge at one end towards the latch at the other. A shape repeated at the base where the uprights, 45mm square and 25/15mm flat, splay out a little at the bottom, the thick and thin bars widening on different planes. The design is very much more subtle than immediately meets the eye. Above, the top verticals curve inwards towards a small central diamond shape.

A later frameless gate *River Gate* has verticals held by two horizontals. At the base the vertical bars are straight but gradually widen out and undulate with extraordinary sensitivity, as they reach towards a pointed top.

Both these gates are so deceptively simple that they belie the great care and thought which must go into them.

Other gates are more solid *Plate Gate*, size 1.12 x 2.20m, made of 12mm steel plate, with forged fittings, is in two parts each relying on cut out voids for their patterning. The two parts are joined at the centre with three broad short tie bars riveted across the opening. A single thin flat rod forms a *dog bar* (for a Jack Russell!) in the centre. Another gate to use broad uprights 80/8mm flat, has them fixed with rivets between two narrow ovals; a difficult procedure owing to a tendencey to distort. The verticals have a distinct texture outside the oval, but within they are left plain. This texture is not one of ridges, such as smiths often produce under the fuller of the power hammer. The majority of his work is forged between two flat

Above: Latch detail on Ovals gate. Below: Pool Gate. Far right: Base fastening of a gate. Right: Gate of 1983. Far right above: River Gate.

Photographs Charles Normandale

plates and it is these that have been allowed to give the irregular mottling; he rarely changes his power hammer tools. Yet another example of the subtlety of these deceptively simple gates.

Another technique he uses is that of *opening up* broad flat verticals to form a pattern and a visual opening. *Pool Gate* is a frameless gate held by two horizontals where all but the two outer bars are twisted, half of them one way and half the other, to produce a circular opening.

The same idea was used to make a gate for a site exposed to the north wind; the suggestion of an infill of glass was rejected as presenting various problems. A better solution seemed to be to use iron in a way that would deflect the wind. From the front the gate is fairly open in appearance but the broad verticals of which it is composed have all been given a twist at 45% so that from an angle it appears to be almost solid. The device gives privacy to a window and protection from the wind. There is a minor patterning at intervals by notching on the side of the verticals and a more open section calls attention to the position of the central latch.

Charles Normandale is well known for designing gates of classical simplicity. They are well proportioned and well balanced; unadorned and unlaboured. In short, they are modern gates of extreme distinction. A sundial too, and a well cover have been reduced to essentials and the simplest of forms. His art is one of elimination that leaves not the smallest unecessary detail. One of his maxims is *less is more*. In a way it sets its own standard; there can be no covering up of imperfections here—when the work is so simple it must be perfect.

In 1984 Charles won an open Art Competition for a work to embellish the North Wall of the Great Hall of the Institute of Chartered Accountants in Moorgate Place, in the City of London. The judging panel included Sir Hugh Casson, Lord Hutchinson and William Whitfield who were also considering submissions by textile designers, painters, sculptors, and other artist blacksmiths.

It was a very large hall 60ft x 18ft and Charles has written:
"I knew that in view of uncompromising dimensions and details of the room, that to design something successful it would have to be very powerful". [1] The whole of the North Wall was filled strongly and rather monotonously with vertical fenestration, and shutters that closed at night when functions were being held. Another element that influenced the choice of design was that there were already some admirable but complex paintings and tapestries in the Hall, by artists such as Piper and Paolozzi, and he was

anxious to do nothing that would conflict with these works.

Some of his early thoughts when formulating the design were the possibilities of introducing curves to counteract the strong verticals of the shutters; or perhaps a flamboyant chandelier to distract from them, or even a chain mail curtain to mask the whole wall. In the end he felt that the metalwork ought to appear as an integral part of the building itself, as if it had been there from the start, and he decided on what has since been described as a massive perforated frieze.

It runs horizontally across the whole wall; it does not come into competition with the other pieces of art in the room, having no colour and no obvious detail, and the design is simple and strong enough to stand up to the verticals behind it. Basically it is panels of

Far left: Well Cover.

Below : Ovals Gate. Subtly textured outside the oval, beneath flat plates, and plain within.

Photographs by Charles Normandale.

12mm plate with voids cut into them, alternately three vertical rectangles and four horizontal rectangles. Its attraction lies in the forging and texture, the curved raised edges around the openings and the slightly dished sides of the panels. The total weight of the piece is 1¾ tons and the length 60ft. For the actual competition he had made a ¼ size model.[1 & 2]

Another strong part of the design is that of the holders that join the panels together and fix them to the

Below: The Great Hall of the Institute of Chartered Accounts. General picture showing the long table and the vertical lines of the wall.

Far left: Detail of one of the holders that join the panel to the wall. The simple shapes are lifted into excellence by the raised sculptural edges of the plate.

Photographs by Charles Normandale and Chris Fairclough.

wall. It is typical of all his work that there is no applied design, all the shapes, although decorative in themselves, are governed by the techniques and necessary solutions to installation. The holders are forged from 100mm square (4inch solid); first a neck was fullered near one end and this was drawn out to form the stem and then bent back at an angle.

Charles was assisted in the making of this piece by Terry Clark—"The power hammer was in constant use and our sledging techniques never had a better opportunity to improve".

The final culmination was collaboration with David Kindersley, Glass Designer and Calligraphist, who was commissioned to provide a backdrop to the whole, in clear and coloured glass, in which he retained the vertical lines of the shuttering.

The piece was installed in September 1985—the problems had been overcome and they felt a great sense of achievement and ultimate satisfaction.

Competitions are contentious, some smiths find them too nerve-racking and to enter unsuccessfully demoralising; but Charles has written: "I hope this will encourage other Artist Smiths to enter competitions and if necessary to stick their necks out and not to compromise—have the courage of your convictions and you will get a great charge."

Charles Normandale was a demonstrator at the "First International Festival of Iron" in Cardiff in 1989. His two hour demonstration piece was very much a tour de force—he made a massive, man-high, pair of scales with striker assistance from Julian Coode and Saraj Guha. The following year he demonstrated in America for the ABANA Conference.

It was also in 1989 that he made some impressive gates to Cranleigh School in Surrey, 5.200m wide, 3.100m tall. These were heavy gates, the main verticals were made of 40 x 25, the back style 50mm square, and the horizontal bar near the top 100 x 25. The gates themselves were mild steel but the decorative elements, which were brought forward from the gate, were in stainless. Curving elements, forming a cresting at the top represented cranes; while lower on the gates large *Winchester Crosses*, the emblem of the school, were brought forward and showed up to particularly good effect when the gates were open.

Other commissions were a massive gate for a Stud Farm in America for Mary Tyler Moore, well known for her connection with MGM Television. There was work of a more traditional nature for the Broadlands Estate, large candlesticks for the Belfry Golf Club, as well as a mild steel and bronze handrail for Parham House.

Now in 1993 there are changes afoot at Wheelydown Forge. A house within a few yards of the forge is to be extended, and Charles, with his two children, will be moving in.

I recently visited the forge to find it is really a little group of flint walled barns with brick quoins and weatherboarding ends to the walls of the forge. Slate and tiled roofs, except for the forge itself where the roof is sheathed with plates of iron. Beyond the forge an unmade track leads upwards through a field of Maize. In another direction I looked out, past swallows balancing on telegraph wires, towards the distant curving form of Old Winchester Hill Fort. Charles had been held up at a meeting and eventually rode into the yard in black leathers, on a Harley Davidson motorcycle.

Far left: Detail of the gates for Cranleigh School.

Photograph by Charles Normandale

He told me about recent commissions, as diverse as 13th century style ironwork all over a wooden chest for the Tower of London, and other ironwork for Hampton Court Palace (he still does traditional work if required); and, in complete contrast, the simplest possible abstract standing sign for Broome Manor Golf Complex near Swindon, where a cut out circular shape denotes a golf ball, and an added oval, the green, is bisected by a long thin cut between steel plates for the hole marker.

Below: Screens in the Crypt of Rochester Cathedral.

Left: Detail of these screens.

Photographs by Charles Normandale.

Some time before, he had collaborated in making a computer designed video, from scores of his ironwork drawings; in which computer generated graphics produced finished illustrations looking exactly as if the ironwork had been completed and placed in position in its environment. Though he did not think it was an experiment he would repeat.

In 1991 he designed and made five screens in mild steel and bronze, glazed with smoked and toughened glass, for the Crypt of Rochester Cathedral. The Crypt was built in 644, so the installation had to be sensitively done. The whole project was made at the forge taken in pieces to the site and installed in the various arches. These of course are all different sizes, shapes and levels.

The main verticals are 40mm sq jumped up at the bottom whilst tapering on the diagonal to the crook at the top. Two bronze forgings are riveted on the point. The door was similar but using 50mm sq. The verticals are held to the horizontals by forged clips. These horizontals support the glass and are infilled with limed oak.

The whole concept gives a private area for prayer in one of the best examples in this country of a vaulted ceiling.

Less prestigious, but more unusual, was a commission to fill holes in a ruin with security screens. In Stanmore, North London, the parish church of St. John the Evangelist has two churches in one church yard. The old one was consecrated in 1632, and is said to be the first English church to be built in brick. It is now a picturesque ruin, open to the sky, or as Pevsner has it "one of the best ruins in the county". The brief was for security screens in

the broken down walls. The grilles are some 4m high and 4m wide. Bars 60mm square taper and curve outwards as they reach the top.

One of his recent works that gives him greatest satisfaction is a pair of Lightning Conductors for London EC1 in Aluminium Bronze. Massive curving forms, smoothly polished, are set on heavily rusticated stone near the base of the building to support the conductor rod.

What marks out the work of Charles Normandale, and has led to his own distinctive and individual style, is his commitment to using traditional techniques to form contemporary design. The elements of the design are almost wholly produced by the construction. This leads to bare strong uncompromising design.

Sources and Notes

1. Charles Normandale "Institute of Chartered Accountants Commission 1984-5". *British Blacksmith* 41.

2. Amina Chatwin "Design and the Blacksmith". *The Anvil's Ring* Vol 12 No 4.

Above: Lightning Conductor. Left: Small Security Spikes at Stanmore.
Photographs by Charles Normandale.

PETER PARKINSON

Left: Peter Parkinson at a Forge-in.

Was born in 1942 in Oswestry, and from the age of eighteen studied at the Royal College of Art for four years on an Industrial Design Course. [1]

From 1964-66 he was an Industrial Designer with London Transport in the architects department. Mostly he was designing in metal work including early signs, barriers, and systems for the Victoria Line. An awkward job in 1965 was providing a reasonable looking facade to a line of mixed dispensing early micro-wave machines, to provide food for drivers at a London bus depot.

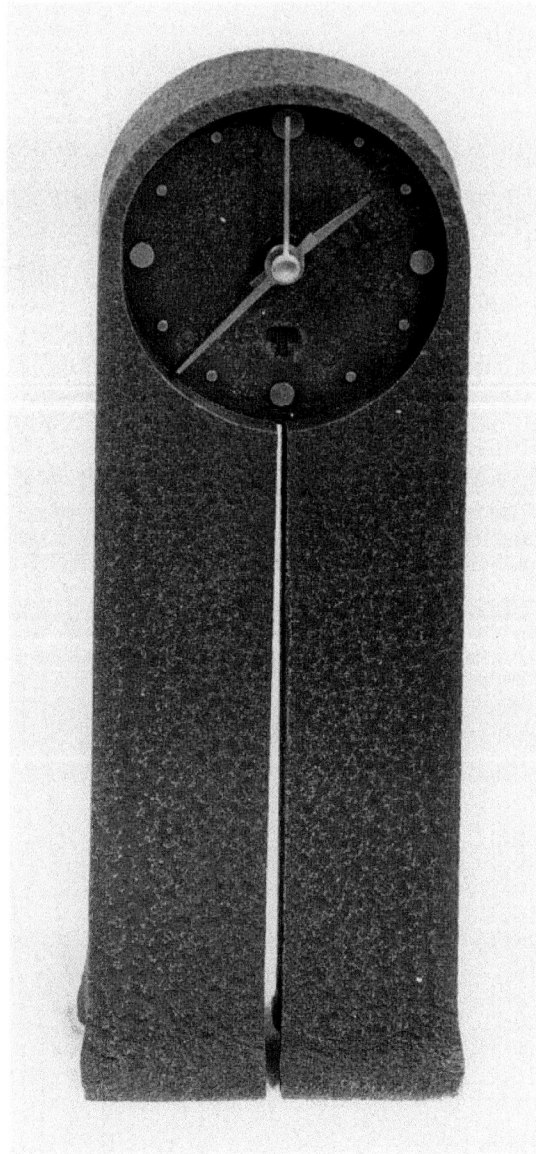

In 1966 he moved to Allied Ironfounders at Sunbury on Thames where he was designing room heaters, cookers, baths and kitchen equipment.

He left in 1968 to become a Part Time Lecturer at Guildford School of Art, and Full Time the following year. In 1970 the school became the West Surrey College of Art and Design, with fine new buildings at Farnham. He was appointed a Senior Lecturer initially teaching Industrial Design, then later developed a BA (Hons.) Metals Degree Course.

From 1976 onwards he took various design commissions including major consultancy work with Mitchell Beazley (Publishers) Ltd.

Following an initial inspirational contact with Blacksmithing through inviting Guiseppe Lund to teach a workshop at West Surrey College, Peter attended the first Crafts Council Forging Iron Conference at Hereford in 1979. He also acquired blacksmithing work experience at Richard Quinnell's Rowhurst Forge. The following year he was at the International Conference. It was also in 1980 that he set up his own forging workshop and joined BABA. At first he showed his ironwork at small local craft and minor art exhibitions, but in the years since then has shown work in major ironwork exhibitions, both in this country, and in Europe and America.

It was after showing at a small Art and Craft show at Thursley, in September 1981, that he received a commission for a number of candleholders for a large 15th-16th century Sussex farmhouse. The owner was restoring and extending the house and had commissioned a local firm of architects and interior designers, to undertake the work. Peter was approached by the architects and, after discussions, was subsequently

Far left: Clock in forged mild steel, 12 inches high.

Photograph by Glynn Clarkson.

commissioned to design and make a number of other pieces for the building, including a large chandelier for the Great Hall.

As it would be possible to view the chandelier both from the ground and a gallery it seemed important that each

Above: Chandelier for Great Hall of Sussex farmhouse.
Photograph John Knight.

viewpoint should be interesting, and if possible dramatic. Peter was given a very graphic elevation drawing, and he initially worked on his design by placing tracing paper over the drawing in order to judge the basic form and dimensions that would best relate to the space.[2] He presented three alternative designs and was pleased that it was the most ambitious that was chosen. It was a large spreading circular canopy, from which a faceted column rose upwards into the high timbered roof. The actual making began in September 1982.

It had been Peter's original intention to make the canopy from segments of profile cut 6mm plate with the edges upset to form a ridge. He decided, however, to use 3mm plate to reduce the weight. This was more difficult to work, as the thin edges had to be upset hot and the metal tended to buckle. Peter has written:

"The canopy was technically the most difficult part to make, since its form derived from the assembly of 36 segments, and errors in the flat profile or bending would have resulted in uneven gaps, which would not show until I had put the entire thing together. Accordingly I made a full size elevation drawing, calculated the circumference at a number of points and divided these figures by 36, which enabled me to plot the true profile of the segments on the flat . . .

"The segments were finally bent cold over a former, the first of a number of special tools made up for the job. It was not until I had bent about ten of the segments, that I could be sure that my calculations were correct (surprisingly they were)."

A problem arose in getting the canopy into the building, when it was discovered that the farmhouse door was both narrower and lower than Peter had been told.

The upper column was constructed of 50mm steel tube which formed a spine to support hoops carrying the faceted column structure and the candleholders. Completed in early December, the hall was scaffolded and a team of people assembled for the installation, including a professional yacht rigger.

It was not until it was in position that Peter was able to see the pieces of the chandelier together for the first time, since his workshop roof had been too low to accommodate the whole assembly.

It is far from the usual expectation of a chandelier—not exactly fragile and glittering. It weighs six hundred pounds, is 15ft high and 7ft diameter. When the owner's little daughter first saw it, it was obviously not what she had been expecting. She pronounced it "Horrid—like a big black flower". However, on reflection Peter took this as something of a compliment.[2]

Also in 1982 Peter Parkinson was one of the blacksmiths featured in the travelling exhibition "Six British Blacksmiths". One of his exhibits was particulaly impressive; a rectangular table of great simplicity of line, relying on its technique of assembly for the design impact. Four straight legs, contrary to the usual procedure, come up through the table top and, volcano-like, the flat top rises to meet the squared off heads of the legs. He produced this distinctive feature by punching a square hole in the table top, from below, using a special little jig with a large square hole in it; so that the metal was dragged down into the cavity and produced the *volcano* shape.

The Annual BABA Conferences for 1982-4 were organised by Peter at the College in Farnham, and in 1984 took as its theme "Design and the Blacksmith". This included six case histories in which smiths each discussed the design, origin, development and making of one of their recently completed works. The final lecture on design was a masterly summing up of the subject by Peter himself. He sought to define the difference between the *decorated* and the *decorative*. He contrasted slides of a late 19th century stove, covered with pattern or in other words *decorated*, with objects of intrinsic beauty of form such as bronze-age axe heads and microlith arrow heads which were in themselves *decorative*. He discussed optical illusion, symmetry and the asymmetrical; the neat balance of black letter print; scale; the tradition of Celtic design; and the changing styles of fashion—such as Rococo. He questioned the well springs for inspiration— nature and close up photographs of plants— paths already trodden by Fritz Kühn and Samuel Yellin with such great effect.

Peter was receiving very varied commissions. In 1984 a pair of 6m wide gates for a private house in Bahrain; the following year the North Door Gate and Altar Screen bars for the church of St. Peter and Paul, Albury, Surrey; and in 1986 Tree Guard Railings for a

Left: Terrestrial and Celestial Globes for the entrance hall of the new Commonwealth Development Office.

Photograph by Peter Parkinson.

pedestrian scheme in Albert Square, Manchester—made by Richard Quinnell Ltd.

It was also in this year that he received his first major architectural commission, which he says taught him a lot about fixing ironwork into buildings. A former WRENs barracks, first built in 1830, was now to house a new Craft Gallery for Portsmouth City Museum and Art Gallery, and four internal security grilles were required over the windows.

Also in 1986 he lectured at the ABANA Conference in Flagstaff, Arizona; and was an invited Guest Demonstrator at the First World Congress of Blacksmiths in Aachen, Germany.

He completed a major commission in 1989— Terrestrial and Celestial Globes for the entrance hall of the new Commonwealth Development Office in Bessborough Gardens, London. The building was a new construction with a Regency façade; the architects were Chapman Taylor Partners. Peter was known to them because, some years before, John Taylor the senior partner had purchased a sundial from him for Ruthin Castle, from an Oxford Gallery Garden Exhibition.

The letter heading for the Commonwealth Development Office featured a very stylised map of the world, composed of large dots arranged in a grid pattern and this gave Peter the idea of using flat headed rivets to depict land masses on the terrestrial globe and stars on the celestial globe. At first it was his intention to use nickel silver, which would have etched slightly under the effect of the chemicals used to colour the globes. Finding this unobtainable at the time he settled for stainless steel which, in the end, turned out to be a fortunate choice as it increased the colour contrast and gave the completed globes a sharper appearance.

In the construction Peter used spun gilding-metal spheres, each of which he cut into six segments, secured to forged steel. He has written :

"The longest part of the job was the marking out, drilling, de-burring and setting of some 2000 rivets. The celestial globe was a challenge, because I was determined to make it as authentic as possible, although I suspect that the client would have been quite happy with a totally notional scattering of stars. Since all star maps show a view of the stars looking *up* from the earth, it is necessary to reverse this to provide a map of the heavens viewed, as it were, from the outside. To do this, I hit on the idea of taking a star chart from a particularly good library book photocopied on to clear film. All I had to do then was reverse the film and plot the stars from the back."[3]

It was also in 1989 that Peter was awarded a Licentiateship of the Worshipful Company of Blacksmiths. Then he organised a National Student Exhibition of Ironwork called "Art College Forgery", which was mounted with other exhibitions in the Old Library Building, Cardiff, during the First International Festival of Iron; and sponsored by the Worshipful Company of Ironmongers. Colleges of Art and Design were beginning to make an impact on blacksmithing and it would not have been possible to form such an exhibition only a few years earlier; as it was, 161 exhibits, of a very high standard, were drawn from eleven Colleges and Polytechnics.[4]

In 1990 Peter Parkinson won the competition to design and make gates for the new British Library. He was naturally delighted especially as it was the first major competition in which he had achieved first place. However on being summoned to see the architect, expecting to discuss the commencement of the work, he was told that as he had won the competition he would be allowed to make the gates essentially to the design of the architect— understandably he walked out of the meeting.

In recent years Peter has collaborated on several very large commissions with Quinnell's Rowhust Forge. He has been responsible for the design and the Forge has been responsible for the production. One in 1988 was an Archway 11m wide forming an entrance to a new pedestrian scheme in Ivegate, Bradford, Yorkshire.

In 1992 came a Triumphal Gateway 8.5m wide for a public art scheme in London Street, Basingstoke, of fabricated steel and cast bronze. Also a piece symbolising the growth

Above: Forged Mirror.

Peter Parkinson

Left: Equatorial Sundial in mild and stainless steel, 1991.

of the new town at Hemel Hempstead, to be installed in 1993.

In 1990 Peter had designed, and himself made, a hanging metal mobile for the Russel-Cotes Art Gallery and Museum, East Cliff, Bournemouth. This suspended flat cut-outs of objects in the museum, as large as dustbin lids, which had been given attractive colours by patination.

It was in 1993 that Peter resigned his full time lecturing post at the West Surrey College of Art and Design in order to pursue his own designing and making activities. More recently he has undertaken part time lecturing at the Hereford College of Art and Design.

He was a guest lecturer at the ABANA Conference at St. Luis Obispo, California, and, in this country, was Chairman of the Judging Committee for the Royal Anniversary Trust gift for the Queen Competition. (See Hyde Park Gates for the Queen Mother, page 149.)

A recent design has been for an archway in the middle of Derby. It is 8m high and largely formed from simple tube, impressive without being too costly, with motifs inspired from the buildings in the street about it.

He has now won a limited design competition for a 5m tall Public Art Piece in Godalming—a steel column featuring terra cotta pictorial panels, and another major Public Art Commission arranged by Cleveland Arts for a number of pieces as part of a new pedestrian scheme in Middlesbrough. These include another archway and a 6.5m wide screen fence across a side road.

It is not easy to define Peter Parkinson's work; sometimes its very perfection makes it rather impersonal. It is probably the legacy of his years in Industrial Design that have given his pieces a clean-cut smooth elegance, an air of worldly wisdom, which marks him as perhaps the most sophisticated of our modern blacksmiths.

Sources and Notes.

1. Catalogue *Towards a New Iron Age*. Exhibition.

2. "A Chandelier for a Country House" Peter Parkinson. *British Blacksmith* 24.

3. "Terrestrial and Celestial Globes" Peter Parkinson. *British Blacksmith* 53.

4. Catalogue of Exhibition. The Colleges were: Bournemouth & Poole College of Art and Design, Brighton Polytechnic, Clwyd College of Art and Design, Edinburgh College of Art, Glasgow School of Art, Herefordshire College of Art and Design, Lancashire Polytechnic, Loughborough College of Art and Design, Manchester Polytechnic, Plymouth College of Art and Design, West Surrey College of Art and Design.

Below: Triumphal Gateway, Basingstoke, 1992. Designed by Peter Parkinson and made by Quinnell's Rowhurst Forge.

Left: Detail of one of the bronze castings.

Photographs by Peter Parkinson.

DAVID
PETERSEN

I first remember David Petersen at the International Conference on Forging Iron. After five days of having our eyes opened to the wonders of *foreign* blacksmithing, we were taken on the sixth and last day to Coalbrookdale. There we saw the Museum, the Furnace Site, and the Blist's Hill exhibits. Then during the afternoon we viewed a *small* exhibition of new work by British Artist Blacksmiths. I remember David Petersen, who was at that time an Art Tutor and Sculptor, standing in admiration before Jim Horrobin's *Hanging Irons* and saying "Now I feel I can happily go away and leave you fellows to get on with the job".

Perhaps he changed his mind, or perhaps iron *grabbed* him that week as it did so many of us. At all events within two years he was at the 1982 BABA conference carrying under his arm, wrapped in a sheet, a dozen fire tools he had hand forged himself. It was clear that he was already enjoying the malleability of hot iron, though, aware of their shortcomings, he did not have the courage to put them in the show. He had just changed direction in his life and set up his own forge.

In a way it was ironic, being born in Cardiff in 1944, when he left Taunton school, he started work at the City's largest steelworks Guest Keen and Nettlefolds. He was after all the son of Jack Petersen, former British Heavyweight Boxing Champion, and himself of a physique to be a keen boxer and rugby player. Years later he recalled that all he could remember of being inside the steelrolling mills was a feeling of awesome terror.[1] He remained there only one year vowing that never again, willingly, would he work in a place so noisy, dusty, smelly and dangerous. Now here he was working with steel again and by his own choice.

After he left GKN he went to Newport College of Art, Gwent, from 1961-65, where he studied fine art; then to London University in 1965-66. He then became a sculptor for MGM Films at Elstree Studios working on "2001".

The following year he was Head of Sculpture at Harrow School of Art until 1970. He then worked as a part-time lecturer in both London and Newport, until he was appointed Lecturer at Newport College of Art in 1972. He became Senior Lecturer in the Faculty of Art and Design at Gwent College of Higher Education 1974-78. During this time he was Visual Artistic Director to several Festivals in Wales, and became in 1976 Chairman of the Association of Artists and Designers in Wales. After leaving Gwent College he joined Dyfed College of Art, where he became head of Sculpture in 1981.

The decision to leave the teaching profession had come at the right time, the Dyfed College was changing to become a College of Design, and there would no longer be a place for Fine Art. This clinched what must have been already in his mind. It is a move that he has never regretted

One reason why he became interested in blacksmithing was that when making metal sculptures from *found objects* he realised that the articles he was incorporating into these works, while being each unique, all had a uniform quality about them—once he understood that they were forged he knew it was a process he must learn.

He has come to realise that St. Clears, a little west of Carmarthen, where he set up his forge is one of the most beautiful places on earth, and he has written:

Above: David Petersen in 1984.

"It's very important to me, where I live and work, as I derive much energy from the immediate environment both in my life and into my work. The daily routine and the changing seasons provide an essential base for my creative well being. Living in a rural community also provides a necessary buffer and distance from the intellectualism of the Art World."

One of his first commissions was a mobile wind vane for the top of a bandstand in Gwent Square, Cwmbran. In collaboration with Theo Crosby of Pentagram Design, and based on his plan, David Petersen designed seven flat ravens on disced metal *Moons* to rotate beneath the points of the compass. The discs were gilded to represent the phases of the moon, and the whole was topped by a larger raven which also rotated. It was the name of the town that inspired the design—Cwmbran in Welsh means the Valley of the Ravens.[2]

Basically David taught himself to forge; he watched others demonstrate, read books, and much appreciated the help and advice he freely received from his fellow BABA members. He certainly learnt fast, and it seems incredible that only two years after the conference where he did not have the confidence to display his group of firetools, he sent a most outstanding piece to the exhibition of the 1984 BABA Conference at Farnham.

It was a wall hung memorial to the artist Graham Sutherland and had been commissioned by the curators of the Graham and Kathleen Sutherland Foundation Trust. It was to be sited above a doorway in Picton Castle, Rhos, Nr. Haverford West. I find it one of the most beautiful examples of modern forging that I have ever seen. The design is completely contemporary, yet the work is carried out wholly in honest traditional blacksmithing techniques. The forging was entirely by hand, David did not even own a power hammer at the time. It depicts a sea bird caught in a thorn bush (the great crescent shaped thorns so reminiscent of Graham Sutherland's paintings) and symbolises the artist's fascination with the Pembrokeshire landscape and the commitment he came to feel for a much loved area. The background mirrors his frequently used scheme of composition of a horizontal landscape superimposed with a circular motif. The simple but descriptively forged

contours of the bird, the way the tail and the one particularly long thorn break the main outline, adding interest and balance—the movement as the bird first finds himself caught by the thorns—it is a sculpture that quite exceptionally succeeds in arresting and holding a moment of drama. No artist could hope for a more sympathetic memorial. It would only be possible to pay homage of this nature in a medium other than the one originally used by the painter, and David Petersen's own artistry has made iron an exceptionally happy choice.

The following year David was commissioned by the University of Wales Institute of Science and Technology, with the assistance of funds from the Welsh Arts Council, to make a large steel dragon for the top of the Bute Building in King Edward VII Avenue, Cathays Park, Cardiff. No one knows better than the Welsh what goes to make up the constituent parts of a mythological dragon—the head of a crocodile, the body of a lion, bat wings, claws of an eagle and tongue and tail of a serpent. Shaped pieces of forged plate were welded on to a steel armature and the whole finished dragon weatherproofed and painted. Being a Welsh dragon the final colour was of course red. This beast who weighs approximately one ton, holds an amulet embattled—the cogged badge of UWIST. It was hauled into position by a crane, 70ft up, on the morning of 5th February 1985, where it joined no less than 300 dragons already in Cathays Park![3]

The Mametz Wood Memorial to the 38th (Welsh) Division. Vallé des Gallios, Mametz, Somme, France. 1987.

Photograph by Bronwen Petersen.

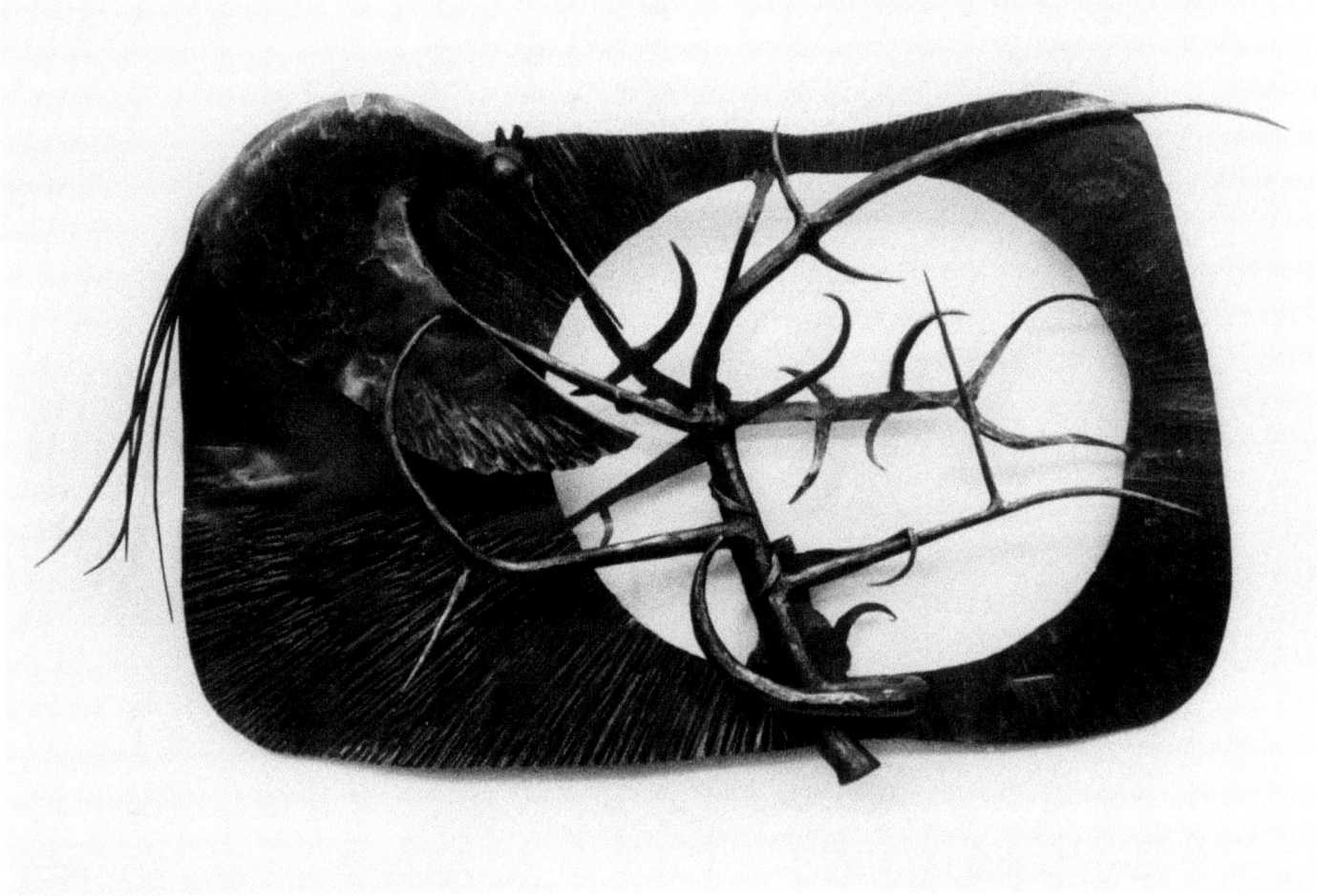

A very similar dragon, 6ft high, was later made by David Petersen as a memorial to the 4,000 men of 38th (Welsh) Division who died in July 1916 at Mametz Wood on the Somme in the first World War.

1986 saw the making of 30 full size Flamingoes for the National Garden Festival at Stoke-on-Trent, commissioned by the Arts Council of Great Britain.[4] To make the Flamingo bodies, motor-cycle petrol tanks were utilised as they were exactly the right shape. The heads were forged from used tank shells, from a nearby shooting range, and the legs were forged from reinforcing bar as the pattern and texture very much resembles Flamingo legs!

Indirectly the flamingoes led, some years later, to the commission of a Crane for the City Park development at Cornbrook, Manchester, by London and Metropolitan plc. It was discovered that the area had been known since 1322 as Cranes Brook. Cranes, or more likely Herons, had made their home there until in the mid 18th century until the brook was diverted to make way for a canal and the Cranes left.

The developers wanted a landmark that would be visible, on the skyline over a wide area; the crane was made, in mild steel, to stand on top of a sixteen metre high brick obelisk. David completed the four metre high sculpture in fourteen weeks and has succeeded in making 5 cwt of steel appear to defy gravity, as the crane launches itself into the air preparatory to flying over the City. Although designed to withstand the elements, and high winds, the Cornbrook Crane is both slender and graceful—a highly successful stylised bird abstraction.[5]

The actual construction was something of a nightmare. It was necessary to balance the whole weight very carefully. The legs are solid forged bar welded and bolted to a heavy frame, which is connected to reinforcing bars within the 35ft high column. The remaining structure of the bird is hollow section thick and thin wall tube; while the wings are forged from solid 25mm. The dished plinth is stainless steel and the dissimilar metals produced problems when the legs came to be welded into position. The bird was designed to flex and move a little in the high winds that swirl about it.

Above: The memorial Wall Sculpture to the artist Graham Sutherland, now in Picton Castle.

170

When the BABA Council was contemplating the organisation of its 1989 Conference members were very much wanting to open up the event to the public, more than had been the case on previous occasions. When David Petersen agreed to become Chairman of the co-ordinating committee, he felt that no where would be more suitable to hold such a meeting than Cardiff, a City built on the important elements of Coal, Steel and Water. He wanted also to open the eyes of Welsh smiths to the rebirth of creative ironwork then in progress. Also at the back of his mind was the wish to try and give back to BABA, through his own time and work, some of the help he had received from members when he had most needed it.

In his hands the Conference became the First International Festival of Iron, drawing in delegates from all over the world and sharing blacksmithing with the general public through forging stations for demonstrations set up in the streets in Cardiff City Centre. He set his sights high and it was a wonder that he survived the incredible work load he took upon himself to ensure its success. He spent months finding sponsors, organising demonstrators and chairing meetings; and when the event arrived he seemed to be everywhere, formally welcoming city dignitaries, and even finding time to play traditional Welsh music, together with his wife Bronwen, to accompany the Welsh dancing. (For a report on FIFI see page 49.)

It was also in 1989 that David was commissioned by the Monks of Belmont Abbey to design and make a sculpture of their patron saint, St Michael defeating the devil, to go in a stone niche 62ins x 46ins x 13ins and 36ins off the ground situated in an entrance hall.

Saint Michael is portrayed as a figure not far removed from most people's idea of a saint, wearing armour with a shield and wings, but instead of a fiery sword he carries a blow torch. In the Bible St Michael is depicted as slaying a dragon with seven heads; David chose instead to show the seven deadly sins representing the evils of contemporary society. An overweight man lolls slothfully on one elbow, surrounded by the attributes of Anger, Greed, Lust and Envy. David has said that "I had trouble with the last sin of Pride, until, that is,I signed the sculpture!"[1]

Unveiled in the Whitechapel Road in October 1989 was a 23 ft hand forged metal arch

commissioned by the London Borough of Tower Hamlets to commemorate Altab Ali, a Bangladeshi clothing worker who was stabbed to death by fascists ten years previously.

David spent a considerable time researching Bangladeshi culture and the history of the anti-racism movement before designing the arch.

The sculptural arch, which weighs a ton, has both Eastern and Western influences. On special occasions, like weddings, it is a Bengali custom to go through an arch decorated with ribbons. This sculptural arch, with its echoes of Eastern architecture, is hung with ribbons that look as if they are dripping with blood. The arch has become a symbol of anti-racism in the East End.

Another major work completed in 1989 was a sculpture commissioned by Allied Steel and Wire as a gift to South Glamorgan County Council for the foyer of their new headquarters building in Cardiff's docklands. It was not without its problems; the first design was rejected as it was considered too ornate for the situation and it was also thought that visitors might trip over the base. It was therefore back to the drawing board,

Above: Saint Michael and the Seven Deadly Sins. Sculpture.

Photograph by R.P. Ivan Page

with David researching afresh and coming up with a completely new design.

The final solution is an abstract wall hung piece based on the history of the site of the new building. It had earlier been marshalling yards where coal was loaded into hoists and transferred to coal ships for transport, the original wealth that led to the subsequent growth and prosperity of the county of South Glamorgan. Coal is represented as abstract wagon shapes queuing to be loaded; the water of the docks is suggested by verticals, the masts of ships, and their wavy reflections in the water below. Coils of *rope* between the masts and the wagons, represent the winding gear of the coal mines at the pit head. It is a very powerful and impressive piece, 30ft high x 8ft wide and 18ins deep, and weighs ¾ ton. Forged from 40mm solid bar and mild steel plate, it took a team of four, assisted by others, six months to make. David and two of his sons, Aaron and Toby, were joined by Andrew Rowe. It seems almost incredible that it was not until half way through making this piece that David discovered that it was intended to position a radiator in the middle of the wall! After many meetings he agreed to lift the lower central part of the sculpture, but insisted that the radiator be installed flush with the wall surface and that the central panel of it should be finished in marble to match the wall.

It would not have been possible to make such a massive piece if David had not expanded and built a new forge and studio in 1988 to house new equipment including two power hammers, one of them a 3 cwt Alldays and Onion. Today there is an altogether wider outlook and the name of the forge is now Petersen Studios. The previous forge and workshop have been adapted for wood and stone carving; and a ceramic studio and store has been enlarged. David draws and works on maquettes in an inside studio, which is also equipped for painting and printmaking. Another larger studio doubles as a lecture room and can be used for *life* classes if needed. A hot glass studio has been set up so that projects of mixed media are now possible.

A major commission in 1990 was a Forged Screen Sculpture for Trinity College, Carmarthen, sited in the foyer of the Halliwell Centre. It is of an heraldic nature with a shield and an open book, finished in black, below the spiny red wings of a dragon. It

Above: Wall Sculpture "Coal, Steel and Water" 1989.
Photograph Davis Lewis STP Photography. ASW Holdings Plc. ©

draws together the threads of College life; an empty scabbard beside an inkpot signifies turning towards wisdom, the masks of Comedy and Tragedy represent drama and a Welsh harp, music. The support is the ladder of ambition, while the celestial crown around the dragon's neck relates to the religious foundation of the College.

If I have given the impression that one commission neatly follows another in leisurely progression I must make it clear that this is by no means the case.

Hazel Moore has left on record an account of two weeks spent working at the Petersen Studios in the Spring of 1992, in which she found that everything seemed to be happening at once. She soon learnt that: "a late start matched with a late finish was normal allowing Dave design time in the morning before starting practical work." Flamingoes, Pelicans and goat sculptures seemed to be everywhere: "This second day marked the beginning of the late nights, finishing at 8 p.m., and also Dave began to show signs of mad frenzy and panic, with only days to his one-man show, with sculptures still to be designed and made, besides an archway which had to be completed by the following monday for delivery to London, but which hadn't been started due to bad weather!" Two days later "Thursday brings chaos and mayhem . . . as the spray painting of 20 flamingoes begins Dave's mood climaxes in the middle of the first batch being sprayed. I've since learnt that his impression of John Cleese is normal, being the result of Smoothrite drying in the spraygun . . . faster than our ability to move flamingoes around the workshop! I spent the afternoon painting flamingoes' legs accompanied by Bronwen, finishing at 8.00 p.m."[6]

Returning two weeks later there was a panic clean up of the main workshop ready for a visit by a group of mentally handicapped people; followed next day by hours of demonstrating. Two days later they were recreating the sounds of a foundry for a local BBC radio station who had missed the casting of torques David had designed and made for the Celtic Film Festival. Work has been known to go on all night; when replicas of the Capel Garmon Firedogs were being made the smiths, feeling themselves getting into the minds of their Celtic forebears, worked with such enthusiasm and commitment that they sometimes went on through the night and into the early hours.[7]

Although David Petersen may often give the impression of the complete maverick Welsh smith, he makes the point that although the technique of forging fascinates him, it is always secondary to his creative need to make sculpture. He is still a sculptor who makes sculpture even if it is in forged metal.

A major commission in 1992 was to make a 3.5m steel figure for the Ebbw Vale Garden Festival. David attempted to combine the concept of the well known figure of the Minoan Snake Goddess from Knosses, one of the oldest of household goddesses, with the Welsh Divine Queen Rhiannon (of the Mabinogion) from Celtic mythology.

The materials used relate to the heavy industrial immediate past of Ebbw Vale. Two rivetted industrial steel buckets form the stepped skirt and recall the cauldrons often used by the Celts as votive offerings, such as the *Gundestrup* cauldron. A heavy riveted *grab* becomes a bra for two orbs, which in turn become the exposed breasts of the Minoan Goddess, and the bra straps become forged steel *ribbons* flowing in the wind. Perhaps it is old fashioned of me to be worried by the lack of a head. In its manufacture and construction the welded and forged metal involved all four elements—earth, air, fire and water—enabling, in celtic belief, the appearance of the fifth element—magic. It is designed to represent the celtic understanding of the earth's regenerative energy.

A 17ft high entrance arch was also made for the Garden Festival; work went on outside in a winter of snow and rain since it was too large to work on inside the workshop. It combines one of the oldest greetings in the world, that of "Welcome", with the most modern available technology. It is coated with Savinite, in Spring colours, a Cathodic protective coating material originally developed by Huntings Industrial Coatings Ltd, Manchester, for use on the exposed metal surfaces of all the NASA space shuttles. It is guaranteed to heal its own scratches and to prevent rust for 50 years.

Now in 1993 David is working on a large female figure based on Branwen the Welsh Princess. It will weigh about 4 tons and will be 25ft high; mostly welded but partly forged. It has been commissioned by British Steel and British Gas to be situated on a traffic round-about in Margam Park, Port Talbot.

It seems as if David Petersen has been extraordinarily successful in bringing together all the strands of his career and his art. The whole outlook at the Petersen Studios now progresses towards encompassing a wide range of the arts, including work in films and television. All his sons, Aaron, Gideon and Toby (the latter particularly enjoys forging) have now qualified in the Arts. The Studios are open to students and it is seldom that there are not at least three on the premises. They join David and Bronwen, their daughter and sons, in working towards their ultimate aim—to arrive indivisibly at Fine Art and Fine Craft.

Sources and Notes

1. "David Petersen—a profile" *British Blacksmith* 53.

2. "Cwmbran Windvane" *British Blacksmith* 18.

3. "UWIST Dragon" *British Blacksmith* 35.

4. *British Blacksmith* 41 p12.

5. "Crane Flies North to Cornbrook" *British Blacksmith* 59.

6. Hazel Moore "Hazel in Wales" *British Blacksmith* 64.

7. David Petersen. "The Capel Garmon Firedogs" *British Blacksmith* 63.

MELVIN PINNOCK

and the Nailbourne Forge.
Martin Reeves & Julian Coode

It was the seminar held in conjunction with the "Towards a New Iron Age" exhibition in 1982 that opened Melvin Pinnock's eyes to modern ironwork design. Later he would write: "I can remember walking down the stairs of the Victoria and Albert Museum after the seminar . . . thinking to myself 'I have the equipment ready to go. As soon as I get back I am going to design something new'.

"I recall my amazement that I had been playing around with fire and anvil since I was twelve, and yet I had never given thought to non-traditional design of the kind that I had just been seeing. Yes, so amazed that I was embarrassed to own up to the fact, even to myself. How could I have thoroughly enjoyed a hobby, and then started on a career, missing something so fundamental?" [1]

Inspired by the seminar, the exhibition, and the first copy of "British Blacksmith" that he had ever seen, Melvin returned to his home in Canterbury ready to start work with a fresh and new enthusiasm. Sharing the experience that day was young Martin Reeves who was to become Melvin's apprentice and later, his colleague.

I first saw their work in September of that year at the BABA exhibition at Farnham (see pages 39 & 42) and wrote about it again in succeeding years.

As a boy Melvin had enjoyed outdoor practical pursuits. He completed his schooling at the Frank Hooker School in Canterbury, leaving at seventeen with only two paper qualifications of note, A levels in Art and Metalwork. He came of a musical family, and his brother Trevor is Director of the English Concert Orchestra. Melvin was the only pupil allowed to tune the school's guitars (he had perfect pitch) and played both the classical and electric guitar. In his final year or two at school he became known as 'The Duke' from arriving each morning in the nick of time with an air of lordly detachment. It was an appelation that he continued to merit. Although he was friendly there was always an air of quiet withdrawal about him, a slightly abstracted look as though his mind was working out something else.

His working life began in the workshops of Early Keyboard Instruments at Lyminge, near Folkestone, under the direction of Richard Clayson and Andrew Garrett. He was soon making hinges, locks and other items of metalwork in the fashion, and using the techniques, of the seventeenth and eighteenth centuries.

His metalwork for harpsicords was well received, not only at Lyminge but by other instrument makers further afield. So it was that he was able to set up business on his own using one of a pair of garages at home. He built and operated not only a forge but also a furnace in which brass and other metals could be cast. Most of his work was small scale and his beautiful turned tuning jacks are treasured possessions in many parts of the world.

Above: Melvin in 1984.

Photograph
Nailbourne Forge.

Far left: Some of the small brassware on which the firm was founded.

Photograph Melvin Pinnock.

Melvin had an almost instinctive grasp of the properties of materials and unfailing ingenuity in devising solutions to engineering and mechanical problems. It had led him, at the age of 15 or 16 to design and make a gear train (in which the most obvious feature was a bicycle wheel) for his new lathe—once he had first mastered the relevant mathematics; and later in life to make or contemplate such things as an on-the-spot planking device to cut up fallen tree trunks.

These were interests that were shared by Martin Reeves. At the age of 15 he made, with Melvin, a land yacht and it was this project that first introduced him to Melvin's workshop. He became a frequent visitor and was keen to learn the craft of blacksmithing. When he left school he became Melvin's apprentice and from then on shared every aspect of his work.[2]

Their largest commission in a modern style, in the early years, was a spiral stairway in the Canterbury Centre, a medieval church that had been converted to public use for a charitable organisation. Perhaps Melvin still had nagging doubts—was he right in proposing a modern style for such an old building. He took a sample baluster and sought the opinion of Robert Paine, architect, who offered nothing but help and reassurance, convincing him that he was doing the right thing for the building.

The balusters had the clean simplicity of all Melvin's modern designs, and the treads fanned out, supported by the most elegant of flat brackets. It avoided the all too prevalent scrappiness of so many modern spiral staircases, made by blacksmiths. It was their first major work in a public place.

Melvin joined the BABA Council, sometimes wrote in "British Blacksmith", and at the 1984 Conference gave a most informative and helpful lecture on "Draughtsmanship and Presentation". He showed work from preliminary sketches to the completed design. It was so arranged that the prospective customer could see his site as it was, and then by overlays, the site with the proposed work superimposed on it. He made it clear how important it is to offer the design in a professional manner, whether to a client or in competition.

In 1984 a move was made to more spacious premises, at Court Hill, Littlebourne, four miles from Canterbury, which Melvin felt were close to ideal. It was about this time that they were joined by Martin's brother Duncan. Here they were able to create a workshop, and office and even a garden, where they could play croquet in the lunch hour. Nailbourne Forge (as Melvin had named it after the intermittent stream near-by), became a place not only of hard work but also of laughter, music (from Vivaldi to pop and jazz) and unceasing banter.

To survive financially while all this was going on meant that they had to turn to doing any type of metalwork, including fabrication, casting, and structural ironwork for builders and vintage car parts. However the time came when Melvin felt able to specialise in his main interest—forged iron; although to a certain extent this was tantamount to taking a cut in wages while still financing the purchase of the new workshop and covering an alarming amount of overheads.

Far left: An Ivy Leaf Table made by Martin Reeves in 1984.

Below: The Land Yacht in action.

Family Photograph.

Left: The Spiral Staircase in the Canterbury Centre.

Melvin Crow

On the plus side—all three were committed, determined and hard working; and they had some unusually good clients, more like patrons than customers. They were also fortunate in having an accountant/book keeper who could tell them just where they stood financially at any time.

They worked in both traditional and modern designs. An example of the former was a fine 18th century style panel for the Riverside Development, Richmond, for architect Quinlan Terry. Some of their work utilised elements of both types. A round-headed gate had a graceful design of vine leaves and a bunch of grapes in the upper part; while below where traditional dog-bars would have been, the forged bars were elongated, waved and finished at different heights. The whole was unashamedly welded together and given the finishing touch of a delightfully creative *tendril* latch. Melvin always saw the latch as the first point of tactile contact between the gate and whoever was about to go through it, and believed that the contact should be a pleasant one.

For a gate to a dark and tree-lined drive they

felt something rather theatrical was required; the design has almost a hint of opening curtains and a cresting of leaves at the centre top.

In the ancient church of St Martin's, Canterbury, there is a wrought iron cross made by Melvin. Some years ago the Altar Cross had been stolen. It was replaced by a strange piece of driftwood, a wooden cross like a vine, so simple and poor that it seemed to speak to people. Finally it became so old that the Vicar asked Melvin to copy it in wrought iron.[2]

Completely contemporary and uncompromising was a gate for a modern bungalow, where shaped uprights were fitted into a simple plain top and bottom horizontal bars by the use of Z shaped joiners, devised by Melvin. This system was also used in a later gate, where the shaped uprights had been developed into a *flame* design of great subtlety.

Melvin was a keen photographer and kept a bank of photographs of the work they made. In this way inquirers could get an idea of the designs that excited them and would, hopefuly, be infected by their enthusiasm. His attention to detail was meticulous and the Forge steadily built up an enviable reputation for quality of design and workmanship.

He commissioned Rachel Reckett to make a sculpture of a blacksmith at work, with the idea of placing a larger version on a wall in front of the workshop. She produced three blacksmiths forging (see page—) but the final piece was never made as there was not enough room on the wall.

In 1989 Melvin wrote an article for the "British Blacksmith" on the forge, which was now well established. It had two hearths, one small with a concentrated blast, which was most used. The other had a continental, double-bottom blast ideal for long heats and large work. There was a finely tuned 1 cwt spring hammer for delicate forgings as well as heavier work. The workshop was very adaptable with equipment that could be moved about as required; steel work benches on wheels, a leg vice on a stand, and a circular saw on wheels. The large MIG welder could be wheeled to a job or to the two ton levelling block just outside the door; when not in use it was kept under a workbench out

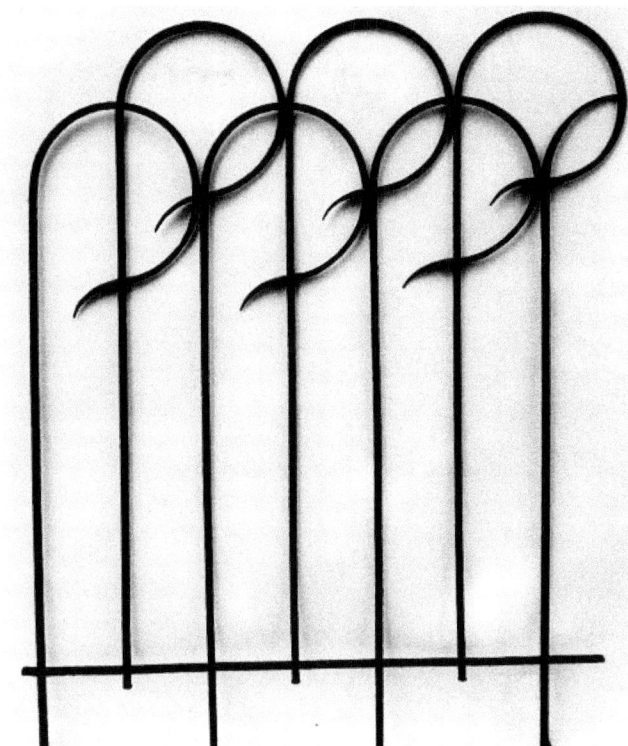

of the way. There were various engineering machines and a powerful hydraulic press.

Melvin found that the three of them rather conveniently came to specialise in different aspects of the work. Martin particularly liked forging, while Duncan was the one for accurately cutting and marking out materials as well as welding and finishing. Melvin was often to be found at his drawing board or receiving prospective clients in the office. He also did much of the fitting together, tool making and jig making. All, however, could interchange their work and, fortunately in view of what was to come, Melvin and Martin shared the administrative work.

Above: Balustrading of 12mm square steel.

Photograph Melvin Pinnock.

Below: Leafy gate for a dark drive.

Photograph Melvin Pinnock

They were taking on a lot of art metalwork for a furniture designer and the need arose for a woodwork area where special patterns for castings could be made.[1] They had already added an adjoining workshop to complete their occupancy of "Builders Square" at Court Hill.[2] At this point they were joined by Mark Fuller, a Royal College of Art graduate sculptor, who became the main art metalworker.

There were now three of them full time and one part time. There was a regular young Saturday helper who placed on record his impressions of the workshop with a short poem:

The Forge

The forge is a really nice place
With Melvin, Mark and Co.
I leave at five oclock
At five oclock I Go.
The pay is the best bit
2.50 if I am lucky.
There is only one drawback
I get very mucky.
     Michael McCullock (aged 11)

Melvin was looking forwards with anticipation. He was excited by the developments at the forge particularly the idea of having a sculptor on the premises. He wrote in the Spring of 1989 ". . . with my knowledge of casting and Mark's skill in three dimensions, even I can't guess what it will lead to!"[1] If only this could have been the case—but the time left to Melvin was to be all too short.

Melvin had many interests, in 1985 he had taken time off to make a five-week trip, with friends, across the Sahara. Sitting outside his tent, listening to tapes of the English Concert and looking at the blazing stars in the desert sky was an experience that led him to buy an astronomical telescope and join the South-East Kent Astronomical Society. He was also a member of the executive committee of the Stour Valley Society and one of the last things he did was to help organise the setting up of a massive boulder in the Greyfriars at Canterbury to mark the completion of the Stour Valley Riverside Walk.[2]

Then there was photography, silversmithing, and music, but above all there was sailing. Over a long period he was an active member of the Herne Bay Sailing Club, where he preferred cruising to racing. During the Summer of 1990 the weather was good and he spent a lot of time sailing.

On Sunday morning September 9th, Melvin called on some friends in Herne Bay, and over coffee discussed where it would be best to keep his boat for the winter. Also that morning he was talking to a former Commodore of the Sailing Club and his son, who was a weather forecaster, about when it would be best to move the boat off moorings for the Winter. They left him looking "utterly relaxed and at peace with the world".[2]

Melvin went to his boat, moored a quarter of a mile offshore, and never returned. He laid the table ready for a meal and must have then intended to swim. Six days later his body was found washed up on the beach. It became clear at the inquest that he must have

Below: Melvin's 'Flame' Gate shown at the Sotheby Exhibition.

Photograph by Glynn Clarkson.

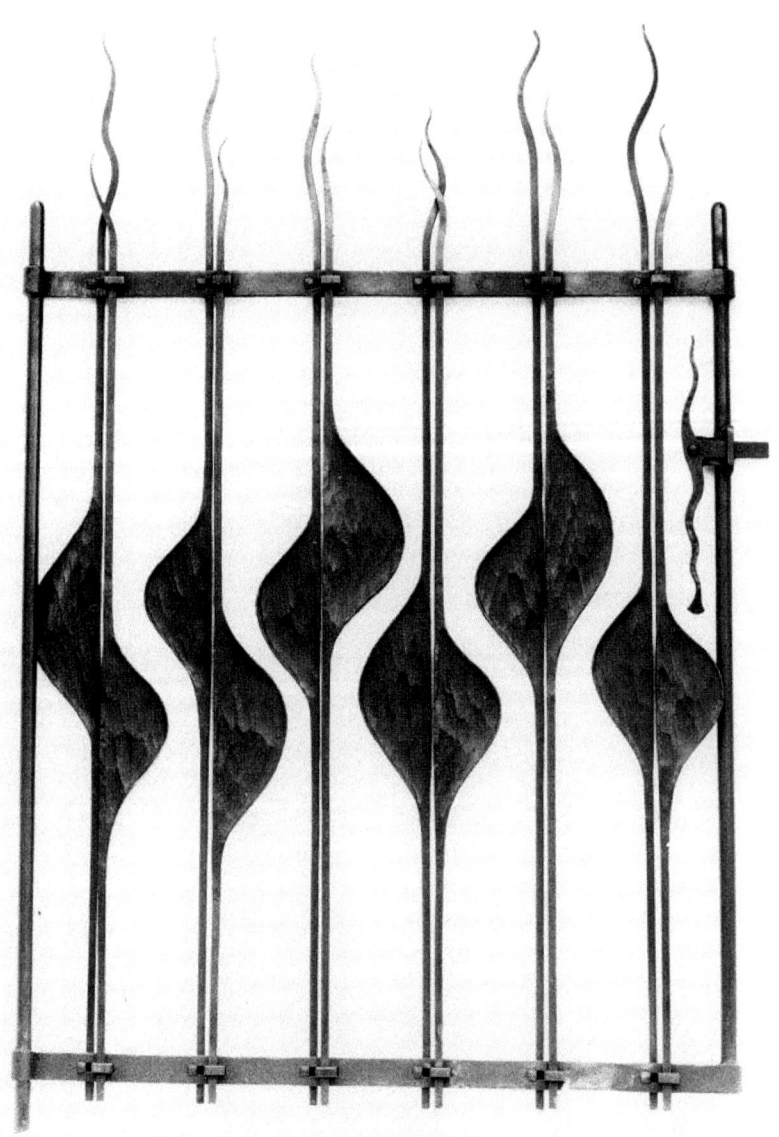

suffered a cardiac arrest immediately on diving in, as there was no water in his lungs. It was a hot day but the water was cold and being alone at the boat there was no one to give him assistance.

Melvin was paid a singular honour by the Worshipful Company of Blacksmiths, who sent to his parents, a hand-painted plaque of the Company's coat of arms inscribed with his name the only sort of recognition that could be offered in respect of one deceased.

In BABA we mourned the loss of a friend. He had done much in his thirty-six years but one felt that he still had so much to give, and death is sad when it comes too soon. The following September I stood in front of his *Flame Gate* exhibited in the Sotheby display, with its deceptive simplicity and subtly flowing pattern, and it only served to emphasise the great loss we had sustained by his tragic death. I met his partner Martin Reeves looking at the exhibition. He had not had time to do any forging for it himself as it had been necessary to give himself wholly to running the business, but I was very pleased to hear that he had been joined by Julian Coode.

Julian had been apprenticed to Terrence Clark for four and a half years. In 1984, after CoSIRA courses over a two year period, he was awarded the Worshipful Company of Blacksmiths Certificate of merit; for a piece of best quality and design, for a modern cross. He then went, as a journeyman, to Germany and spent fifteen months with Paul Zimmerman. It was the first time he had worked with such an artist, and Paul's friends were glassmakers and artists, so that Julian felt that while he was there his eyes were opened for the first time to a wider world of art. He then returned to England and spent six months working at Quinnell's Rowhurst Forge.

He then did a one year Foundation Course at Farnham West Surrey College of Art and Design, and gained a place on the 3 Dimensional Design course, at the end of which he won a prize for the best degree show at Farnham from the New Ashgate Gallery. This enabled him to travel to Russia with David Petersen to meet Russian blacksmiths; and to do a week's teaching at a college in Farnham.

Above: A Gate with Grapes designed by Melvin Pinnock. A new form for an old theme. Note the delicate "tendril" latch. This is an unashamedly electric welded piece.

Photograph by Steve Silk.

Ribbon Gate, designed and made by Martin Reeves, inset into detail photograph showing the latch with the Nailbourne stamp. Texturing done under a 70ton hydraulic press in 150mm 'bites' between spring steel negatives of a bar prepared with a power hammer.

Photographs by Melvin Pinnock.

This page left: Barrier in forged mild steel. This was a railing approached in a different way. It was within a gap in a wall (which ran below it and on each side) see diagram. Made in 1991 by Julian Coode.

Photograph by Julian Coode.

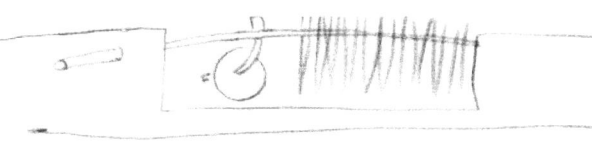

Elevation

Plan

By December 1992 Martin and Julian formed a partnership, purchased the forge from Melvin's parents, and started their own business.

Martin had been involved with making a number of very large hanging signs for Euro-Disneyland, all of different types and designs. Then together they made twenty large forged sign brackets for a Dutch Shopping Centre. In 1992 Martin won a prize for a grille at the Young Artist South East Exhibition sponsored by South East Arts; and together they gave a forging demonstration in the town centre of Dover.

I hope they will have good fortune; and that we shall see interesting pieces from the forge in the years to come.

Sources and Notes.
1. Profile. Melvin Pinnock *British Blacksmith* No 52.

2. *Remembering Melvin*. Privately printed booklet 1990.

Left: A Gate in forged steel, 1993 by Julian Coode. This commission came from a client seeing the Barrier piece at the Hannah Peschar Gallery Sculpture Garden. A gate was required along similar lines.

Photograph by Julian Coode

WALENTY
PYTEL

I first met Walenty Pytel in April 1993 when he was still living at Terrace Hall, Woolhope, Herefordshire; his home for thirty years. It was deep country I was driving through, the road was getting narrower, rougher and muddier all the time, then it broadened out again and the hedgerows were full of bluebells and white Campions. The morning mist began to rise and pale sunlight to lighten the rather grey day. The house was long, half-timbered black and white, old and beautiful. A BBC radio and television van was parked on the gravel drive and I pulled up alongside.

I tried knocking at the front door, a young sapling was growing through the floor of the porch and entangling itself in the door knocker; it was obviously too elegant to remove and somehow the door had the air of not being much used. I made my way to the nearby workshop. It was delightfully pastoral; petals of apple blossom falling to the ground outside the door and the whole folded about with the soft sounds of sheep. Walenty Pytel had been giving an interview for radio, because there is a lot of media interest in his latest piece of sculpture; now he turned to welcome me. He comes forward hand outstretched—a friendly face wreathed in a shock of unruly whitening hair.

Inside, the workshop is largely filled with a sculpture of Dolphins. Three Bottle Nosed Dolphins each 7 or 8ft long, about life size, swim in a close knit group. As I move around the sculpture I discover the most delightful baby Dolphin swimming in the centre, a little towards the back, protected on all sides by the adult fish. Walenty feels strongly about the need for conservation of certain species in the world today; this is his effort to call attention to the plight of the Dolphins for whom many people feel a particular sympathy and a special need to work towards their protection.

The sides of the fish are formed of curved vertical steel bands that vary in width—the narrow gaps between the sheets as visually important as the solid forms. The welding together is all carefully thought out; it is not a case of using whatever width comes to hand,

but, all the time, of creating, balancing, patterning and shaping.

The open circles of the Dolphin's eyes give far more life than a fixed eyeball could achieve; as one moves around the sculpture so the eye space is filled with light and shade, according to whatever is seen behind that space.

The Dolphins can be taken apart to make transport easier. One, mounted on a stand, really takes the weight of the others; each fish is welded to a hollow tube about 3 ½ins square. This pushes in or out of the other parts of the group. The interior of the Dolphin bodies, like an aeroplane wing, are criss-crossed with angles and braces to obtain extra strength. They also contain fixed tubes for the insertion of the joining tubes. The whole concept for such a large piece is one of engineering. Walenty obligingly removes one of the Dolphins and stands on top of it, jigging up and down, to demonstrate its strength.

When completed the sculpture will be dipped in a bath of warm hydrochloric acid to remove rust and then zinc dipped. In this way all the interior of the piece will be protected, as well as the outside. It will be finished with several coats of synthetic lacquer, ending with steel blue. Named *Forever Free* it is designed to have a fountain splashing beneath it.

Walenty Pytel works in many sizes, a sculpture may be as small as three or four inches or as large as 45ft high; though on the

Above: Walenty Pytel working on 'forever Free'.

whole there seems to be a tendency to work on a larger scale as time goes by. On the floor of the workshop lie sheets of brown paper on which he has drawn out the head of a Griffon, for whom just the head and neck is about five feet long. For a large sculpture he makes a welded steel model and then scales it up to the required size, which may take many months to complete. He learnt, the hard way, that this was the only satisfactory method for success. When he was working on the Woodpecker for Bulmers' Cider factory he thought he could copy it by eye. Working from steps and ladders in his workshop it looked a perfect enlarged replica, only when he took it outside and stood back 100 yards did he find it was completely out of proportion and he had to start all over again.

It has taken twenty-seven years of learning and development to bring him to the expertise he enjoys today. During that time he has created what was, certainly when he began, an absolutely unique form of sculpture. He is always making small table sculptures, usually of birds, which may take only a matter of days to create. These are made to commission or for sale in the gallery his wife runs in conjunction with her interior design shop, Wyebridge Interiors, in Hereford. What he most enjoys, however, is to have three or four large works under construction at once, so that he can go from one to another, working on them as he pleases. If he needs real relaxation he will walk down to the river, with his black Labrador, and spend some time fishing. Doubtless it is here that he sees and studies many of the birds that will be the models for his work.

Walenty Pytel was born in Poland in February 1941. His father was in the Polish army and his mother was a nurse. They lost everything during the war. The family was re-united by the Red Cross in Italy at the end of the war, and then came to England.

From the age of fifteen he trained at Hereford College of Art obtaining the National Diploma of Design in 1961. This training in graphic design led him to work in a commercial publishing firm in London, McLaren and Son, until 1962. In the following year he decided to return to the country, where he married Mary Spencer, and moved to Woolhope. They have a son, Jeremy, and a daughter, Catherine. He opened two studios specialising in graphic design and, for the

next four years, taught part time at Hereford College of Art. Here his subject was window display and paper sculpture. There was something of a vogue for paper sculpture at this time and it was used commercially in many applications. Admiring his work in paper, a friend asked him to make a pheasant in copper. In a way, to transpose the clean precise shapes of cut and bent thick paper to metal was a very natural evolution.

Left: The Bulmer Woodpecker in Hereford.

Below: The young Dolphin swims in the centre protected on all sides by the adult fish.

At first he took sheets of metal and riveted and soldered them together. There was a certain angularity about the work and the sculptures lacked the flow and continuity that would characterise his later work. As his sculptures developed he found they did not have sufficient strength, and he realised the need for other techniques. He used mild steel sheet and became a proficient welder. The gauge of sheet he uses today may be anything from 1/16th to 1/8th of an inch and the very fact of bending it gives added strength. The nature of the sculptures began to change; by allowing the molten metal of the welding to run down the sides of the model the outlines became softer, adding still more strength which gave many more possibilities of design.

His work on welded steel sculptures created a new form of metal art, and led inevitably to emulation; before long he was judging competitions of welding at agricultural shows.

Throughout his career he has been best known for his sculptures of birds. He so well captures the characteristic outline and form of the various species that, although his works are more stylised than naturalistic, each bird is immediately recognisable—Tawny Owl, Corn Bunting, Dipper, Partridge, Falcon, Osprey and a host of others—a Coot runs across the surface of water to take off and Ibis display, their long necks bending backwards with their beaks raised to the sky. In 1973 he made a Parrot for Le Perroquet Restaurant in the Berkeley Hotel, London; and there are some of his bird sculptures in Juliana's Discotheque in Amsterdam and Bahrain. One of his best known works must be the Woodpecker for the headquarters of Bulmer ciderworks Eign Street, the A438, in Hereford. One of his finest major sculptures *Take-off*, three Egrets rising into the air, at Birmingham Airport, measures 28ft, and was commissioned in 1985 to commemorate forty years of peace in Europe.

The birds have been joined by beasts; in 1975 he made a Wild Boar for Chanel Perfume, Paris. Sometimes the beasts are mythological like the 25inch Unicorn commissioned by Princess Anne in 1979 as a gift to the Portuguese Government. He has recently completed a 10ft equestrian statue of a warrior on horseback.

Probably Walenty Pytel's best known work is the Jubilee Sculpture standing in New Palace

Yard, Westminster, outside the Houses of Parliament, beneath the tower of Big Ben. After a lengthy search, it was Walenty's design that was chosen by Members of Parliament and commissioned by them and the Department of the Environment; it commemorates the 1977 Jubilee Year of Her Majesty the Queen. It is a group of six beasts, representing the Commonwealth. The largest at the base include a magnificent unicorn and a fiercely clawing lion; there are two small birds and a beast above, and the whole is topped by a golden crown. The work achieved universal acclaim:

"The Commission was a triumph for Pytel, who is considered one of the most promising young English Sculptors". *Daily Mirror*

Below: Mythological Bird with detail of head.

Cadbury Ireland Ltd

Peggy Richardson.

"The sculpture is an impressive piece of work and when unveiled to the public will almost certainly be hailed as one of the finest pieces of metal work in this country". *Western Daily Express*.

"Pytel uses rough naturalistic or severely stylised surfaces with skill". *The Guardian*.

It is unfortunate that the need for security now places the sculpture outside the range of the general public. Two models were made for M.P.s and one sold at Christies.

It is interesting to compare the completed work with the maquette. The roughness

produced by the welding which forms an intrinsic part of the surface in models, does not have the same impact on larger forms. By the sheer nature of the technique small sculptures usually have more lively surface detail and greater variation of texture than the large works.

One of the reasons his sculptures are so decorative and creative is that flat surfaces, fine rods round in section, and empty spaces, all combine in equal importance, to create a descriptive form. The negative spaces are always as important as the positive metal; sometimes a series of straight ladder-like spaces form part of the structure, and at others varied sizes of round or broken voids enrich the surface giving a net or lace-like effect. These textures are frequently overlaid with blobs and bosses of welding that add a jewel-like quality of great richness. Today his sculptures for the home, of small birds which are highly finished with several coats of synthetic lacquer, have as much the look of jewels as sculptures. Particularly as they often perch, fleetingly one feels, on finely drawn stems or on bunched groups of twigs as jagged as needles and reminiscent of mineral crystals. Perhaps this is a lead to his future work as he expresses a particular interest in working towards compositions of animal and bird subjects with plant and tree forms.

He occasionally creates abstract sculptures; there was one tall and narrow piece in the workshop composed of hundreds of intricate shapes and rods. These works are suitable for wall mounting. One very fine abstract mural

Above left: Abstract Wall Sculpture for Cadbury Schweppes plc, Dublin.

Above right: The 'Fosser' sculpture. 45ft. high, for J.C Bamford Ltd, Uttoxeter.

Far left: The Jubilee Sculpture in New Palace Yard, Westminster.

Photograph Walenty Pytel.

Far left: Exotic Bird. In recent years the birds tend to be integrated into a more complex surround or "branch".

Above right: Fish.

Photographs by
Walenty Pytel

was made for Cadbury Schweppes plc Dublin office. It is 15ft long and consists of decorative wheel forms and thin interlacing rods, placed both vertically and horizontally, with the bias mainly towards the horizontal.

An abstract sculpture in the round he made for the Uttoxeter factory of J.C.Bamford Limited, was no less than 45ft high—said to be the largest metal sculpture in Europe. Called the Fosser Sculpture (from the Latin fosser to dig), it is made from parts of JCB earthmovers. He began by dismantling a number of plastic toy trucks and diggers before assembling them into a model to inspire the finished sculpture. In a creation of this size a man is lost and insignificant if he sits in one of the great monster-like clawing "hands".

At the other end of the scale, for private collectors, Walenty produces limited editions of bronze sculptures, highlighted with 9 carat gold and set on bases of Italian marble, cast from his welded mild steel originals. Walenty Pytel is a member of The Guild of Master Craftsmen and The Royal Society of British Sculptors. Exhibitions of his work have been shown in Spain, France, Germany, the United States of America and Japan, as well as in this country.

As I say "good-bye" I look up at a sculpture of a Cormorant on a very high pole in front of the house; Walenty points out some pieces of hay hanging from it. Perhaps it is symbolic of the easy integration of his life and work with the birds and beasts around him that a sparrow has built her nest inside the body of the metal bird.

For an illustration of the 'fosser' sculpture see page 185.

Below: Both sides of a small jewel-like bird.

RICHARD
QUINNELL Ltd

and The Rowhurst Forge.

Richard Quinnell has already featured in "How it all began" (pages 33 and 35) because he played an important part, largely in an organisational role, in the rebirth of creative smithing in this country.

It was before he was born and World War II was still in the future when his father, living in a beautiful old medieval house on the outskirts of Leatherhead, set up blacksmithing in the outhouses at Rowhurst. He wanted to produce light fittings for his electrical showroom in London, and he employed one smith, John Donelly.

The business expanded to a full blown enterprise in 1946 with about a dozen young men trained by the original smith and making such things as candlesticks, letter-racks and coffee tables, under his supervision. It was wrought ironwork, very traditional, and of high quality. They were, in fact, manufacturing wholesalers and supplied to retail stores all over the country. In 1953, when Richard was thirteen, his father died and his mother took over running the business.

The making of Richard Quinnell into a smith was a long gradual process of assimilation. From the time he was *eye level to an anvil* he was taking an interest in the familiar workshop, and as he grew older he was continually learning the craft from the smiths. He worked solidly in the business for one year before going up to Cambridge to study Zoology. After graduating in Natural Sciences in 1963 he made the decision to join the family firm.

There was another branch to the business— the production of decorated porcelain door furniture, for which they found a ready market in Australia. Owing to a severe crash in the economy of that country, a total embargo was placed on the import of non-essential goods, and this precipitated a crisis for the firm. The position was serious and was a major reason for Richard's greater involvement

Above: Richard Quinnell in 1980.

Fortunately he was successful in selling off the porcelain branch and was then able to concentrate on developing the ironwork side of the firm. He decided to upgrade the products and concentrate on one-off commissions, restoration, and custom made architectural ironwork. This was only possible because, although the work force was small, it was highly skilled.

Restoration was always an important part of the work and the firm has probably restored more 18th century gates and screens than any other contemporary firm. There were more than a dozen really important examples, mainly in London and the home counties, including railings and balustrades at Clandon; others were further afield, as was the Bakewell screen at Chillington Hall and gates at Bowood. Much of it was for the National Trust and the Historic Buildings Department of the Greater London Council.

Many of the 18th century gates in the Ham and Richmond areas owe their continued existence to timely restoration by the Rowhurst smiths; among them those of Petersham House, Marshgate House and Ormeley Lodge. They were fulfilling commissions throughout London; there was a delightful Chinoiserie "Viewing Platform" in the grounds of Kenwood House; a bronze balustrade for the Guildhall at Kingston-upon-Thames; and a number of works for architects, Sir Basil Spence, Fitzroy Robinson and partners, and Pentagram Designs, as well as many others.

The work of the firm was always broadening; they had fabricated a sculptural sundial in Aluminium for Guildford Borough Council and the Prudential Assurance Co. Ltd; and made the National Emblem and grilles in wrought iron and aluminium for Malaysia

House and security grilles and insignia for the Kuwait Embassy, London.

Neither was their work any longer confined to this country. There was a gate for a house in Capetown; they produced the Royal Coat of Arms for the British Embassy in Rome (Sir Basil Spence) and the British Embassies in Caracas and Pretoria (H. Truscott); while there were a number of commissions for the Bahamas (Robjohn Melich and Robjohns, Clarke & Co., and Melich/ The Studio).

1975 was the year that they set in place the newly made Corona on the top of Greenwich Royal Observatory; the 19th century original having been destroyed during World War II.

The year was something of a watershed. Surprisingly perhaps, in view of all the activity and success, Richard felt that an element was missing. The ironwork that the firm made was based on traditional designs, as he said: "It never occurred to us that we could work in any other style, or initiate designs of our own—it also fitted our belief that we were the last of a breed and were working with a dying craft. I honestly thought that we were the last firm of blacksmiths in the world."

Such was his disillusionment that he felt he had wasted half his life, he felt isolated and alone, and was on the point of giving up the business. It was at this time that he was invited to America, to demonstrate at the ABANA conference. His first instinct was to say "No", then he decided to spend the second part of his life saying "Yes" to opportunities. A whole new world of smithing opened up, BABA was formed and British ironwork would shortly be set on the path of the great revival. (See "How it all began" page 33.)

As far as the firm was concerned there was also an opening up geographically. 1976 saw the beginning of a large amount of wrought ironwork for the Middle East—ornamental balustrades, stair rails and gates, and a wide variety of metalwork for royal palaces in Oman. As well as a Minaret balustrade and dome finials for a Royal Mausoleum in Jordan. With other work for Bahrain and Dubai.

The Rowhurst forge does not confine itself to forged work but also restores cast iron. Richard feels that some of the most beautiful

Above: Steel Architectural screen for the former front entrance of Unilever House, Embankment, London.

pieces ever to pass through his hands were two Winged Lions, cast in Paris at the end of the last century. They were in danger of breaking apart through internal corrosion, but were restored and now grace the portico of a villa near Venice. Nearer home, there was the "Strawberry" stair at Strawberry Hill, Twickenham, and the "Golden Gates" to Ascot racecourse.

Three members of the firm had work chosen for the "Towards the New Iron Age" exhibition at the V & A in 1982. Richard showed his newly made *Isolink* an abstract sculpture made of mild steel, hot formed and fabricated, flame metallised with zinc and painted; now installed at Sunbury Cross on the M3 west of London. Also, tongue in cheek, his quirky *Big Chicken Gate* like an enormouse piece of chicken wire. Ronald Eastman showed a section of a modern car barrier, and Ian Lamb a group of three modern forged grilles.

Ronald Eastman was born in California, USA

"... I honestly thought we were the last firm of blacksmiths in the world."

188

in 1932 and trained with Quinnell Ltd, becoming foreman blacksmith in 1961. Among more traditional works for which he has been responsible are the gates and screen for Liverpool Anglican Cathedral and the arboretum gates for Bowood House, Calne. He also made a fabricated steel archway screen, finished in bronze, red, and gold, for the former front entrance to Unilever House, Embankment, London, designed by Theo Crosby of Pentagram Design and detailed by Richard Quinnell.

Ian Lamb was born in Montrose, Scotland in 1934, and apprenticed at Richard Quinnell Ltd. He worked on the Greenwich Royal Observatory Corona and made the ship weathervane on top of the Bristol and West Building Society on Broadquay in Bristol. In 1984 he won the Addy Taylor Trophy with a fire grate of simple solid bars whose acute bending produced all one could require of an object intrinsically decorative in its formation; it was also unusual in that the inner and outer form was held in tension by the front and back rods, rather then being fixed to them.

One of his more recent works was a railing for Lancaster Magistrates' Court and an Altar base for the Roman Catholic Church of the English Martyrs in Streatham. It was designed by architect Derek L.S. Phillips. Upward curving steel arms, mirror the raised arms of a priest when elevating the sacrament, and uphold an Altar Table of a single slab of limestone. The arms were made from U shaped channel rolled to a curve and fitted together to form a 76mm square. An aluminium strip was applied to each face to give the subtle effect of moulded section. They were completed by gilding which is lit by down-lighting concealed in the stone top. A stone base stands on a richly coloured flamingo carpet and from a distance down the church, the whole Altar seems to float in space.[1]

Eamon Kenward, who worked seventeen years with the firm, spent several years on commissions in the Middle East; on one occasion with other younger members of the company, Chris Bush, John Allen and Matt Galpin. One of his balustrades was made for a house in Del Mar, California, of twisted and fitted steel sections forged and turned brass. It was painted and gold plated and measured 5m x 1m. An unusual candle bowl he showed at the 1982 BABA exhibition is shown on page 40.

Alan Puddick together with Eamon Kenward made a gate in forged and fabricated steel and steel tube for Anvil House offices for an industrial forging company in Dudley. He was awarded a bronze medal by the Worshipful Company of Blacksmiths for his restoration of the wrought iron gates to Chillington Hall, originally made by Robert Bakewell.

He was the senior member of the team of Rowhurst Forge smiths who made the Swan gates for St. Hugh's College, Oxford, for its centenary in 1986. They are situated on Canterbury Road at the entrance of a new carriage drive.

The gates were designed by Lawrence Whistler, well known as an engraver of glass. Swans are one of the emblems of St. Hugh and Whistler devised a design of singular grace and beauty. They are his first work for iron and were originally conceived as small pencil sketches. Two swans glide on water against a background of reeds, while the lower part of the gates show the reflection of the swans. The plumage, with bold swirls and flourishes, is in the style of Calligraphy—the art of beautiful writing; bringing out the firm curves and the thick and thin lines made with the pen.

A full size drawing was prepared to show the way in which the subtle lines expand and taper along their length. Applied gilding, indicated in red chalk by Whistler on the drawing, emphasised these variations. Each piece had to be hot forged by hand because every bar varied in section throughout. The many intersections between bars had to be very precisely fitted and the need for symmetry demanded extremely accurate assembly.[2]

Another member of the team is Barry Walton, the finishing specialist; he has been responsible for this very important aspect of

*Top above:
Fire grate, held in
tension, by Ian
Lamb.*

*Above: Candlestick
by Matt Galpin.*

the work for over twenty years.

In December 1982 Richard Quinnell and his wife Jeanette (Jinny) opened the *Fire and Iron Gallery* as an extension to the Rowhurst Forge showroom. For several years they laboured somewhat in the face of adversity as the M25 severed the family land and caused much disruption by its building so close to the forge. It has now become an internationally known gallery for the display of Ironwork by leading smiths from all over the world.

The establishment of the gallery led by 1985 to a new venture *The Fire and Iron Design Group*, an informal grouping of creative designer-blacksmiths working in conjunction with Richard Quinnell Ltd.

Many modern smiths lack both the work force, space and special equipment needed to produce large architectural commissions in a limited time. This becomes possible by working with Quinnells and reduces the strain on their administration, financial and production resources, while still enabling them to work in close supervision with the work they have designed.

Already by 1984 James Horrobin's screen and grille for Richmond House, Whitehall, had been produced on this basis (see page 139). Another major work made in co-operation was the Epithedron or tomb-canopy over the remains of the head shrine of St. Hugh in Lincoln Cathedral in 1986. The work was designed by David Poston, jeweller, and the main elements forged by Alan Evans (see page 107). Secret structural joints needed to join the pieces were made by Richard Quinnell Ltd who also precision machined the long tapered spires in stainless steel. It is an altogether impressive work that adds emphasis and importance to the partly ruined stonework of the shrine.

Peter Parkinson worked with Richard Quinnell Ltd for his entrance archway to a pedestrian scheme in Ivegate, Bradford in 1988, and his *Triumphal Gateway* for

Above: The Swan Gates for St. Hugh's college Oxford. Designed by Lawrence Whistler.

Reproduced by kind permission of the Principal, St. Hugh's College, Oxford.

Basingstoke in 1992. There was also collaboration for *Tree Guards* in Albert Square, Manchester: and Quinnells commissioned Peter to design the *History Tree* for Hemel Hempstead.

Jinny Quinnell died in September 1988 at the tragically early age of 47. She had done a tremendous amount to set up the early BABA conferences and gave much time and energy to furthering the craft. Her courage and bravery, over a period of three years, in coming to terms with cancer was a shining example to everyone. A Trust Fund was set up in her memory, by Richard and their children, Lucy and Peter, which provides travel bursaries for craftspeople in mid-career, and supports palliative care projects for the terminally ill.

In the following year Richard Quinnell was awarded the MBE for his services to blacksmithing which he regarded as very much an honour to them both, and to Blacksmithing as a whole.

Further collaboration by the *Fire and Iron Design Group* were the gates for Harrow Baptist Church, designed by Alan Evans (see page 108); and on the gates to the Russell-Cotes Art Gallery and Museum in Bournemouth, the decorative masks were by David Petersen.

In 1990 the United States Air Force (USAF) award was won by the Rowhurst Forge against worldwide competition. The design *concept* was by the landscape consultants, Atkins Sheppard Fidler, based on the shoulder badge of the USAF Guided missile squadron based at Molesworth, but all detailed design and practical detailing were by Richard Quinnell and John Cullin. The beast, constructed of overlaid steel plates, stands 3m high. Perhaps the Griffin is not quite as bellicose as he appears; I am told that,

secretly, in the pommel of his sword, he conceals a Campaign for Nuclear Disarmament badge.

A recent work by the Forge, designed by Cardew and Godfrey, has been low rails, in an informal style, of arches interlaced with stems and leaves for Dorchester Abbey precincts. Also the top finials, balls, and weather vanes made for the impressive classical cupolas (which house extractor fans) on Quinlan Terry's redevelopment of Richmond Riverside in west London. In the spring of 1992 angular signage was produced for the Bilton centre in Leatherhead, and gates with ironwork made by Ron Eastman and repoussé copperwork by Ian Lamb, for the Bishopsgate Institute.

Above: The 3m high Griffin at Molesworth USAF base.

Photograph © RCHME Crown Copyright.

A work I find very attractive is a *Tree of Life* made for Bournemouth Hospital Appeal on which hang golden apples bearing the names of donors; this was such a success that it was followed by two others.

During a visit to the United States in 1993 Dick Quinnell and Pauline Prowse were married *over the Anvil* by Mack Beal, Blacksmith, sculptor and Justice of the Peace. The ceremony took place in the open air at Jackson in the White Mountains of New Hampshire. The rings were forged nickel/steel Mississippi Meander Damascus, lined and rimmed with gold, made by Jim Wallace, Jim Cooper, Steve Yusko and Dick Quinnell himself. Richard has celebrated the event in his own way with a sculpture *You and I* now showing in the Fe Exhibition.

Today Richard Quinnell's daughter Lucy is in charge of the *Fire and Iron Gallery*, and the two delightful little boys to be seen running about in the garden and yards are Richard's grandsons. Already Tom the eldest, aged seven, is hammering in the forge—the wheel has turned full circle.

Sources and Notes

1. *British Blacksmith* Number 46.

2. *British Blacksmith* Number 42.

Above right: The 'History Tree', Hemel Hempstead, 1993.

Photograph Peter Parkinson.

Right: Tree for the New Bournemouth Hospital Appeal, 1989.
Photograph Richard Quinnell.

RACHEL
RECKITT

Rachel Reckitt is an artist and sculptress who came comparatively late in life to working in iron. Her father was an architect and she was born in St. Stephens near St. Albans. She is particularly well known for her wood engraving, which she studied under Ian Macnab at the Grosvenor School of Modern Art between 1933-1937.[1] She was elected a member of the Society of Wood Engravers about 1938.

Rachel is small and white haired and usually has two large dogs at her side. The last person one would expect to work in iron. She lives where she was brought up in a long house on a hill between the Brendon Hills and Blue Anchor Bay in West Somerset. It looks over rolling hills to distant moors. It was her parents who planted what is now a tremendous spreading Cedar, that fills the vista beyond the garden where fields sweep down to steep wooded valleys. They also created the Japanese Maple Garden, a riot of reds and golds all summer. It must have once been a house where the châtelaine could live in leisure and watch gardeners at work; but those days are no more.

I remember once arriving and finding Rachel shepherding a recalcitrant herd of sheep out of her front drive; another time she was carting muck. Morning and evening she walks up to the fields to check on the bullocks, her dogs at her heels. Until recently she kept a horse so that she could ride and exercise the dogs. Years ago she owned a Dingo, an Australian wild dog; terrorising the villages was one thing, but the fear of it killing sheep was another, and it had to go. After lunch you might find her resting in the old conservatory, sitting beside a window-sill of potted geraniums, bright with the sunlight streaming through their crimson petals, in front of a window that opens out into the garden, overlooking the shrubbery, and the distant Cedar. This part of the house is hung with Wisteria and double doors open on to a long narrow water-channel garden with a little pool at the end, filled with yellow Irises and a statue.

Twice a year there is a frenzy of weeding and the house and garden are opened; to local children for a party of old time dimensions, and again in early Autumn for a wine and cheese evening. This raises money for the local church, with a group of first class musicians playing outside on the terrace. Rachel is an active member of the congregation of the nearby church. She carved delightful angles on the altar screen, for which her mother made the embroideries. Later she made a brass cross for the bell turret.

Above: Outside and inside Rachel's workshop.

Between these activities she is likely to be in her little wooden workshop near the side of the house where, early in Summer, the ground near the kitchen door is bright with great clumps of satin-red Oriental Poppies, backed with the golden blossoms of Laburnum. Here, she heats the iron in a small hearth of fire brick, operated by propane; rather precariously balanced on top of an old oil drum.

It was when Harry and Jim Horrobin were working the forge at Roadwater, not far from her home, that she began to study forging and welding with them. It would not be true to say that she had never worked in metal before —but not to any extent. After leaving the School of Art Rachel made a number of Inn signs using a metal relief technique which she had to invent as she went along. She used sheet tin or aluminium mounted on wooden cores. Fifty years of wind and weather have not loosened or corroded them and they only occasionally need fresh coats of paint. Indeed in Roadwater itself can still be seen an inn sign on the wall of *The Valiant Soldier* which she made in tin when she was nineteen. There are also in her home several found-object sculptures of old plough coulters, which seem to sail like so many yachts across a smooth sea.

The large screen to the bell tower in the church at Old Cleeve was a joint project. Jim Horrobin and his students, from an evening class, made the ironwork screen, which held full length figures of the Virgin and Saints painted by Rachel. She had begun to work in strip aluminium and the figures of angels on the overthrow are early examples.

Above: One of the Angels in the church at Old Cleeve.

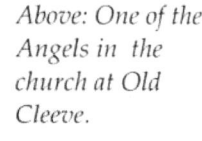

The earliest of the works in aluminium strip simply have the form built up with unchanged width of metal, on a shaped outline. Later, as she came to work with mild steel the sculptures achieved a far more descriptive form, by using sheet cut into many more varied shapes. This change can be clearly seen by contrasting the rearing horse with a horses head shown in the photographs.

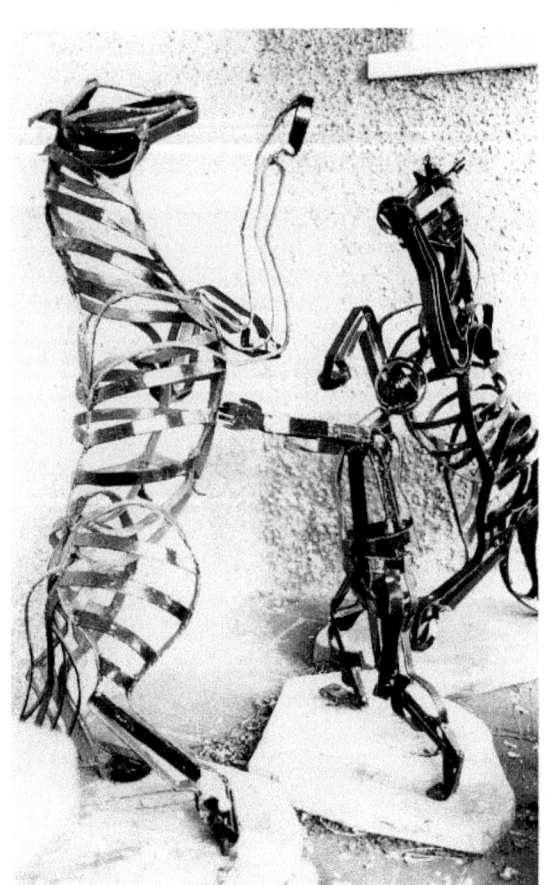

Left: A Figure with Two Horses made with aluminium strip.

Right above: "The Valiant Soldier" Inn sign.

Right: Found object "sculpture" made of plough coulters.

It was when she started building up the sculptures with pieces of mild steel sheet, shaped and forged, that her work took a great step forward. *Worshipping Figure* shown in the BABA exhibition of 1982 (see page 40) used this technique. Also about this time can be placed the *Heron* which she made for the top of a summer house in the garden; it seems to be reaching up as though just about to take off.

Rachel found she liked working with small pieces of iron, where the material is built up directly to produce an immediate result. In this it differs from sculpture using clay or

plaster where the model must pass to other hands to be cast into bronze; and of course is quite unlike wood or stone carving where the process is one of removing material rather than building it up. The making of sculptural figures in forged iron, as fine art, can so often appear facile or unconvincing, but her work could never fall into this category. It is undoubtedly her many years of study and dedication to painting and sculpture that make her metal sculptures so convincing. She knows and understands the underlying form of figures both human and animal. She would be the first to admit that her blacksmithing skills are limited. It is the veracity and creativity of her metal sculptures that lifts them into art.

In 1983 she was making rather larger figures and often using forged angle iron, as in *Woman and Child*. The following year

Above: Horseman with detail of horse's head.

Far left: Heron.

forging, intended to be enlarged as a wall mounted sign for the Nailbourne Forge, commissioned by Melvin Pinnock. The vigorous action of the smiths grew out of studies she had first made for a wood engraving after seeing Freddy Habermann and Vaclav Jaros forging.

By 1989 she was working on a larger scale still and showed *Woman Planting Rice* at the BABA exhibition. Perhaps it was the crouching figure of Eve that gave rise to this work. It was later augmented to *Three* Women *Planting Rice*; it was not high, since the figures are bent almost double, but covered a large area. Colour was also introduced into the work, a dark green on the inner sides of the black iron.

About this time she also made a very decorative statue of St. Nicholas, for a stone niche in the church of St. Nicholas at Withycombe. This was painted in bright colours and, in part, gilded.

In 1991 she used more subtle colours of russet, beige, greys and soft green for a garden statue of a life size *Roe Deer* with a rose in its mouth—apparently their favourite food! Quite large and varied flat mild steel shapes have been forged and welded to make up the hollow body, and the head looks back over its shoulder in a wonderfully enquiring way—

". . . *who* has been eating your roses!" The work was commissioned by Dick Quinnell. In 1986 several of Rachel's works had been shown in the "All Women Exhibition" at the Fire and Iron Gallery in Leatherhead.

Blacksmith which had just been completed, was shown at the BABA exhibition. She then made a group of three *Deer*, a private commission for setting in a woodland garden.

Adam Discovering Eve was completed before August 1987, two figures with a great deal of movement and an almost disturbing vivacity. Also at this time she made a relief sculpture of three blacksmiths

Left:
Woman
and child.

Right:
Saint
Nicholas.

Below:
Three
Black-
smiths.
Photograph Melvin Pinnock.

Source Note.
1. Albert Garrett *A History of British Wood Engraving.* 1978.

MICHAEL E. ROBERTS

The wonder is that Michael was ever able to become a blacksmith at all. In his late teens he spent four years in a wheelchair in hospital. One matron told him in no uncertain terms that his body would never be strong enough to even try to be a blacksmith.

Michael was born in Bolton in 1942 and his mother died soon after. Up to the age of five he was very largely looked after by his Godmother, in Bolton, whose family had a steel works in Swansea. His grandfather, who was an inventor and a very good copper metallurgist, took a great interest in him. He also loved craft work. He worked closely in his metallurgical interests with Eric Smythe and it was through this connection that at the age of 6 Michael was adopted by a Gloucestershire family, Pat and Sam Keochlin-Smythe. He grew up with another boy in the care of the family; their nephew whose father was a prisoner of War with the Japanese. Together they shared the experience of boarding school, where Michael was academically handicapped by being partly dyslexic, a condition not fully understood at that time. He was also left-handed which was then treated as being something of a crime. At sport, however, he excelled and won most of the cups on Sports Days. Towards the end of his schooldays, however, he began to be increasingly aware of great tiredness, which would later be accounted for by the development of a kidney disease.

From the time he was seventeen he was very anxious to go into metalwork, though his family thought a career in agricultural would be more appropriate. Meanwhile he went on several trips taking stock abroad; one of them to South Africa. He then spent a year in New Zealand and it was there, while herding stock on horseback, that he was finally overcome by chronic kidney disease and flown back to England. This was the beginning of the four years in a wheelchair and the complaint that still affects his life very adversely from time to time.

The head of Michael's adoptive household,

Sam Keochlin was a Swiss businessman, and Michael has written "To say that he had a great influence on my life is an understatement." Through him Michael spent five years in Switzerland, during his twenties, and for 3½ years of them trained as a welder in Basle.

During his spare time he began to visit German, Austrian and Swiss blacksmiths. He greatly appreciated the modern designs of their ironwork and was also impressed by the surroundings in which they worked.

Back in England he started the uphill work of trying to be a blacksmith; knowing that if necessary he could always fall back on his skills as a welder to earn a living, or augment, his income.

He was working in an old Nissen hut, 8ft high and 32ft long, on family land, on the Cotswolds. During the first four years in business the only metal work he could obtain was repairing farm implements and building farm trailers. Something then happened that changed the direction of his work. Foot and Mouth disease came to the farm where his Nissen hut was located and farm repair work ceased.

Then as so often happens, when one door closes another opens. While he was in Switzerland he had taken a six month course on fireplaces; now he heard of a farmer friend who had a smoking chimney. The outcome was that work making firebaskets and fireplace hoods of steel, copper or brass gradually became the mainstay of his

Above: The Anvil Barn Forge at Miserden on the Cotswolds.

197

business. He might make anything from 3 to 30 a year, varying in price from £500 to £3000 or more. He once got stuck up a chimney for 6 hours, and feels he well understands the feelings of a child Victorian chimney sweep.

Michael seems always to have been drawn to working with non-ferrous metals. He began to forge copper, brass and aluminium, but found that these metals have many requirements that are different to forging iron and steel. It was a very fustrating business. He has written: "There was more non-ferrous in burnt shards on the floor than finished pieces on the anvil. There were more than a few windows broken in the Nissen hut as I vented my frustration by throwing hammers at the windows. Strangely enough I found replacing the glass quite soothing."[1]

The reasons for most of Michael's problems are to be found in the highly complicated metallurgy of the non-ferrous metals. Copper has a natural affinity to combine with other metals with the result that today there are several hundred copper alloys commercially available. Bronzes are basically copper-tin alloys and Brass alloys are essentially copper-zinc, but there can also be inclusions of lead. In every case the make up of the alloy will affect the way in which the metal needs to be worked and what it is suitable for making. Zinc in any alloy if over heated will burn off in dangerous fumes.

Because all these metals melt at a lower temperature than iron the first and foremost requirement is that they should be worked at a lower temperature. Michael explained some of the things he has leart, the hard way, for success in forging non-ferrous metals. For instance Copper should not be too hot for working under the power hammer. Equally in working brass it is only under the flatter that one has any control over it, and because of the ease with which over plasticity can occur, fullering is harder to control and can very easily break the bar by going straight through it. All these metals are, in fact, only at the correct forging temperature for a critically short period of time.

Brass dislikes hot air coming into it; the very best way of heating non-ferrous metals is in a temperature controlled gas fired furnace.

Some brasses work easier than others. Some can be worked cold; though one should be careful of working cold brasses especially in

sheet form. One of the problems is that both Brass and Bronze can be *hot short*, that is brittle when heated. Michael found that if he forged a piece of brass on a cold anvil with a cold hammer it was likely to fall in half. To some extent this problem could be overcome by heating a longer length of bar in the hearth, than it was intended to work (thereby forming a *shock-absorber*) and using a heated anvil and hammer.

Brasses containing up to 36 per cent zinc are known as Alpha brasses and have excellent cold working qualities. Beyond 37 per cent zinc, there are the Beta brasses which have excellent hot working qualities. Muntz brass (copper 60 per cent, zinc 40 per cent; melting point 1650°F) is used for brazing rods and hot forging. When lead is added to copper-zinc alloys they become suitable for machining.[2] Hot stamping brass and best forging brass, which is a very pure metal, Delta SI or equivalent are the best to use for forging.

Today's modern phosphor bronzes have great resiliency, hardness and fatigue endurance, but they are hot short or brittle when heated beyond red heat. Special alloys are obtainable for casting.

From his years in Switzerland Michael was aware of the International Exhibitions of

Ironwork which were organised at Lindau every four or five years. He was fortunate to have work accepted for the 1974 exhibition and used most of his savings to make the trip. It was a big breakthrough for him; he was showing alongside Paul Zimmermann and other European smiths that he admired. It was the first time that most young German smiths had been allowed to exhibit; wholly free forging was not allowed, but disciplined modern work, splitting, and drifting, was encouraged. The later work of Fritz Kühn on experimental forms and his *Chicken Breast* grille (illustrated p 11 in "Towards a New Iron Age" catalogue) was a potent influence on a new generation of smiths. Michael admired, and was influenced by, the work of Achim Kühn, Hermann Gradinger, Otto Schmerler, Oscar Hafen, Peter Schindler and Water Suter; and he returned to England inspired by, but determined not just to copy the European work. He knew that he had to look for and find his own style. He did not like the decorative blacksmith work he saw being made in England in the early 60s because he felt strongly that one should make

things and shapes of the era in which one lives; though he believed our forebears were right in one thing—they made beautiful things and they made them well. [1] He was inspired by his Cotswold surroundings, the stone walls and flowers about him. Fascinated too by desert flowers, that could survive in extreme heat, and by *modern*

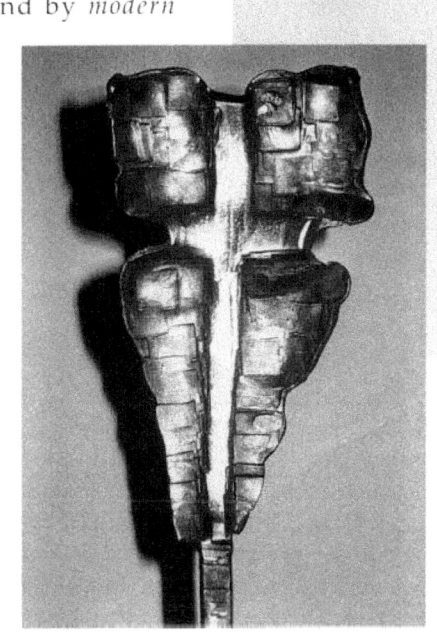

Michael Roberts

Above: Bronze Candle Sconces.

Left: Grave Marker.

Far left: The Angel Gate.

forms—the shapes of large trucks and cars.

By the end of 1975 Michael had succeeded in doing a deal with the local Squire for a derelict barn at Miserden. One of the few things it did have was an enormous three-phase transformer, just what he needed for the TIG welding. For the next five years he became a builder in his spare time—he wanted pleasant surroundings to work in, a clean shower and toilet, and a kitchen for tea breaks—in a place that looked in keeping with a Cotswold village. He can still remember the words of the planning Officer in 1975, "You're only a blacksmith Mr Roberts. What are you trying to do, build a palace?" Well, today in his beloved barn he has all the space and facilities one could need as well as a showroom and office above. There were problems about noise which led in the end to him being forbidden to open any doors or windows, so now he has four *Smog-eaters*.

Michael went to the International Conference on Forging Iron in 1980 where one of the things that most amazed him was to hear that Samuel Yellin had been forging bronze, brass and aluminium, monel and copper in the 1920s! Two things especially stand out in Michael's preferences—he most enjoys the challenge of forging in non-ferrous metals and just as he enjoys flower arranging, so he also enjoys display and arranging exhibitions. He joined BABA and over the years has done much to change the face of the associations' exhibitions—working long and tirelessly, often until exhausted, in the search after a perfect presentation. He also helped greatly with the ABANA exhibition in 1984; he went first to one of their conferences in 1982 and has been to every one since until 1992. He believes the American smiths have taught him to have fun in his work.

In the early years his staples were kitchen and fireplace utensils in brass and copper, skimmers, ladles, forks and firetools. He also made a lot of bowls and small wall plaques with incised patterns.

He particularly enjoys working with iron when it is designed to show flowers and plants to advantage. In 1983 he combined a handrail, up some garden steps, with a support for roses in a Briar Rose design. He has worked a lot for gardens and in 1985 made an Angel in bronze for Morton Court. It stands in a 500 year-old wall and is designed to be seen from inside the garden, so that the frame does not show, from which position it is particularly effective. A simple but convincing figure with just the right amount of stylisation. The base of the gate, which represents the hem of the skirt, curves forwards. In some ways he was striving towards a three dimensional effect or what he very logically prefers to call four sided.

This was also a feature he used in a pair of double gates for Aldershot in 1987-88, each leaf 8ft high x 3ft 9in wide, curves forwards at the bottom rail. He was also bearing in mind that curving produces strength just as the more curves one puts into a car body the stronger the thin shell becomes. He based the design on Elizabethan embroidery, particularly *Black Work*. Many of the motifs common in this work have been incorporated into the gate—foliage fronds, lilies, and other flowers, acorns and oak leaves.

Both sides are well finished with details, the foliage at the base for instance occurs on each side. The inner side of the uprights of the gate are scalloped and leaflike tendrils hold the edges and then, turning back on themselves, twine round the leaf and stem. The centre joining edge is scalloped in the same way as the partially *flat work* gate in the Hungerford Chapel at Farleigh Hungerford Castle. The whole gate is composed of luscious curving forms, there is not a single straight line. The cost was £19,500. For the work Michael used £4000 worth of aluminium bronze and £400

Above top of page: The 'Elizabethan' Gate. Photograph Michael Roberts

worth of abrasive wheels. Joints were electrically ground down to be invisible. Very carefull attention was given to making the gates as permanently corrosion free as possible.

In 1993 Michael made a very beautiful shell-like flower holder for Sue Artus, representing Great Britain, to use at the InterFlora World Championship in flower arranging in Sweden. For the first time in twenty-five years Great Britain was the winner, and he is now making sculptural stands for her to use in demonstrating in the U.S.A. He is also currently busy making a number of iron flower and candle table stands, each about 3ft high, for wedding receptions and banquets in Warwick Castle.

Sources and Notes.

1. Michael E Roberts—"A Profile". *British Blacksmith* 58.

2. Oppi Untracht *Metal Techniques for Craftsmen*. Robert Hale & Co. London 1969.

Michael Roberts

Above: Gates for Holt Court, 12' high and 11' wide. Each leaf weighs ³⁄4 ton. Security overthrow. Steel and gold leaf.

Below: Grave Memorial, later patinated green. The objects symbolic of the life story of the person.

Michael Roberts

ANTONY ROBINSON

Left: Antony Robinson just after finishing the Winchester Gates.

Antony Robinson was born in April 1935 in Earley, near Reading, Berkshire. When he was thirteen the family emigrated to Australia where they lived near Melbourne. After he completed his schooling he was apprenticed to a plumber. This was when his association with metal began ". . . I soon came to enjoy immensely working with lead, knocking up the most complex shapes for roofwork." It was at this time also that he began to learn the art of sheet metal development and worked in sheet copper and steel.[1]

In 1958 he returned to England and in the following year met and married his wife Marie, to whom he is deeply devoted. They have four children, two boys and two girls. He soon found that plumbing was not a very exciting job in this country and took various other work connected with metals. He worked for the aircraft manufacturers Handley Page, and for Hoffmann and Burton in Henley.

In 1964 he began to learn a new trade as a blacksmith with Bob Bridgeland near Reading. He also went on a CoSIRA course under the direction of Pat Collins, and later studied with Tommy Tucker. It was a brave move as his children were young and he was still trying to establish a stable life for his family. He had been making ornamental ironwork for six years by the time he started his own business at Mortimer, near Reading, in 1970. Five years later he moved to his present house and forge at Stanton-upon-Hine-Heath, Shropshire.

Tony's grandfather had been a blacksmith on the Great Western Railway and he firmly believes that in coming to blacksmithing he had entered on his ancestral craft. His father had been a man of considerable ability and boundless creativity. So it was that he began to feel he was finally coming to his true development.

In 1974 his eye was caught by a magazine article which mentioned that there were no new designs for gates, though this was referring to wooden gates. It certainly started a train of thought because that same evening he drew up three new designs for forged steel gates. He decided to abandon the traditional smithing forms that he had been taught. He wanted his designs to be on a completely new basis—they had to have a meaning for their existence. This was a concept that was almost unheard of in this country at that time.[2]

"My first gate therefore had to be the beginning. It also had to symbolise the basic structure of a man, in fact myself. This gate was impossible to realise until 1980, when I made it for the Lindau Exhibition. The other two designs I drew up that evening were an even further breakaway. They were the first signs, as with the Lindau gate, of my inhibitions being broken down. These made another mental gateway through which I passed. Venturing into this unknown territory was for me exciting, and the fustration at not being able to realize these designs then was unbearable."

The second gate design used plant forms, the female figure, and contemporary variations on traditional techniques, and the third design included bronze plaques let into the structure. At this time Tony had no knowledge of contemporary development of forged metal design in Europe or elsewhere, and it was not until he attended the Experimental Workshop in Hereford in 1979 that he realised these three designs were sound. Here he saw modern ironwork for the first time, and was brought into contact with other smiths who were putting new meaning into their work. When

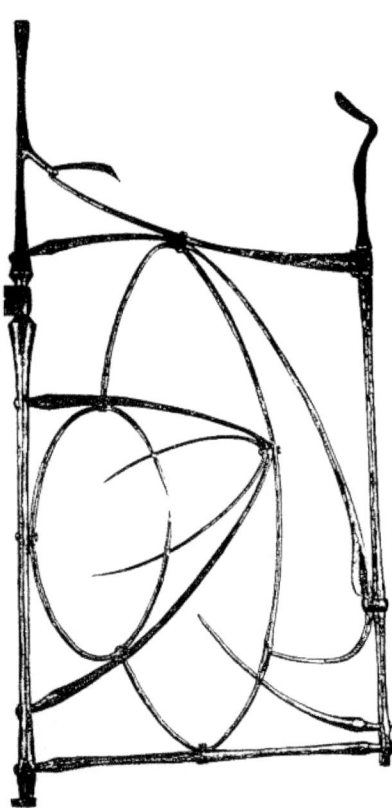

Above: The symbolic 'Man' gate made for the Lindau exhibition in 1980.

he heard Simon Benetton talking about the art of iron he was deeply moved—even to tears. The following year at the International Forging Iron Conference he was a flamboyant figure, in his colourful *Magicians* waistcoat, and his work was firmly moving into modern design.

He has always been fascinated by the bright quality of stainless steel and some of his earliest modern works were flowers forged out of this metal. Not flowers as earlier blacksmiths had made them—these he usually stuck, on long stems, in groups into the grass, where the petals were so filled with movement and life, that they seemed to flutter, like silken poppies, in the wind. He is on record[1] as remembering Simon Benetton speaking of *the flowers in the field*, so perhaps there is a connection here—his art is always indivisable from his philosophy and his emotions. Philosophy, music and religion are key elements in his work as in his life.

It was also now that he began to make candlesticks, which had all the grace of nature, where steel twisted into leaves. He made abstract sculptures and forms that seemed to have an element of the human; but this was to be on-going and really developed over the next few years.

In 1980 he was invited to enter the limited competition to design gates for the V & A gallery. As the gates were to be situated between the music and ironwork galleries his design expressed "the renaissance of the spirit of mankind through music and metalwork". He incorporated female figures in the frames and bird and tree forms in the jambs and lintel. But this is history and we know that the commission went to Jim Horrobin with a very different design.

It was only a year later that he was again invited to take part in a limited competition. This time it was by the Hampshire County Council and they wanted a design for gates, with grilles above, to fill two pointed archways in the great Hall of Winchester Castle. They led into the adjoining newly built Crown Court and were to commemorate the wedding of Lady Diana Spencer to H.R.H. Prince Charles.

It was a tremendously important moment for him in more ways than one. Not only did the subject strike a cord in his emotional and philosophical outlook, but on a more mundane level, making experimental sculptures and entering competitions was not paying the grocery bills.

"I knew that this was it, that with this competition I should make it, or be finished with forging as I had had no work of any consequence for over 18 months and was ready to sell up. So from the very beginning the Winchester job had a special meaning and was, I believe, a true answer to my prayers.

"The design evolved in two ways; first the unusual experience of thinking of the main design motif while speaking with Michael Morris, the architect, on the telephone. This was a coincidence, because on visiting the Hall for the first time to see what was involved, I found the design almost identical in shape, painted all over the wall by the archways. The second was about two months of working the design out and preparing the maquette, and folio of drawings. These drawings were window mounted on board, and enclosed between stainless steel covers with brass hinges and clasps. This reflected the medieval history of the Hall with the late twentieth century Court. Preparing all this called for much disciplining of my impulsive nature. The design was chosen, and between tears of relief and joy I offered a prayer of thanks. The strain had been intolerable."[2]

In 1983 I knew that Tony was at work on the gates and I asked if I could call and see them. So it was that one day in the Spring ". . . I drove north into Shropshire. After the Motorway, country roads gave way to narrow lanes leading into the heart of the countryside. Stanton-upon-Hine-Heath was hardly more than a group of houses. I stopped at the village shop to enquire the way to the Blacksmiths—round the corner down a mud strewn lane past a farmyard; I knew I had arrived when I saw a garden planted with angular figures and forms of iron rising above the hedge. Confirmation appeared in the shape of an extraordinary door in an old stone building. Its wood was encrusted with years of paint, peeling away like the textured bark of a tree. The door was surrounded with a frame of beaten copper, and boasted a

Above: "An extraordinary old door . . . its wood encrusted with years of paint peeling away like the textured bark of a tree . . . surrounded with a frame of beaten copper . . . and a handle forged into strange shapes . . ."

handle of enormous dimensions, forged into strange shapes made from some piece of rusting iron which had once formed part of an agricultural machine. The door was locked and the key long since lost, so Tony Robinson led me into his spacious forge through large sliding doors at the back. No cobwebs or dust in this workshop, most of the tools by the hearth gleamed as brightly polished as silver, and the protective cover of the power hammer was characteristically and carefully shaped and ornamented into a pattern. Tony Robinson's workshop epitomises the thought and care which goes into his work.

"Much of the shop was taken up by two leaves of a gate, each 14 feet long, lying flat on trestles; while standing up as high as a man, a semi-circular shaped fabrication of steel, pointed at the top, reflected back the warm glow that gleamed from the hearth fire and the light from the shining tools. Tony was about half way into making two pairs of gates for Winchester Great Hall. By installation, Autumn of 1983, he would have laboured almost two years—two summers and one winter.

"A visionary he may be, but only a man with his feet firmly on the ground could have completed the immense workload the gates represent. He determined to create them not in mild but in stainless steel, some six times more expensive and needing nearly three or four times more physical effort to work. He chose the metal because he felt the situation, the finest medieval aisled hall in the country, demanded the best—a jewel-like quality in the material of the 20th century. He believed, even if no maintenance were carried out, they would last a thousand years—a fitting work for the ancient town of Winchester, where in the cathedral the St. Swithin gates are the earliest surviving iron grilles in Europe.

"The concept, the design and most of the work was Tony Robinson's, but he did have occasional voluntary help from other friends; from Freddi Brandli, a Swiss; and Peter Duis and Franz Taucher, German smiths. Both the Robinson sons, Edmund and Simon, gave a lot of assistance, and even his wife, Marie, was called upon to help with the oxy-propane torch in the later stages.

"Each gate weighs almost fifteen hundred weight. The first job was to forge all the vertical elements of the design from 4" x ½" and 4" x ¾" bars which had been sheared

from plates. Only about 18 inches in each seven foot length could be heated at one time and forged on the Goliath Power Hammer. The verticals on the hinge sides of the gate were curved into deep channels and house the pivots. These gave more trouble than any other part of the gates; the length being such that it was difficult to keep the vertical straight, there was a distinct natural tendency to twist. The channels and the moulded form at the base were formed in specially made swages with round bars of various diameters to act as top tools beneath the force of the sledge hammers. A kind of basic repoussé work in ¼" plate!

"The front edge of the verticals facing the centre of the gates was diagonally cut into with a 9" Wolf angle-grinder, and forged upwards to hold more than 400 scroll shapes which form the chief element of the design. This was achieved by electric arc welding and

204

These were welded together and form the pattern to the back of the grille. In front of these ovals, a series of vanes or wing shapes beaten from 14 gauge sheet culminate into a central form where the two meeting triangular shapes have been opened out into the initials C and D (for Charles and Diana) and the date 1981."

"The design on the back of the gates is quite different from the front, with verticals of the framing forming the dominant pattern. Throughout the gate, welds are placed, in almost a butterfly pattern, to give added strength to the whole. The gates swing on taper roller bearings in the Purbeck marble steps and Nylotron bushes at the top of the transomes of the grilles.

"The long tapered handles are 11'6" long, forged from 2" round steel. After the birth of Prince William, Tony Robinson made a key (to operate the lock) in the form of a trumpet incorporating the initials of all the Prince's names into a pattern at the top."

"Antony Robinson sought to make ironwork for the year 2000 and in some indefinable way he has succeeded. While the gates are completely in sympathy with their medieval surroundings and in some ways reflect the ironwork of that period, there are elements which are

produced textured discs which considerably enhance the impact of the design and are in some ways reminiscent of the small moulded or swaged, decorative features used on medieval iron grilles. (See illustration on right.) The scroll shapes, which fill the front of the gates, change in emphasis as they rise and grow larger and more leaf-like, sweeping upwards and outwards, as they near the top. Above, fixed metal grilles fill the pointed arches of the openings. The background to this area is formed of ovals of 1½ " x ¾" steel made into a loop on the brick, welded and then placed under the power hammer to slightly flatten—especially towards the ends.

compatible with the space age. The great triangular shapes, like shields (or as the Medieval mind would have said the wings of angels), which fan out across the tympanum would not be out of place in some space age odyssey. They are majestic gates for a processional way which epitomise not only earthly power but spiritual aspirations. These are gates we need not be ashamed to have produced in the same age that saw man first walk upon the moon. Perhaps the most surprising thing of all is that this massive work came not from some large business with many workers but from one man's tiny country forge."[3]

"The gates proved to be far more expensive and the work far harder than Tony could have anticipated. But he was much assisted by British Steel who, on seeing the completed job, donated the materials. Another important contribution was from E.S.A.B., the international welding company, who supplied a seemingly never ending supply of free consumables. The work of forging the stainless steel was immense, both power hammer and men were working to their limits. The three-dimensional forging at the base of the gates had to be done by hand, which meant that two strikers would be working at full swing while taking the whole blast of heat from a white fire about 2' 3" square. As each part was made it had to be ground and polished. Once he was able to look back on the work, Tony has said: "The memory here is one of constant maximum pressure hour after hour, day after day . . . ."

"The trickiest job of all was to get everything square and true. I found with all the precautions taken and checks done again and again, when the gates were released from the jig they twisted a little. The stainless, when forged and fitted in the way it was done, only concedes what it thinks it will, and retains it's own identity. So we both worked together, each giving a lot to each other and yet determined to retain something of our original selves. With all seriousness this involvement with my material is total . . . ."

"The grilles are fixed in the arches with Rawlock bolts, 8 to each grille. The grilles were hoisted by block and tackle and bolted up a couple of weeks before the gates were taken to the Hall. The gates were installed in a matter of a few hours with the computer aided forklifts from Lansings of Basingstoke; very professional and precise. All I needed to do was assemble the bearings and bolt up the hinge pins. We all then just stood back and looked and looked.

"The whole work is in reality two different sets of gates and grilles as viewed from two buildings. I knew this had to be so at the beginning. I should like to mention here the work done by Michael Morris was lacking in no detail and he was the perfect link man, organiser and backup etc., extremely cool and calm. Just what I needed . . . ."[2]

The Worshipful Company of Blacksmiths awarded one of their rare Silver Medals to Antony Robinson for his achievement. Delegates to the BABA conference at Farnham in 1983 were taken to see the Winchester Gates and Alan Dawson has written: "The highlight was certainly the trip to Winchester to see Tony Robinson's magnificent gates in the Great Hall. We all entered the dim interior and stood in awe as the gates were revealed in all their glory as the lights were raised like a sunrise." [2]

Whereas the straight lines of the verticals of the Winchester Gates are visible from the back this shows very little from the front, and this is characteristic of all Tony's works. Apart from a few designs for railings, one length of which was shown in the Six British Blacksmiths Exhibition in 1982, one is hard put to find any straight lines in most of his work—all are graceful flowing curves. I have already mentioned that he was beginning to make things based on leaf forms, and this was something that evolved from 1982 onwards.

He made bowls of stainless steel which took their form from individual leaves. The one shown in the BABA exhibition for 1983, still seems to me the most beautiful of bowls—the forged rough inner surface contrasting with the smooth shiny brilliance of the edge and the leaf stem curving over into the most graceful of handles. It is indeed an exquisite work of art.

Under his hands the human form became gradually capable of metamorphosis, growing out of the curving form of leaves or wings.

He seems to have been fascinated by the concept of *Winged Victory* and a series of sculptures at the time played upon that theme. As early as 1982 there began to be simple C shapes whose upper part divided into wing forms; and in the following year there was a similar sculpture but with more refining of

Left: Railing made in 1982 with rarely used straight bars.

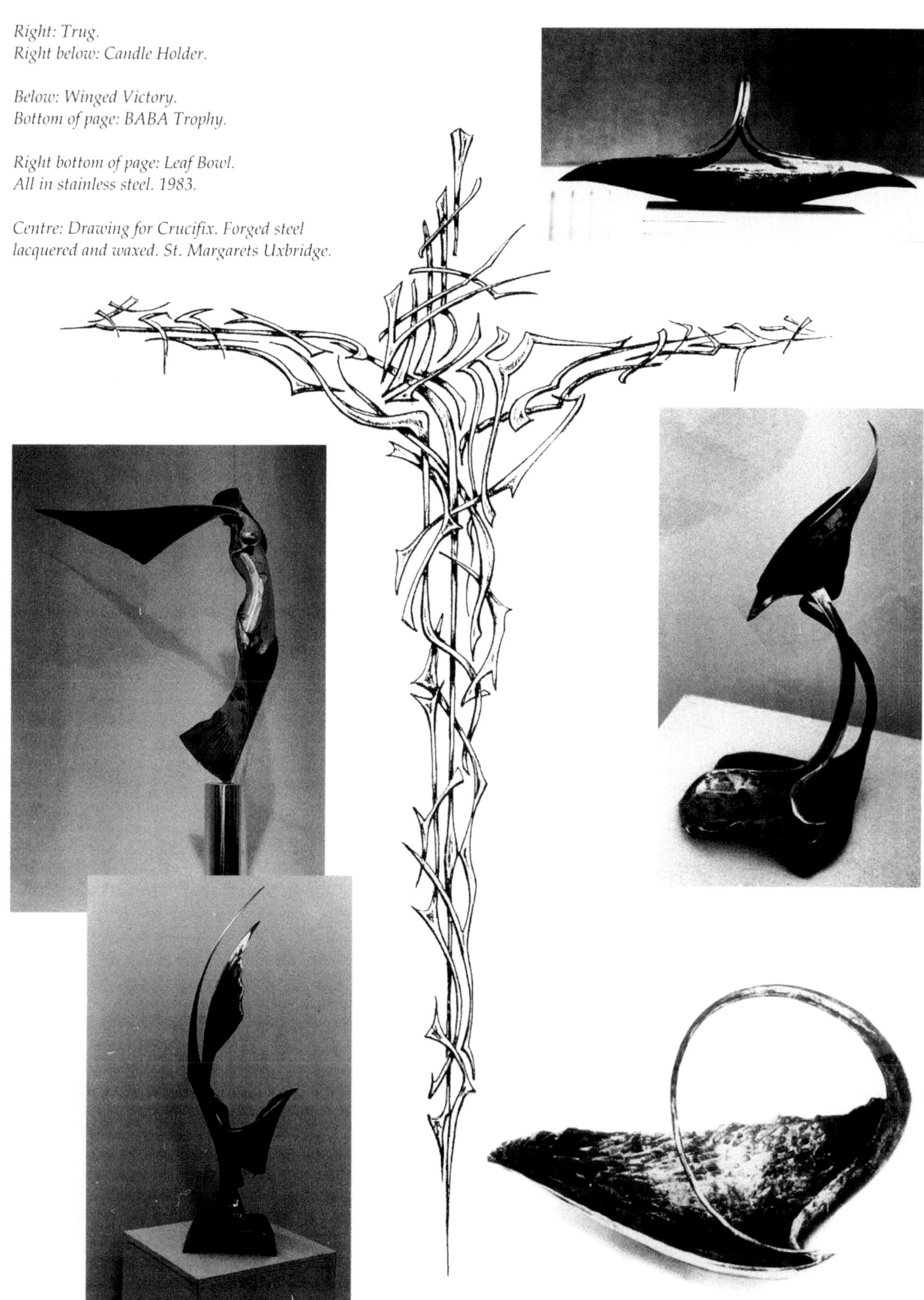

Right: Trug.
Right below: Candle Holder.

Below: Winged Victory.
Bottom of page: BABA Trophy.

Right bottom of page: Leaf Bowl.
All in stainless steel. 1983.

Centre: Drawing for Crucifix. Forged steel
lacquered and waxed. St. Margarets Uxbridge.

the firm elegant gleaming shapes, more apparent movement in the steel. The trophy made for BABA in 1984 seemed a combination of the leaf and human victory forms. A small *Torso* was made for Rachel Reckitt and an enormous *Winged Torso* was forged as a demonstration piece for ABANA in 1984. The large graceful sculpture *Auferstehung*, which literally translates to "Thou shalt rise again", made for the Friedrichshafen Exhibition was also part of the winged victory theme. Always these pieces were made in the most intractable of materials—stainless steel. The Friedrichshafen Town Council purchased this sculpture and it still stands at the edge of the lake. It represents the victory of eternal life over death, and is closely linked in the makers mind with Mahler's Second Symphony.

This was also the metal that he used when in 1989 he made *Our Lady Queen of Peace*, an imposing eight foot high figure that was made for an exhibition in the ruins of Much Wenlock Priory. It is a subtle concept, as if a cloak wraps round an invisible figure. Only stylised hands in benison are clearly portrayed. Where the face would be the shadows of the cloak hood cast its non-existence into darkness.

The stainless steel, used for the Virgin, symbolises her purity; she stands on a serpent crushing it beneath her feet, as he coils about the scrap metal plinth, representing the chaos of the world. This sculpture is now in Tewkesbury Abbey, at the far eastern end, opposite the blocked up doorway that was once the entrance to the Lady Chapel.

Tony would dearly love to have won the commission for a work in Hereford Cathedral. A Christ in Majesty that would have soared above the newly sited Altar table, on crossed arches whose outer ends would have been fastened on each of the four pillars of the crossing. The figure, of stainless steel, would have been some fifteen feet high, looking down into the Nave, with downward outstretched arms; while behind it candle-flame shaped rays would have centred, like a halo on the head, with narrow beam spot lights highlighting the representational face. He saw it as evoking in the Cathedral the presence of the Holy Spirit; something which the late Bishop John Eastaugh felt was lacking and who, before his death in 1988, spoke of the need for a prominent representation of joy in the Cathedral. He put so much thought and

prayer into the design that he was devastated when it was not chosen—because it was thought to be too powerful.

Perhaps he is most fulfilled when working on ecclesiastic commissions, but when there is no religious theme it is his philosophy that inspires his work.

In 1983, assisted by his son Simon, he made the *Eternity Gates* for Dudmaston House, Shropshire. It leads from the garden into the former stable yard and was commissioned by Sir John and Lady Labouchere at the time of their Ruby wedding anniversary. They have a great interest in modern art and there are many fine paintings and sculptures inside the house.

In the design for the gates Tony Robinson sought to show "the world we live in and its place in God's creation—the Universe with its ever increasing circles". Curving lines grow up on each side, like a tree of life, and plant forms sweep over at the top in reference to Lady Labouchere's great love—the garden. The close set bars at the centre represent the pathway of life and rise up with "a tunnel-like feature at the top centre, indicating the time of transition from this temporal earth to the spiritual life after death". [4] These gates are, perhaps of all his work, his favourite. He found great empathy with Lady Labouchere who appreciated the meaning of the gate even before he had explained his pencil drawing. Seldom can there have been such

Below: The "Eternity Gates at Dudmaston".

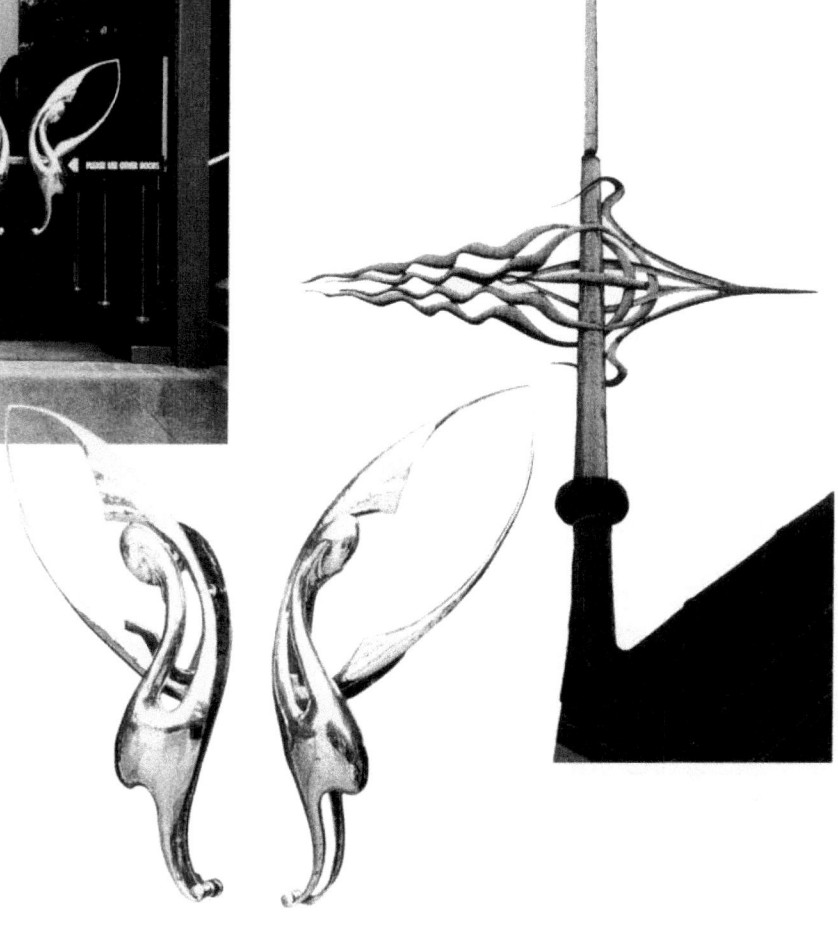

rapport between the person who commissioned the work and the artist who made it. The gates are sparingly gilded and are now showing a soft bloom of spring green algae on some of its forms, which adds considerably to the effect. Tony was so anxious that nothing should break the smooth sweep of the design that the dropbolts are concealed behind the backstyles, and can only be seen from the back.

Nearby, in the garden is his sculpture made entirely of wrought iron from "Blist's Hill", with an *Oliver hammer* thrown in for good measure. It symbolises the town of Ironbridge, which is not far distant, and its history; not only are the old industries of Coalbrookedale remembered but there is also the indication of a resurgence of a positive future.

In 1986 Tony made massive door-handles and two weathervanes for the Swan Theatre in Stratford-on-Avon. He was a brilliant choice for the commission and the graceful swan-like shapes of the handles are absolutely typical of his style; while the rippling shapes of the weathervanes mirror the gently moving waters of the nearby river Avon.

It was 1990 that saw the making of a very fine screen *The Oceanides Screen* for a private commission at Lake Bluff, Illinois, U.S.A. It is a powerful wave design showing the curving surf of an incoming wave and the dragging out of receding water. It is 25ft long and between 6'6" high at the front end and 8' at the other. It took about five months to complete the work and install it on site. It has a unique sliding mechanism, moving on a

Above: The Door Handles for the Swan Theatre, Stratford, with detail.
Top Right: One of the two weathervanes for the same theatre.

kind of trolley below ground, and a front castor wheel fitted to prevent digging in under the weight of snow and ice. (See page 210.)

Strongly idealological Antony Robinson binds his work closely into his religion and his philosophy of life. The grace of his forms and the rich gleam of his chosen metal combine to give his work a rare and exquisite quality.

Sources and Notes.
1. "Profile—Antony Robinson". *British Blacksmith* 19.

2. Antony Robinson "The Winchester Great Hall Gates". *British Blacksmith* 28.

3. Amina Chatwin "Anthony Robinson's Winchester Gates". *The Anvil's Ring* Vol.12 No 3.

4. Personal communication.

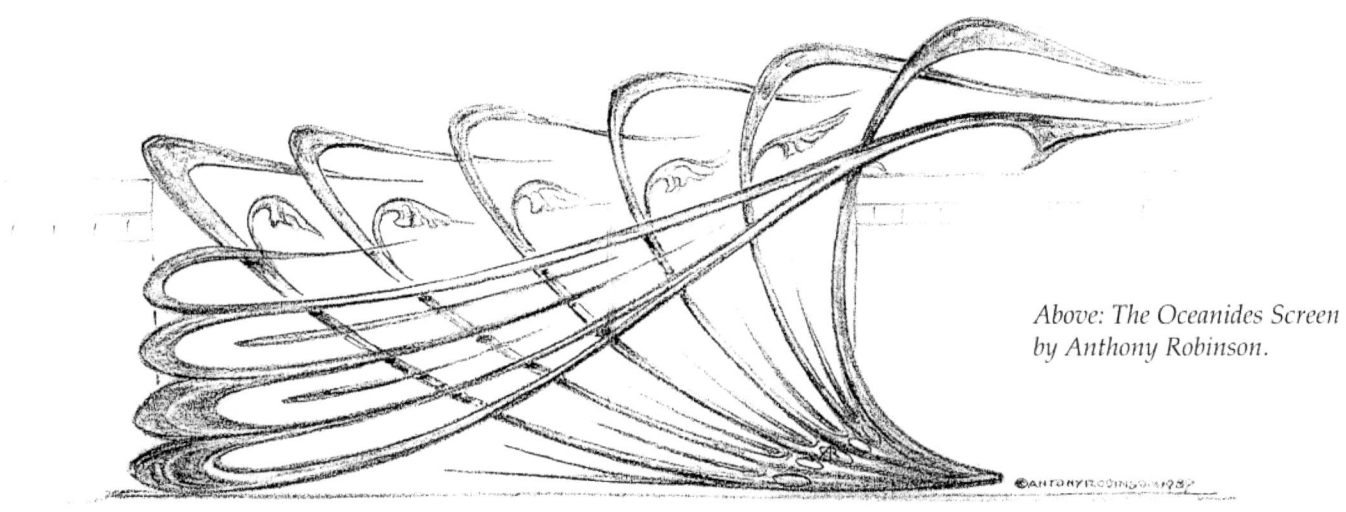

Above: The Oceanides Screen by Anthony Robinson.

INDEX

ABANA 33 113 121 133 159 167 188 200 208
Adam brothers 5
Adamson Lesley 140
Age of the Locksmith 2 74
Ahrends Burton and Kokalek 126
Albert Square Manchester 165
All Women Exhibition 196
Allen John 189
Allied Ironfounders 162
Allied Steel and Wire 171
Altab Ali Arch Whitechapel 171
Andrews Jack 24
Angle Iron deflected 119
Anglo European College of Chiropractice 144
Anvil House Offices Dudley 189
Art College Forgery 166
Art Deco 9 10 103 136
Art Nouveau 7 8 10 17 69 99
Arts & Crafts Movement 10 11 14 111
Arup Associates 135
Asda Store Roehampton 124
Ashbee Charles Robert 13 14
Association of Artist and Designers in Wales 168
Atkins Sheppard Fidler 191
BABA 92 130 149
BABA Conference 1982 Farnham 168
BABA Conference 1983 Farnham 155
BABA Conferences 1982-4 Farnham 164
BABA Conference 1984 Farnham 169
BABA Conference 1985 Coalbrookedale 45
BABA Conference 1987 Hereford
BABA Conference 1989 Cardiff 49 171
BABA Exhibition 1982 38 94 189 195
BABA Exhibition 1983 41
BABA Exhibitions 200
BABA Farnham 174
BABA Foundation week-end 155
BABA trophy 68 208
Back-blast forge 82
Bailey Ivan 26
Bainbridge-Reynolds W 11 13 34

Bakewell Robert 4 62 187
Barber Ryan 144 147
Barbican 62
Basildon Park 90
Basingstoke Gateway 166 191
Bath and West Show 68
Beal Mack 192
Bealer Alex 33
Beaven & Sons Gloucester 106
Bede College 69
Belfry Golf Club 159
Belfry Hotel Wishaw 103
Bellows design (simple) 68
Belmont Abbey 171
Benetton Antonio 29 148
Benetton Simon 30 36 203
Benettons 77 119
Bennie Elspeth 52
Bent Richard 61-63
Bergmeister Manfred 72 148
Beursplein 10 12
Bidgood Jane 144-6
Bilton Centre Leatherhead 181
Bishop Auckland Town Hall 70 71
Bishopsgate Institute 191
Black Hamish 50 77
Black Sean 149 152
Blackie Walter W. 20
Blair Claude 34 37
Blist's Hill 46
Bollards 70 124
Booth Adam 21 61 64
Borders Regional Council 66
Bottom-blast forge 82
Bournemouth Hospital Appeal 192
Bournville Art College 68
Bowood House 187
Bradmore House 147
Brandli Freddi 204
Brandt Edgar 10
Braque 75
Brasses 198
Bredohl Manfred 45 50
Bridgend Roman Catholic Church 117
Brighton Pavilion 102
Brimsfield Glos. Gates 107

Bristol and West Building Bristol 189
Bristol University 140
British Artist Blacksmiths Exhibition 168
British Blacksmith 174 175
British Embassy Caracas 188
British Embassy Rome 188
British Embassy Pretoria 188
British Forged Metal Sculpture 50
British Gas 173
British Library Competition 166
British Steel 173 206
Broadgate Development 110 111
Broadlands Estate 159
Broadway Centre Hammersmith 147
Broome Manor Golf Complex Swindon 160
Bruno's Wine Bar Whitehaven 93
Building Centre 37 62
Building Design Partnership 127
Builth Wells 62 63
Bulmer's Cider factory 183
Burrell Heather 54
Burton Richard 126
Bush Chris 189
Butler Reg 76
Cadbury Schweppes plc Dublin 186
Calder Alexander 76
Cambell Marion 37
Camberley Shopping Centre 102
Canary Wharf 145
Canterbury Centre 175
Capel Garmon Fire Irons 1
Capel Garmon Fire Irons replicas 173
Capricorn Architectural Ironworks & Design 56 58
Car barriers 125
Car Park Cupar Fife 53
Cardew and Godfrey 191
Cardiff Bay Development 50 115
Carillon Court Ealing 143
Caro Anthony 50
Carter Ron 36
Casson Sir Hugh 111 157
Cast iron restoration 188
Castle Park Bristol 113
Cauldron Chains 1

Caversham Hotel Reading 103
Celtic Film Festival 173
Ceolfrith Gallery 32 132 140
Chanel Perfume 184
Championship Challenge Trophy 68
Chapman Taylor Partners 166
Charles Rennie Mackintosh Society 20 23
Charleston Gazette 122
Chatsworth 1 151
Chattanooga Foundation 24
Chelmsford Cathedral 142
Chelsea Flower Show 140
Cheltenham Art Gallery & Museum 81 111
Chester 3
Chichester Cathedral 1
Chillida Eduardo 75
Chillington Hall 187
Chop and bend technique 107
Chop and twist technique 109 110
Churchill Hotel London 96 101
Churchill Travelling Fellowship 152
City and County Museum Lincoln 67
City Park Manchester 170
Clandon Park 90
Clark Terrence 39 42 46 52 86-91 105 112
    159 179
Claydon Architectural Metalwork 12
Claydon Clamp and Connection 121
Clayon Knot 123
Clayson Richard and Andrew Garrett 174
Cleveland Arts 167
Cleveland Gallery 124
Coalbrookedale 140
Colbert Ivan Yates 54
Cole Hector 32 36 45 46
Commonwealth Development Office 166
Compangnons de Devoir 26
Computer use 114 127 146 161
Conference 162
Coode Julian 44 46 88 179
Cooper Jim 192
Copper 198
Corbusier Le 79
Cordaroy Bill 43 52 54
CoSIRA 34 92 94 119 149 202
Cossons Neil 34
County Agricultural Shows 62
Crafts Council 104 140
Cranleigh School 159
Cranston Catherine 15
Creed John 61 66 76
Crosby Theo. 101 169 189 189
Crowcombe Church 129
Crown Reach Development 133
Crownshaw Peter 58
Crummy Mike 58
Cullin John 191
Cupernham Junior School 62
Cwmbran Gwent Square 169
CZWG 128
Daily Express Building 101
Davies Brothers 140
Dawes Brian 97
Dawson Alan 32 35 38-9 42 45 55 66 92-
    103 206
Dawson Nelson 11
Day Colin 36
Day Frank 129
Debenham House 13

Department of Transport specification 126
Derby arch 167
Design and the Blacksmith 164
Design Solution 97
Donelly John 187
Dorchester Abbey 191
Dorchester Hotel 103
Dorman Long Steelworks 69
Dorothea Restoration 136
Dorset Craft Guild 150
Dorset Rise Blackfriars 143
Doverhay Studios Porlock 136
Dudesek Jan 44 45
Dudmaston House 208
Duis Peter 204
Dyfed College of Art 168
East Kent Astronomical Society 178
Eastaugh Bishop John 208
Eastman Ronald 188-189 191
Ebbw Vale Garden Centre 173
Ecumenical Church Milton Keynes 112
Edinburgh Festival Fringe 52
Edinburgh Market Street 65
Edinburgh Playhouse Theatre 65
Edinburgh Scottish Gallery 66
Edney William 4
Edward IV Chantry 3
Edwards George 34
EEC Crafts Exhibition 64
Eleanor Grille 2
Elsom, Pack and Roberts 141 147
Elstead Forge 155
Elwood A.W. 34
Emm M 40
English Martyrs Church Streatham 189
Estonia etc 52
Euro-Disneyland 181
Evans Alan 32 33 36 79 81 95 104-116
Exhibition at Pezenas 77
Experimental Workshop at Hereford 202
Farrell Terry 126
Fe Exhibition 53 192
Feddon Matthew 58 111
Federal Reserve Bank 24
Festival of Light 51
Finnegan Jimmy 65
Fire and Iron Design Group 190 191
Fire and Iron Gallery 36 52 101 190 192
    196
Fireworks Exhibition 52 64
First International Festival of Iron Cardiff
    64 159 166 171 159
First World Congress of Artist Blacksmiths
    Aachen 153
Fitzroy Robinson and Partners 187
Flat bars squeezed 119
Floch le Igor 50
Fly-press use 124
Foreshore Development South Shields 101
Forge-ins 50
Forging between plates 156
Forging Contacts Exhibition 62
Forging Links Competition 64
Forging On Exhibition 66
Fortune Tim 41-43 46-47 57
Fountain Screen 3
Frank Hooker School 174
Friedrich Christoph 50
Friedrichafen Exhibition 208

Frodingham Steelworks 51
Frost Cara 55
Fuller Mark 178
Galpin Matt 43 189
Gardner John Starkie 11
Gardner Starkie Ltd 134
Gardom John 4
Garnier Pierre 10
Gas Forges 82
Gaudi Antonio 8 9 148
Geddes Sir Patrick 21
Gerakaris Demitri 48
Gili Katharine 50
Gimson 112
Glades Bromley 102
Glasgow Garden Festival 64
Glasgow School of Art 7 13 15-22 52 66
Gonzalez Julio 75
Goodden Robert 23
Gosport Borough Council 62
Gough H.R. 11
Gradinger Herman 36 140 140
Great Yorkshire Showground 50 52
Gressenhall Rural Life Museum 52
Griffiths Derek 40 54
Grosvenor School of Modern Art 193
Grunewald Theo. 46 117-118
Guard's Chapel St Pauls Cathedral 43
Guardian Royal Exchange 95
Guest Keen and Nettlefolds 168
Guha Saraj 46 59
Guild of Master Craftsmen 186
Guildford Cathedral 91
Guildford Borough Council 187
Guildford School of Art 162
Guildhall London 62
Guimard Hector 8 99
Gwent College of Higher Education 168
Gwylt Alan 32 33
H R H The Prince of Wales 36 97 203
Habermann Alfred 29 36 42 44 49
Habermann Alfred Jun. 47
Habermann Vera 47
Hafen Oscar 45 199
Hammer Warming 112
Hampshire County Council 203
Hampton Court Palace 3 4 160
Handicraft Guild of 13
Handley Page 202
Harrow School of Art 168
Hatchlands Park 90
Havinden Jolyon 53
Hawkins David 56
Hawkins Neil 56
Heavy Metal Exhibition 62
Hefaiston 90 153
Hemel Hempstead History Tree 167 191
Henry V Chapel Westminster Abbey 2 74
Henshaw Charles 65
Hepworth Barbara 112
Hereford Cathedral 208
Hereford College of Art 183
Hereford College of Technology 23 62 64
Hess Dominic 136
Higgins Ney Design Unit 104
Hill House Helensburgh 20
Hill John 58
Hill Stuart 32 33 35-6 119-128
Historic Buildings Council GLC 187

Historical Metallurgy Society 23
Hobbs Robert 83
Hoffmann and Burton Henley 202
Hofi Uri 50
Holy Redeemer Church Pershore108
Holy Trinity Brompton 108
Holy Trinity Sloane Street 11 12
Holzbacher Werner 155
Honeyman & Keppie 15
Hopper Graeme 54
Horrobin Harry 129 193
Horrobin James 30 32 33 36 38 44 79 82
    112 129-137 168 190 193 203
Horta Victor 8 32
Horvath Jaques 134
House for an Art Lover 22
Hughes Tom 43
Hungerford Castle 200
Hunter Price Partnership 89
Huntings Industrial Coatings Ltd 173
Hutchinson Lord 157
Hutchison Robert 53
Hyde Park Corner 145
In Business Challenge 64
Innes John 110
Inspiration and Context exhibition 78
Institute of Chartered Accountants 157 158
International Centre for Wildlife Art 139
International Conference on Forging Iron 23
    32 66 92 132 140 150 168 199 203
International Exhibition of Ironwork
    Friedrichschafen 153
International Experimental Workshop 36
Ironbridge Gorge Museum 30 45 140 140
Ivegate Bradford Arch 166 190
J.C.Bamford Ltd Uttoxeter 185-186
Jack Alan 138-9
James David 46 47 49
Jaros Vaclav 29 36 42 44
Jarrow Church 74
Jobst Arno 133
Johnson & Co. 53
Johnson Philip 52 61 65
Johnson Roger 2
Johnson Shona 52 65
Joist Sculptures 108
Jong de 10
Joyce Tom 45
Jubilee Sculpture New Palace Yard 184
    185
Jujol Jose. Ma. 9
Keith George 97
Kensington Palace Barracks 127
Kenward Eamonn 40 60 189
Kenwood House 187
Keochlin-Smythe Pat and Sam 197
Kilner Lennox 55
Kindersley 159
King Peter 43
Kingdons Yard Winchester 153
Kington Louis Brent 33
Knight Alan 72 104
Knowles Craig 58
Komine Takayoshi 50
Kühn Achim & Helgard 36
Kühn Achim 10 14 27 28 50 77 80 199
Kühn Fritz 27 28 35 50 79 81 129 199
Kuwait Embassy 188
Labouchere Sir John and Lady 208

Lakeside West Thurrock 102
Lamb Ian 36 40 189 191
Lancaster Magistrates Court 189
Lansings of Basingstoke 206
Latham Associates 135
Leach Ben 132
Leeds College of Art 66
Leeds County Arcade 135
Legge Adrian 52
Leghtone Thomas de 2
Leicester Screen 110
Lewis Richard of Rotherham 111
Lincoln Cathedral 109 190
Lincoln Design Competition 70 71
Lindau Exhibition 72 140 199
Liverpool Anglican Cathedral 189
Liverpool College of Art 66
Liverpool Street Station 124
Livery Companies 62
Livewire Competition 64
Lloyds Building 79
Lock Stephen 109 111 134
London Transport 162
London University 168
Longdens 11
Loughborough College 92
Lund Giuseppe 31-33 35 37 140-148 162
Lyle David Architect 37 134
Lynn Chadwick 76 77
Mackintosh Charles Rennie 7 13-22 29 74
    80 111
Macnab Ian 193
Malleson Michael 43-46 149-154
Mametz Wood Memorial 169
Marchal Serge 26 36 77
Margetts Paul 51 61 78
Margrie Victor 23 34
Marks and Spencers Chelsea 148
Marshgate House 187
Martin Hugh and Partners 97
Martyr's Public School 15
Masson Claire 43
Matisse 75
Maurach Jurgen 45
May Susan 55
McLaren and Son 183
Metals Degree Course 162
MGM Films Elstree 168
Middlesborough Inland Revenue 69
Mila Building 10 11
Military Hospital Utrecht 127
Miller Daniel 45
Miller Lindsay 32
Minories Gallery 32 36 119
Mitchell Beazley (Publishers) Ltd 162
Mitchell Denys 32 33 66
Modern methods of technique and design
    82
Moebius Eric 36
Moisio Kauko 48
Moore Hazel 52 173
Moore Henry 75
Moore Mary Tyler 159
Morgan W.E.C 34
Morris Singer Foundry 143
Morris William 10
Munkembeck and Marshall 135
Museum of Archaeology Cambridge
    153

Museum of the Iron Age 153
Nash 102
National Blacksmiths Competition
    Committee 62 63
National Diploma in Design 66
National Garden Festival 170
National Trust 187
Nelson Judd 33
Nettlecomb Court 133
New Ashgate Gallery Farnham 179
New Court Building Woodgreen 127
New Iron Age Exhibition 62
Newport College of Art 168
Non-ferrous forging 198 199
Normandale Charles 41 42 44 50 88 111
    155-161
Norris Bill 43
Oakes Bob 50
Oakes Carol 52
Oberon Peat 51 52 61 69
Old Cleeve Church 193
Onos Juan 8
Organic Logic Exhibition 78
Oriel House Connaught Place 134
Ormeley Lodge 187
Ottawa Exhibitions 144
Outcasting technique 127
Overs Richard 42 43
Paine Robert 175
Paley Albert 24 25 33 48 50 66 77 78 81
    142
Palmer David 55
Paolozzi 157
Parham House 159
Parkinson Peter 32 36 40 42-3 44 79 162-
    167 190
Pascal Serge 26
Pasta House Restaurant 93
Pay Peter 77
Payne Steve 60
Pearce-Higgins Caroline 23 34 35
Pentagram Design 101 169 189
Petersen Aaron 172 173
Petersen Bronwen 171
Petersen David 32 49 52 82 155 168-173
Petersen Gideon 173
Petersen Jack 168
Petersen Toby 155 172 173
Petersham House 187
Phillips Derek L.S. 189
Phospher bronze 198
Picasso 74 75
Picton Castle Rhos 169 170
Pinnock Melvin 39 42 44 174-181 196
Piper John 157
Piquet Charles 10
Plate cutting119
Poillerat Gilbert 10
Poirier Bill 51 57 60
Police Administration Centre 134
Pomfret Henry 46 47 48
Portsmouth City Museum and Art Gallery
    165
Post Modernism 111
Poston David 109 190
Powell J.K. 69
Prentice Ian 97
Preston Hall Museum 69
Prince's Square Glasgow 95-100

Princes Quay Hull 102
Propane hearth 114
Prowse Pauline 192
Prudential Assurance Co Ltd 187
Public Record Office Kew 113
Puddick Alan 189
Pull-out technology 122
Pytel Walenty 182-186
Quaker Meeting House Painswick 104
Queen Elizabeth Gates 145-6
Queen Mary and Westfield College 127
Queen's Cross Church 20
Quick fix system 98
Quinnell Jinny 191
Quinnell Jinny Trust Fund 191
Quinnell Richard 33 -36 45 54 92 109 112
    135 187-192
Quinnells Ltd 162 179
Quinnell's Rowhurst Forge 166
Rachel Reckitt 38 40 61 177 193-196
Reckitt Rachel Award 64
Reeves Duncan 46 175
Reeves Martin 42 175
Regency Period 5
Reiter K23 pneumatic hammer 104
Richmond House Whitehall 134 190
Richmond Riverside Development 176
    191
Rickard Gino 140
Ridler Gabrielle 136
Ripple or Moire patterns 120
Rivergate Centre Peterborough 62
RMJM 127
Robert Emile 8 9
Roberts Michael 32 38 41 42 197-201
Robinson Antony 32 33 43 46 68 88 109
    140 148 202-209
Robinson Edmund 204
Robinson Marie 204
Robinson Simon 46 56-7 109 112 204
Robjohn Melich, Robjohns Clarke & Co.
    188
Rochester Cathedral 160 161
Roeland Leenes 127
Rogers R. Partners. Architects 79
Romsey Abbey 62
Ross Roland 155
Rowe Andrew 43 46 97 172
Royal Academy 43 89
Royal Anniversary Trust 153 167
Royal College of Art 162 178
Royal College of Music 140
Royal Mausoleum Jordon 188
Royal Museum of Scotland Edinburgh 67
Royal Observatory Greenwich 188
Royal Society 108
Royal Society of British Sculptors 186
Royal Welsh Agricultural Showground 62
Royals Shopping Centre Southend 102
Rural Development Commission 52
Ruskin Gallery Sheffield 142-3 148
Russell-Cotes Art Gallery Bournemouth
    167 191
Russell Brian 50 -52 61 70
Ruthin Castle 166
Saatchi Charles 136
Sandle Michael 143
Savoy Theatre 136
Scheeepvaarthuis 10 13

Schindler Peter 199
Schmerler Otto 199
Scotland House School 18
Scott Tim 50
Scottish Metropolitan Properties Ltd 66
Scottish Museum of Fisheries 64
Sedding J.D. 11
Sevenoaks School 72
Shepley Engineering Ltd 97
Sherbourne Abbey 62 153
Shoreditch College of Education 104
Sir John Soanes Museum 136
Six British Blacksmiths Exhibition 36 164
    206
Slimbridge Wildfowl Trust 139
Smith Ivan 32 33 34
Smithsonian Institution 24
Smythe Eric 197
Society of Wood Engravers 193
Sotheby Sale 52
Sotheby's Exhibition 54 69 103
South East Arts 73 181
South Glamorgan County Council 171
Southampton Railway Station 110
Southampton University 140
Sparsholt Agricultural College 62
Spence Sir Basil 187
Spencer Mary 183
Spencer Neil 106
St. Cuthbert Philbeach Gardens 11
St. George's Chapel 3
St. Giles Centre Elgin 102
St. Hugh Shrine 109
St. Hugh's College Oxford 189 170
St. John the Evangelist Stanmore 161
St. John's Methodist church Bloxwich 72
St. Martin's Canterbury 177
St. Mary the Virgin Silchester 143
St. Nicholas Church Withycombe 196
St. Paul's Cathedral 4 36 104
St. Paul's College Cheltenham 72
St. Peter and Paul Albury 164
St. John's Church Cardiff 49 117
St. Mary's Church Slindon 62
St. Mary's Church Wookey 62
St. Paul's Cathedral handrail 108
St. Paul's Church Tupsley Hereford 108
St. Peter Mancroft Church Norwich 122
St. Swithin's Grille 2
Steigler Dorothy 50
Stein Gertrude 75
Stephenson Graham 101
Stevenson J.A.R. 6
Stillingfleet Yorks. 80
Stratton Street London 103
Street G.E. 11
Stretched mesh fencing 126
Strong Sir Roy 37
Sturrock Mrs Mary Newbery 15
Subes Raymond 9
Sun Alliance Cheapside 136-7
Sunderland Polytechnic 70
Suter Walter 199
Sutherland Graham Memorial 169 170
Sutherland Kathline Foundation Trust 169
Swan Theatre Stratford 209
Swan Walk Horsham 102
Szabo & Schenck et Fils 10
Talk-in at Redfield 52

Taucher Franz 204
Taylor Addy Cup 43 87 189
Taylor John 166
Teesland Development Company 95
Terry Quinlan 176 191
Tewkesbury Abbey 208
The British Grate Exhibition 31 132
The Mackintosh House 20
Thedvall Roy 51
Thomson Alexander 15
Three Counties Show 68
Tijou Jean 3
Tilley Mark 54 60
Tobacco Dock 126
Topp Chris 80
Towards a New Iron Age Exhibition 37 72
    132 174 188
Tower of London 160
Townsend David 60
Trees of Iron 93 95-6 150-1
Trinity College Carmarthen 172
Truscott H. 188
Tube public seating 123
Tucker C.A.H (Tommy) 34 35 38 43 129
    202
Tucker David 45
Tuschinski Cinema 10 12
Twists right angle 109
Ulrich Fritz 33
Unilever House 189
United States Air Force Molesworth 191
University of Rochester U.S.A. 78
University of Wales 169
Unknown Political Prisoner Competition
    76
Usher Gallery Lincoln 66
Van der Mey 10
Vicarage Fields Barking 102
Victoria and Albert Museum 1 4 36 119 132
    203
Victoria Plaza 141 143 145-6
Victoria Quarter Leeds 102
Victoria Queen 13
Victorian Ironwork 5
Voluntary Services Overseas 68
Waight David 144 147
Waldorf Hotel 103
Walker Peter 42 43
Wallace Jim 192
Wallsworth Hall 139
Walton Barry 189
Warburton Chapel 3
Warwick Castle 201
WCSHA building 115
Wellington Secondary School 92
Welsh Arts Council 169
Welsh Arts Council Conference 36
Welsh National Opera 50
Wessex Iron Exhibition 62
West Dean 65
West Surrey College of Art 41 43 44 162
    167 179
West Tony 32
Westferry Circus Canary Wharf 144-5
    148
Westminster Abbey 2
Westminster Obelisk 91
Whistler Lawrence 189
Whiteway Stroud 104

Whitfield Partners Architects 37 88 134
Whitfield William 157
Williams Paul 37
Wilson Avril 59
Wilson Henry 11
Wilson Jane 47 57
Winchester Castle 203
Winchester Cathedral 2 112
Winchester Great Hall 36 204
Winchester Great Hall Competition 126
Windsor 3
Windyhill House 19
Wintershall Estate 90
Wise Edward 60
Wootton Anthony 32 33 41 42 46 61 72
Worshipful Company of Blacksmiths 43 62
    63 68 166 179 206
Worshipful Company of Ironmongers 166
Wren Christopher 106
Wyebridge Interiors Hereford 183
Wynne David 145
Wynne Paul 55
Yellin Samuel 24 50 81
Yellin Metalworkers Co. 50
Yett Scottish 18
York Minster 13
Yusko Steve 192
Zanni Augustino 34 35
Zimmermann Paul 44 72 81 152 170 199

NAMES AND ADDRESSES OF BRITISH BLACKSMITHS MENTIONED IN THIS BOOK.

Elspeth Bennie 1/1 96 Bowman Street, Crosshill, Glasgow G42 8LG

Richard Bent Hammer and Tongs, Hawkes Farm, Braishfield, Romsey, Hants SO51 0QJ

Adam Booth Piper's Forge, 4 Victoria Street, Kirkpatrick Durham, Castle Douglas, DG7 3HQ

Heather Burrell 206B Bedford Hill, Balham, London SW12 9HJ

Capricorn Architectural Ironworks (David Townsend) Tasso Forge, 56 Tasso Road, London W6 8LZ

Ron Carter Trapp Forge, Simonstone, N.Burnley, Lancs. BB12 7QW

Terrence Clark Wildfields Farm, Pound Lane, Woodstreet Village, Guildford, Surrey, GU3 3DT

Claydon Architectural Metalwork (Stuart Hill) Unit 12, Claydon Industrial Park Gt. Blakenham, Suffolk IP6 0NL

Ivan Yates Colbert 1 Newton Street, Crewe, Cheshire, CW1 2NG

Hector Cole Couzens Farm Studio, The Hill, Little Somerford, Chippenham, Wilts. SN15 5BQ

Bill Cordaroy Old Farm Cottage, Back Lane, East Ruston, Norwich, Norfolk NR12 9JE

John Creed 24 Auchinloch Road, Lenzie, Glasgow G66 5EU.

Peter Crownshaw St Michael's Farm, St Michael's, Tenbury Wells, Worcs, WR15 8TG

Mike Crummy Tomatin Smithy, Tomatin, Inverness-shire IV13 7YP

Alan Dawson Shepley Dawson Architectural Engineering Ltd Joseph Noble Road, Lillyhall, Workington, Cumbria, CA14 4JX

Colin Day Ironcrafts (Stotfold) Ltd. Road, Stotfold, Hitchin, Herts SG5 4PA

Dorothea Restorations Ltd New Road,Whaley Bridge, Via Stockport, Cheshire, SK12 7JG

Alan Evans Makins, Whiteway, Stroud, Glos. GL6 7ER

Matthew Feddon 42 Wellington Street, Gloucester.

Tim Fortune Filleybrook Forge, Henstridge Trading Estate, Henstridge, Nr Templecombe, Somerset BA8 0TG

Cara Frost Claycastle Cottage, S.Perrott, Nr. Beaminster, Dorset DT8 3HU

Derek Griffiths Ironworks U.K. Ltd, Wheel Business Park, Wheel Lane, Westfield, E.Sussex, TN35 4SE

Theo. Grunewald 2 Clyllan Cottage, Llanharan, Glamorgan CF7 9NH

Saraj Guha Unit 3, Wield Industrial Estate, Lower Wield, Alresford, Hants

Jolyon Havinden Blackford Home Farm, Rothienorman, Aberdeenshire, AB51 8YL

Neil Hawkins 19 Northfield Park, Pilton, Barnstaple, Devon, EX31 1QA

John Hill Daneswood Forge, Danes Dyke, Flamborough, Bridlington, Yorkshire, YO15 1AA

Robert Hobbs Engine Forge, Bath Road, Upper Langford, Nr. Bristol, BS18 7DG

Graeme Hopper Croft Forge, Rough Lea, Hunwick, County Durham DL15 0RH

James Horrobin The Doverhay Forge, Porlock, Minehead, Somerset, TA24 8QB

Robert Hutchison East Lodge, Touch, Cambusbarron, Stirling, FK8 3AG

Alan Jack 111 Old Cheltenham Road, Longlevens, Gloucester.

David James 22 Cransley Hill, Broughton, Kettering, Northants. NN14 1NR

Philip Johnson Ratho Byres Forge, Freelands Road, Ratho, Newbridge, Midlothian, EH28 8RS

Eamonn Kenward Wildcroft Cottage, Rectory Lane, Buckland, Betchworth, Surrey, RH3 7BN

Lennox Kilner The Forge, East Knoyle, Salisbury, SP3 6AJ

Craig Knowles 18 Brookside, Pill, Bristol, Avon, BS20 0JX

Adrian Legge The Hootings, Butterley, Bromyard, Herefordshire, HR7 4NG

Giuseppe Lund Butterfly Farm, Ashurst, Southampton, Hants. SO4 4UH

Michael Malleson Trent Smithy, Rigg Lane, Trent, Sherbourne, Dorset, DT9 4SS

Paul Margetts Field House Farm, Belbroughton, Stourbridge, Worcs. DY9 9ST

Susan May 17 Carysfort Road, London N16 9AA

Hazel Moore 2 Easton Piercy, Kington St. Michael, Chippenham, Wilts. SN14 6JT

The Nailbourne Forge Martin Reeves and Julian Coode. Court Hill, Littlebourne, Canterbury. Kent CT3 1TX

Charles Normandale Wheely Down Forge, Warnford, Nr. Winchester

Willam Norris 71 Fore Street, Port Isaac, Cornwall

Bob Oakes 13 Swan Close, Dunholme, Lincoln, LN2 3SB

Peat Oberon 21 Fairfield Avenue, Linthorpe, Middlesbrough, Cleveland TS5 5HB

Richard Overs Firecraft Unit 1, Brewery Workshops, Cricklade Street, Cirencester Glos.

David Palmer Penrhos, Groeslon, Caernarvon, Gwynedd, LL54 7TS

Peter Parkinson Heathfield House, Shortheath Common, Oakhanger, Nr Bordon Hampshire, GU35 9JT

Peter Pay Hole Farm, Chulmleigh, N. Devon. EX18 7DS

Steve Payne 1/1 96 Bowman Street, Cross Hill, Glasgow, G42 8LG

David Petersen Efail Y Tyddin, San Cler, Dyfed SA33 4EJ

Bill Poirier Riverden, Roadwater, Watchet, Somerset, TA23 0QH

Henry Pomfret c/o Phuthadikobo Museum, P.O. Box 367, Mochudi, Botswana.

Walenty Pytel Harleton, Bromsash, Ross on Wye HR9 7SB

Richard Quinnell The Rowhurst Forge, Oxshott Road, Leatherhead, Surrey, KT22 0EW

Rachel Reckitt Golsoncott House, Rodhuish, Minehead, Somerset, TA24 6QU

Michael Roberts Anvil Barn, Miserden, Stroud, Glos, GL6 7JD

Antony Robinson The White House, Stanton-upon-Hine Heath, Shrewsbury, Shropshire, SY4 4LR

Andrew Rowe 286 Ystrad Road, Fforestfach, Swansea

Brian Russell The Forge, Little Newsham, Winston, Darlington, Durham, DL2 3QN

Ivan Smith Woodside, Sneads Green, Nr. Droitwich

Roy Thedvall Wernnwydd Cwmmpengraig Velindre, Llandysul, Dyfed, SA44 5HX

Mark Tilley 58 Wychwood Avenue, Knowle, Solihull, West Midlands, B93 9DQ

Chris Topp Syndhurst, Carlton Husthwaite, Thirsk, N.Yorks, YO7 2BJ

David Tucker 35 Main Street, Ticknall, Derbyshire

Peter Walker Chapel Cottage Forge, Chapel Lane, Anslow, Burton-on-Trent, Staffs. DE13 9QA

Avril Wilson 20 York Avenue, Hove, E. Sussex, BN3 1PH

Edward Wise Pantiles, Garth Lane, Knighton, Powys, LD7 1HH

Anthony Wootton Roggenhoserweg 5, 87633, Obergünzburg, Germany.

Paul Wynne 102 Fleswick Avenue, Woodhouse, Whitehaven, CA28 9PB

WOOD ENGRAVINGS

on the Title pages and on pages 61, 84 and 85 are from limited editions by Rachel Reckitt (Golsoncott House, Rodhuish, Minehead, Somerset TA24 6QU) from whom originals can be purchased.

PHOTOGRAPHS AND COPYRIGHT

All photographs not otherwise attributed have been taken by the author and are her copyright.

Many of the photographs have been taken by the blacksmiths themselves and/or they hold the copyright.

Other photographers holding copyrights are listed below.

Glynn Clarkson Photography Maple Works, Old Shoreham Road, Hove, East Sussex BN3 7EY

Melvin Crow 9 Sandpiper Road, Whitstable, Kent, CT5 4DP

Robert Elliott Greystone Hall, Gainford, Darlington, DL2 3BL

Chris Fairclough Studio 65, Smithbrook Kilns, Cranleigh, Surrey GU6 8JJ

Ivor Nicholas Photography Westlakes, Asby, Workington, Cumbria CA14 4RR

Tim Porter Hans Hill Farm, Sezincote, Moreton-in-Marsh, Glos GL56 9TB

Andrew Priddy Photography Friday Street, Minehead.

Steve Silk Mill Studio, 17b Stour Street, Canterbury CT1 2NR

Studio 7 Photographers Commerce House, Outer Circle Road, Lincoln LN2 4HY

Alain Surelle 1346 Chemin de Calvas 30000 Nîmes, France.

BRITISH ARTIST BLACKSMITHS ASSOCIATION. Officers change but the Secretary for 1995 is Chris Topp (see address list) Book Dept. Peter King, Rosebank, Plaxtol, Sevenoaks.

"CHELTENHAM'S ORNAMENTAL IRONWORK"

by Amina Chatwin was first published in 1975. The Spa towns of Britain were particularly rich in architectural ironwork but none had such a wealth and variety as Regency Cheltenham. Well received at the time, the book has become something of a classic, which has been called.......*"a masterly pioneer-study of the finest living display of decorative ironwork in Britain"* (Review by the late Michael Rix. M.A.) *"The book.....has much of the charm of a sophisticated scrap-book"* House and Garden. 94 pages 6 x 8¹/₂" (paperback) 160 illustrations and photographs. Second printing still available from Coach House Publishing, The Coach House, Parabola Close, Cheltenham, GL50 3AN. Price £5 including (in U.K.) p&p.

THE AUTHOR:

Born in Cheltenham in 1927 Amina Chatwin has always been on the edge of the Arts. Brought up a dancer, she was also a Licentiate of the Guildhall School of Music and Drama, and worked with the Roel Puppets; a company who made and operated Marionettes as an art form for adults. She studied sculpture to improve her woodcarving skills. Later she taught at the Roel Summer Schools and travelled, with the Director, Olive Blackham, giving lecture-demonstrations at schools and colleges across the country, particularly at the emergency teacher training colleges set up after the war. In later years she became examiner for A Level puppetry in South Wales.

It was while working in Paris that she began to write, by sending reports on the Arts and life in Paris, back to her local newspaper; The Gloucestershire Chronicle and Graphic.

For thirty years she worked in the fashion trade, running her own shop in the picturesque Montpellier area of Cheltenham.

During this time an interest in ancient art led her to archaeology and in turn to industrial archaeology, particularly the history of metals. In 1975 she wrote and published "Cheltenham's Ornamental Ironwork". She has written a number of articles on ironwork, particularly in *The Anvil's Ring* and *The British Blacksmith*. For some years she has been writing a history of ironwork in Britain but interrupted this work to complete the present book.

In 1987 she semi-retired but continued to operate a showroom and mail order dress business for a further five years. She now gives herself entirely to writing.

She is a past Chairman of *The Historical Metallurgy Society*, an international body, and currently edits their HMS News. In 1994 she became President of *The Gloucestershire Society for Industrial Archaeology*.

9781901037265

BV - #0102 - 070524 - C0 - 295/215/16 - PB - 9781901037265 - Gloss Lamination